To Mom
from Jim
May 1972

THE CAPITOL AT WASHINGTON
Before the Great Dome was Built.   (*Ridgway*)

THE
BLUE-CHINA
BOOK

EARLY AMERICAN SCENES AND HISTORY
PICTURED IN THE POTTERY OF THE TIME

BY

ADA WALKER CAMEHL

With a new introduction
and checklist of British blue-china potters by
GEOFFREY A. GODDEN
author of *Encyclopedia of British Pottery
and Porcelain Marks*

WITH 200 ILLUSTRATIONS

DOVER PUBLICATIONS, INC.
NEW YORK

DEDICATED

TO

MY HUSBAND

WHO MADE POSSIBLE THIS BOOK

Published in Canada by General Publishing Com-
pany, Ltd., 30 Lesmill Road, Don Mills, Toronto,
Ontario.
Published in the United Kingdom by Constable
and Company, Ltd., 10 Orange Street, London
WC 2.

This Dover edition, first published in 1971, is
an unabridged republication of the work originally
published by E. P. Dutton and Company, New
York, in 1916. The original Supplementary Chapters A through C are here called Appendixes I
through III. Geoffrey A. Godden has written
specially for the present edition a new Introduction and a fourth Appendix, "List of British
Potters Employing Identifiable Marks on Wares
for the North American Market."
Several of the illustrations were printed in blue
or red in the original edition; all appear here in
black-and-white.

International Standard Book Number: 0-486-22749-9
Library of Congress Catalog Card Number: 73-145884

Manufactured in the United States of America
Dover Publications, Inc.
180 Varick Street
New York. N. Y. 10014

TRANSYLVANIA UNIVERSITY
LEXINGTON, KENTUCKY
(*Wood*)

MARINE HOSPITAL,
LOUISVILLE, KY.
(*Wood*)

CITY OF DETROIT, MICHIGAN

Early Stern-Wheel Steamboat in Harbor. (*Unknown Maker*)

INTRODUCTION

TO THE DOVER EDITION

THIS work was first published in 1916, over fifty years ago and yet it is as interesting and useful today as when it was first written. This is largely because it is as much concerned with the timeless history of the nation as with the pottery which illustrates it, depicting cities and buildings as they were early in the nineteenth century.

So it is that, whereas in the last fifty years the story of British ceramics has been almost completely rewritten, this book on American-view pottery remains a standard work, requiring in its main section no subsequent revision. Within recent times, however, much research has been carried on in England on the Staffordshire potters and their working periods and identifying marks, and it is now possible to add to this new edition (as Appendix IV) details of over eighty Staffordshire potters (or firms) of the period 1800 to 1860. From these details now incorporated in this work the reader will be able to identify and date a mass of Staffordshire blue-printed pottery of the type which was imported into America in such vast quantities.

This book is mainly concerned with the American

views, rather than with the makers of the pottery. It is therefore relevant in this Introduction to redress the balance and to fill in some of the English background to these pieces. With the exception of the potters working in the seaport of Liverpool, almost all the earthenware shipped to America came from the "Staffordshire Potteries" by way of canal and river across country to Liverpool, for export to North America. The "Staffordshire Potteries" were not, as now, the one sprawling city of Stoke-on-Trent but rather a series of separate small towns. In alphabetical order these were Burslem, Cobridge, Fenton, Hanley (and Shelton), Longport, Longton (and Lane End), Stoke and Tunstall.

Within these townships were situated hundreds of small potteries employing in most cases fewer than forty workers. The well-known large firms were relatively few in number, and in general these internationally known concerns did not manufacture designs especially for the United States market. For example, in the 1810–30 period the leading firms of the industry were Wedgwood, Spode and Minton, none of which appear to have made at that period these American topographical or historical designs, although they were exporting vast quantities of their standard wares, decorated with neutral designs which they could equally well sell in England.

The special blue-printed American views were, in the

GEOFFREY A. GODDEN

main, produced by the middle range of Staffordshire
potteries, by those enterprising potters who were striv-
ing to enter new markets and to establish their reputation. While they had the facilities to make good quality
wares, they could not hold their own in the home market
against the established giants of the trade and the need
arose to cultivate new markets and to produce novel designs, especially for the American china dealers.

In reality, we admire and collect this Staffordshire
blue china not so much for the earthenware objects
(which are in the main utilitarian table wares, being
parts of dinner or tea services rather than tastefully designed vases or purely decorative pieces) but more for
the added decorative print. It is not often realised that
the potter who added his mark to the piece had in many
cases no direct responsibility for the print which was
added to his wares. For many of the smaller potters could
not afford to employ full-time the skilled engravers required to produce the many copperplates necessary before
a single dinner service could be printed. The time needed
to complete such a set of engraved copperplates for any
new pattern was very considerable and the expense of
such "retooling" must have been a considerable embar-
rassment for many potters.

To avoid the necessity for the small potter to employ
continually skilled engravers, many of the potters used
the services of specialist engraving firms, either com-

missioning a special new design, or more often buying a ready engraved design from "stock." It is the work of these little-recognized engravers which interests us today and it is most regrettable that their work was not signed and that we know so little about these skilled artists on copper. The designers and engravers were indeed the key skilled hands, for while the workmen employed in the many manufacturing processes could be trained in their craft, the engravers had to have a natural artistic flair. The extent to which these engravers were employed can be gauged from the fact that even the Chamberlain porcelain manufacturers at Worcester sent up to Staffordshire for sets of engraved copperplates depicting special designs.

The firm from which Messrs. Chamberlain obtained their engraved copperplates in 1813 was Messrs. Bentley, Wear & Bourne, a partnership also patronised by Minton at the same period and later by Mason. There can be little doubt that this firm of engravers supplied finely designed patterns to a host of other potters and some of these engravings must have related to the special American views. Simeon Shaw, in his *History of the Staffordshire Potteries,* published in 1829, gives us a contemporary reference to this firm. "In Vine Street, Shelton, Messrs. Bentley & Wear, eminent engravers, have a fine gallery of paintings, including some of considerable value . . . ." This, then, was no ordinary back-street engravers' workshop, but a prosperous concern sporting an art gallery! The principal partner was William Bentley, who was born in 1777 and died in May 1833. The exact date of the partnership foundation is not known but it was flourishing in 1813, as contemporary accounts prove. The local directories list subsequent changes in partnership: Bentley & Wear, c. 1822–33; Bentley, Wear & Wildig, c. 1833; Wildig & Allen, c. 1834–37; and Allen & Green, c. 1837–51. The amount of Staffordshire earthenware decorated by means of the copperplates engraved by these firms must be truly enormous and yet credit goes solely to the makers of the basic pottery, not to the artist-engravers.

Of course, other talented engravers were practising their art in the Staffordshire potteries and it would be tedious to give here a long list of the persons, but mention must be made of some of the more noteworthy: Allen & Hordley of Shelton; William Brooks; Messrs. Green, Sargeant & Pepper of Hanley; James Kennedy of Burslem and Elisha Sherwin of Hanley.

Talented as were these engravers, their main task was merely to transpose a given design onto a sheet of copper, as the first stage in the mass-production of identical copies on earthenware. Often the basic design was copied (after slight amendments to enable the motif to fit a circular plate or other ceramic object) from a published engraving, but rarely were original drawings used, or

INTRODUCTION TO THE DOVER EDITION

the services of a skilled artist or draughtsman employed, such as James Cutts of Shelton, who described himself as a "Pottery engraver's designer."

It is of interest to list briefly the many processes that a humble blue-printed Staffordshire earthenware plate had undergone before it arrived on the American shores as part of a large service, and to calculate the number of persons who would have had a hand in its production. First, we have the basic raw materials which have to be excavated, refined and ground. These materials have then to be mixed in accurate proportions to form a workable and stable body. The resulting mix is then rid of air bubbles and is formed into a plate. This plate is then fired in the biscuit kiln, after which the underglaze blue print is applied to the unglazed but once-fired plate. This decorated plate is then glazed and fired again to fuse the glaze. Subsequently it is checked for defects and if sound, placed in the potter's store. Later it is sorted with other component pieces to form a complete service, which would have been packed in straw and shipped by canal to the port of Liverpool, where it would have been transferred to a transatlantic sailing vessel for its voyage to the New World. This summary is quite basic and takes no account of the all-important method of transferring the design from the engraved copperplate onto the unglazed earthenware. As this book is concerned greatly with these printed motifs, the method of application should be explained.

As already mentioned, the basic design was painstakingly engraved or etched onto the surface of a copper sheet (a separate sheet was required for each of the various shapes that made up the complete service). This "copperplate" was then heated and the thick oil-like blue pigment rubbed over the copper and into the recessed-engraved design. The flat face of the copperplate was then wiped clear of pigment, which remained only in the engraved recessed portions. Onto this charged plate was placed a sheet of special tissue-like paper. The resulting sandwich of copper, pigment and paper was then put in a press, so that the paper took up the pigment from the engraved parts of the copper. This paper was then peeled off and the surplus parts cut away or shaped to fit the particular article. The trimmed paper was then carefully appplied to the object so as to fit the required area, and after being pressed firmly onto the object the inked design was transferred to the unglazed earthenware. The paper then had to be soaked off and the object lightly fired to rid the pigment of surplus oil before the article was glazed and fired again. To apply the design by this basic process, probably no less than six persons were employed and in the production of one completely finished plate at least ten persons were occupied, quite apart from those employed in the preparation of the pigment, the manufacture of the paper and

INTRODUCTION TO THE DOVER EDITION

all the other arts and crafts upon which the potters were dependent.

It is continually a matter of amazement to me that the Staffordshire potters were able to ship to North America complete table services of over a hundred pieces which could be sold at a quite modest amount, one which most families could afford. It is less surprising that the surviving pieces from these Staffordshire earthenware services should now be eagerly collected and displayed in museums and be the subject of books such as this.

1970   GEOFFREY A. GODDEN

The man who will tell the story of a race, a nation, or a period according to the clothing, dwellings, utensils, and everyday art of it will be, I vow, the only true historian of them all, and vividly in his pages the age and people shall live again, though wars and dynasties and that elaborate comedy called politics be but the edges and binding of the book. So let us glorify our hobby, Hobbinal my friend. Is it not part of the true stuff of history? Don't we know that about the doings of eighteenth century English potters rests a nimbus of chronicle as well as of romance?

SIR J. H. YOXALL, M. P.

VIEW NEAR CONWAY, NEW HAMPSHIRE
(*W. Adams & Sons*)

BAKER'S FALLS, HUDSON RIVER
(*Clews*, "Picturesque Views")

LITTLE FALLS AT LUZERNE, HUDSON RIVER

(*Clews*, "Picturesque Views")

ACKNOWLEDGMENTS

In the field of American history, the volumes I have consulted for the story of those years which Staffordshire pottery depicts, comprise a number too great to be severally enumerated. Old letters, diaries, journals, travels, biographies, files of newspapers and magazines, historical records of all kinds, have been pored over. Of notable value among them may be mentioned the daily journal of General Lafayette upon the occasion of his triumphal tour of the States in 1824–5, his keen observations continually comparing the state of the country at that period with its condition half a century earlier when he was a member of its Continental army. Of especial interest also have been Esther Singleton's " Story of the White House," Mrs. Taft's " Recollections of Full Years," and the recent volume, " Walks About Washington," by Francis E. Leupp and Lester G. Hornby.

In the field of ceramics, to those who before me have trod the alluring paths of " old blue " I owe a debt of gratitude: to Mrs. Alice Morse Earle, whose " China Collecting in America " set us upon the trail that leads to poverty of pocket and enrichment of joy and understanding, the book which perhaps has done most to arouse popular interest in those humble and oft-times despised pieces of common tableware which enshrine the annals of our pioneer years; to Dr. Edwin Atlee Barber, of Philadelphia, not only for the assistance which his comprehensive volumes have afforded, but also for the privilege of enriching my own work with the " Index of American Views " and with several photographs from his " Anglo-American Pottery "; to Mr. Robineau, editor of the *Old China Magazine,* for photographic plates and descriptions of historic wares; to the beautiful volume of Mr. R. T. Haines Halsey, upon the historical pottery of New York State; and to the valuable works of Mrs. N. Hudson Moore.

In addition to the public displays of historical pottery which

ACKNOWLEDGMENTS

the Museums and Historical Societies of several of our large cities open to the student, many individual collections have been generously placed at the disposal of the author. My thanks are due first, to the present Mistress of the White House, Mrs. Wilson, for permission to have photographs made of the collection of presidential china which is on permanent exhibition in the lower corridor of the historic mansion; and to Colonel William W. Hart, Commissioner of Public Buildings and Grounds in Washington, for his interest in my behalf. To Mr. George Kellogg, of Amsterdam, N. Y., my thanks are here acknowledged for the privilege of consulting his very complete collection of blue historical Staffordshire, as well as for many photographs of specimens, among them the valuable " New York from Weehawk " and the " New York from Brooklyn Heights " platters, and his rare series of State Arms plates; to Dr. Irving P. Lyon, of Buffalo, N. Y., for photographs of his splendid group of Liverpool pitchers; to Mrs. Francis W. Dickins, of Washington, D. C., for permission to photograph her extensive loan collection of historical pottery in the National Museum of that city; to Mr. Henry Leworthy, of Fredonia, N. Y., for photographs of his rare collection; to Mrs. William Garland, of California, for photographs of the Mrs. Hinman collection; to Mr. W. F. Sheely, of New Oxford, Pa., for photographs; and to Mrs. Randolph Barnes, of Buffalo, N. Y., for many hours of pleasurable and profitable discussion upon our chosen topic, as our individual collections grew.

I wish here also to thank Mr. Brayton L. Nichols, editor of *The Illustrated Buffalo Express,* for critical aid in my literary work, and for the privilege of using material which appeared in that paper; also, the Century Company of New York, for permission to incorporate in this volume material which first was published in Saint Nicholas.

ADA WALKER CAMEHL.

Buffalo, 1916.

INTRODUCTION

"ALL THIS OF POT AND POTTER"

About a century ago the pottery-makers of England, with that keen insight which has given to the British Empire the markets of the world, established a profitable branch of commerce with the Colonies and with the States of the new American Republic, by means of an appeal unique in the annals of trade. They decorated the pottery destined for the new market with faithful views taken from America itself, many of which, by the way, have been perpetuated in no other manner. They reproduced designs from volumes of contemporary prints known as "The Beauties of America," "Picturesque Views on the Hudson River," etc., or, from original sketches out of the note books of English tourists returned from the "grand tour" of the new country. A few of the potters sent their own artists over the sea to make drawings with pen and pencil, sketches in oil, or impressions with the newly invented "camera-obscura" or "camera-lucida" (the beginnings of modern cameras), of scenery bordering upon the wonderful rivers, of mountain ranges, inland lakes, and of the far-famed cataract of Niagara. The artists gratified the civic pride of the dwellers in the new cities by making pictures of their important buildings—state houses, colleges, almshouses, prisons, warehouses, inns, churches, theaters, mansions, etc., as well as of their world-famous enterprise, the "Grand Erie Canal." The English potters did not hesitate to honor the national heroes of the new-born Republic, several of them turning out fanciful scenes of America's pioneers; others, setting aside their own patriotic pride, used portraits of George Washington and of the naval heroes of the War of 1812, together with sketches of engagements fatal to British arms, of monuments raised to Colonial victories, and of Revolutionary battlefields whereon the patriot forces had routed the redcoats.

Benjamin Franklin's portrait and his popular moral "Maxims" and "Proverbs" were eagerly appropriated for pottery display, while the famous visit of General Lafayette to America furnished still another series of decorations. One potter confined his output of American views almost entirely to a group of designs, now rare and valuable, illustrating the coats of arms of the original Thirteen States, and still others commemorated in clay the two marvels of early nineteenth century science—the steamboat and the locomotive.

The pictures thus secured, more than two hundred and fifty in number, were taken to the English pottery works, where, by means of the recently discovered process of transfer printing from copper plates, they were stamped upon dinner sets, tea services, toilet sets, and all manner of useful ware. The potters of Liverpool were the first to put American views upon china, printing, shortly after the close of the War of the Revolution, the portraits of George Washington and Benjamin Franklin upon yellow jugs and mugs and punch bowls. A number of years later, the Liverpool potters produced an almost complete series of portraits of American naval heroes, together with illustrations of the principal engagements of the War of 1812.

By far the greater number of American views, however, went to the group of English hamlets in the county of Staffordshire, which numbers about a dozen and is still known as "The Potteries." Burslem, Cobridge, Hanley, Stoke-upon-Trent, Tunstall, are among the important pottery settlements whence ware was sent to America; while the names of potters which the collector most commonly finds upon the back of his specimens are Enoch Wood, Stevenson, Clews, Ridgway, Stubbs, Tams, Mayer, Adams, Jackson, and Green. A long list of pieces, however, are unmarked, and the makers unidentified. From the year 1783 when Enoch Wood set up his works at Burslem, until about 1850, almost all of the English pottery which was sent across the sea bore views obtained from America, the specimens which now survive being known as "Old Staffordshire." The name of the potter, oft-times his initials alone, may be found upon the back of the pieces,[1] together with peculiar marks (a number of which are illustrated in the supplement to this volume) and scrolls encircling the title of the view upon the face.   Every piece of the same set of dishes was not thus defined, hollow ware such as cups and saucers, sugar bowls and pitchers, being frequently found without a distinguishing mark, the name of the potter then being determined by the border design.

Attractive indeed are the border devices with which the American views are framed, nearly every potter customarily making use of one distinctive pattern.   He might vary the scene within the frame, or he might borrow some sketch from a neighboring potter, but the border around it, as a rule remained peculiarly his own, thereby making of it to-day a ready means of identification.   The border designs, as a study of the illustrations reveals, are composed of graceful combinations of sea-shells and mosses, roses and scrolls, acorns and oak leaves, grapes and vines, or of fruit, birds and flowers in delightful arrangement.   Animals peculiar to the tropics appear in one series, the American eagle perches proudly among the scrolls of another, while one or two of the more intricate patterns bear marked resemblance to the borders found on Flemish tapestries of the Renaissance, or encircling the charming terra-cotta Madonnas of Della Robbia.

[1] See Appendix II.

INTRODUCTION TO THE FIRST EDITION

The rich blue color so greatly admired, which until very recent years has been impossible of reproduction, was first adopted in England early in the nineteenth century, and was an echo of the Oriental blues, as well as of the Dutch Delft, which, owing to Holland's earlier trade facilities with the Orient, presented the first reproduction of that color in Europe. Until about the year 1830, at which time printing upon pottery became cheapened by the process of lithography, blue was almost the sole color in use in the Staffordshire potteries. The color was cheap and flowed easily, and its density hid from view the imperfections in ware and workmanship —blisters in the glaze and marks of the triangles used to separate the pieces in the kiln, marks which may still be discovered upon all pieces of flat ware made in Staffordshire during the first quarter of the nineteenth century. It must be borne in mind that the beautiful old blue dishes so greatly coveted to-day are not of fine material, nor of skilled manufacture, their present value lying in their decorative quality, and in the pictured memorials of early America which they perpetuate— memorials which at the present time are accorded an important place among the authentic documents of history. As the years went by, however, the rich deep blue was followed with paler tints—light blue, pink, green, mulberry, purple, gray, and also black—until at last, just before the Centennial Exposition of 1876, the event which proved to be the rebirth of the Art spirit in the United States, the common tableware of our forefathers had faded to the dull monotony of white.

When and how did the pictured English pottery find its way to the United States? Near the end of the eighteenth century, soon after the close of the Revolutionary War, "sailor-pitchers" and punch bowls made in Liverpool were brought to these shores by sea-captains and sailor-boys and were presented as keepsakes to home friends. By reason of the graceful forms and of the verses and portraits printed upon them, verses breathing of homely sentiment and patriotism, and portraits of celebrated patriot heroes, they were lovingly cherished by New England housewives. About 25 years ago, when keen interest in the preservation of historic china had its beginning, there was scarcely a New England family with sea-faring ancestors whose chimney shelf or corner dresser was not graced with one or more yellow jug or bowl of Liverpool.

The more gayly hued pottery of Staffordshire manufacture was, until as late as the middle of the nineteenth century, shipped to American merchants in large quantities and purchased for daily use by our forefathers and their china-loving dames. They admired the rich colors and the quaint forms, and, as they sipped their spiced brew or fragrant tea, they found added pleasure in looking upon the faces of their beloved heroes, in living over in imagination the great battles, and in marveling anew at the wonderful achievements of peace, depicted upon the specimens before them.

The prices given for the imported ware were so small, from a six-pence to a shilling being the cost of a single plate, that the amounts paid at the present time to possess one of the surviving pieces would amaze our thrifty forefathers as well as astonish the trade-seeking potters who turned them out. Liverpool jugs bearing the portraits of Washington or of the heroes and sea battles of 1812 are worth thirty, fifty, and more dollars, while one hundred dollars are frequently given for a blue plate or platter or pitcher printed with some historic design. A few years ago, the sum of $290 was given for a blue platter picturing "New York from Brooklyn Heights"; at a recent sale, $1000 was paid for a Pennsylvania Arms plate; and not long ago a platter of the "New York from Weehawk" design brought $1225, the highest price yet paid for a specimen of old Staffordshire.

It may be asked, Where are examples of Staffordshire historical ware to be obtained at the present time? It is a surprising fact that search for pieces of English pottery with American views in the country where it was manufactured fails to discover any specimen, practically all of it having been shipped to the market for which it was created. In this country, a large number of pieces which have survived the changes a century has brought to the rapidly developing nation are carefully gathered into the public Museums or Historical Societies of the great cities, or else they are cherished in the no less valuable private collections of china-loving individuals. But there yet remains in country homes throughout the eastern states, in the oft-times careless possession of descendants of original owners, a harvest sufficient to tempt the admirer of "old blue," to lure him into that fascinating quest which *may* be as futile as the search for the pot of gold at the end of the rainbow, but which has for reward, in addition to the specimens secured, a fuller understanding of the formative period of his own nation.

What joy can compare with that of passing a long summer day in the country, driving with horse and carriage or swifter motor (the halcyon days of the spacious tin peddler's cart, which served the earliest in the field of china collecting, alas! are gone), over sun-baked dusty hills and through winding, shadowy valleys, stopping at each low-browed dwelling in quest of old blue china? A debt of gratitude is due the oldtime potters of England for making and sending to these shores such quantities of attractive ware that even yet stray specimens are hidden away under dusty eaves, upon top pantry shelves, or on the high mantels of dark parlors, waiting to be peered out and gathered.

Uncertain as a lottery are the rewards of a china hunt.

INTRODUCTION TO THE FIRST EDITION

One may, after knocking at the door of some "likely" farmhouse, be shown, in place of the "old blue dishes, pewter, or any other old things" humbly asked for, a hair wreath set in a deep gilt frame, or a bunch of faded worsted flowers—memorials of another more recent "Art" period of our history. Or, the seeker of historic relics may make his way to the back door (the true hunter of old china never approaches the front) through the pigs and hens of the barnyard, only to be informed by the woman who opens it, "Old blue dishes? Land, yes! I had stacks of them, but when they got broken I just pounded them up and fed them to the hens!" As he picks his way to the gate he may take a long look at the poultry, until there rises before his vision rows of Easter eggs born into the world bearing the sad love story of Chang and his sweetheart Koong-Shee, or else the benign features of Franklin or of the Father of His Country; surely, "Cæsar dead and turned to clay . . ." has a parallel in the present.

Then the unexpected "finds"! Setting out in search of a Willow platter which neighborhood rumor whispered was "in the low white house on the hill yonder, a part of her grandmother's wedding set," how keen the pleasure to discover in place of the more common pattern, a rich blue platter inscribed, "Landing of General Lafayette,"—and how eager the desire to hasten home with the prize and search for the story it records. The

day we came upon the large vegetable dish with the aqueducts, the canal boats and the four familiar faces . . .
our interest in the sluggish ditch had been but a dull one
until then.　And the big-winged frigates so fiercely fighting upon the yellow jugs, Penn and his Indians, and
Columbus, the battle-monuments and the buildings of
the early cities—how they sharpened our appetites for
hitherto dry facts, and awakened an impulse to unravel
and follow to their source the bright threads of this
alluring and gayly patterned "stuff of history."

The knowledge of a bygone period of our nation's
history acquired from the pleasant study of old blue
china suggests to the mind a comparison with the present era, and tempts a vision, "far as human eye can see,"
of that which lies before.　"We live in a most extraor-
dinary age," remarked Daniel Webster a century ago—
words frequent on men's tongues to-day.　For, as a
present-day historian observes, "Less cumbered by old
traditions than the elder nations, and with a vast continent in front of her, America has marched along the
new roads of history with a rapidity and an energy for
which there is no precedent."　From the twelve million
inhabitants of Webster's time the Republic has increased
to a population of one hundred millions, and the flag
which the century-old tableware pictures displaying
thirteen stars, now proudly flies nearly half a hundred.
To-day, in place of the Mississippi River or the "Shining

Mountains" bounding the western territory of the nation, the dwellers in Alaska, in Hawaii, in the islands of the Far East and of the tropical seas are, like the early settlers upon the Mississippi banks, "fellow citizens and neighbors of those who cultivate the hills of New England." Almost all of the stately buildings displayed upon the old tableware have been swept away by the growth of the great cities, the few which have been spared being at the present time either lost to view as the kernels of imposing modern structures, or else their proportions are dwarfed by neighboring tower-like piles.

Science has taken the past hundred years for her special field, and has marked its pathway with such countless milestones of achievement that the clumsy and fear-inspiring little steamboats and locomotives which the blue plates present as the wonders of a century ago have been at the present time succeeded by the swift moving leviathans of sea and land; and the telephone, the wireless telegraph, the automobile, the submarine, have, each in turn, been cause for marvel . . . until, crowning all marvels, the boon denied Icarus of old, navigation of the air, is a commonplace to those who live to-day. Obsolete as the primitive yewbows of yeoman archers, or as the cumbersome armor and lances of mediæval knights, is the Art of warfare as it is manifested in the old-china battle-scenes of the Revolution and of the sea engagements of 1812, . . . a vivid contrast to the vast European campaigns which at the period of writing are claiming the attention of the world. These century-old sketches of the one time "thin, red lines" of gayly uniformed British soldiery defiling up Bunker Hill, for hand-to-hand combat with the enemy, and of *Old Ironsides* slowly and laboriously kedging her way out of the enemy's reach, have been succeeded by modern photographs, and moving-picture films, of parallel trenches filled with gray-clad soldiers losing or winning battles sometimes without a sight of the enemy; of long-range guns, aëroplanes, and submarine destroyers.

To the western Republic, the hundred years of peace which have been recently concluded have brought such unexampled growth and prosperity that to it as to a "Promised Land" turn the hopes of the folk of Old World Empires, who within its borders seek and find that liberty which was so hardly won by their forefathers—America's pioneers.

As to the place which the future holds for the United States, the prophecy spoken by an early and far-seeing citizen of the Republic is one with the convictions of those who behold her at the present time entering upon a "new road of history": "Humanly speaking, no circumstances can prevent these United States from becoming eventually, and at no distant period, a great and powerful nation, influencing and controlling the other sovereignties of the world."

CONTENTS

PART I
THE COUNTRY AND THE CITIES OF EARLY AMERICA

I   A TOUR OF THE LAND 3
II   "THE CROOKED BUT INTERESTING TOWN OF BOSTON" 22
III OLD NEW YORK 43
IV   THE PHILADELPHIA OF PENN AND FRANKLIN . . 71
V   EARLY BALTIMORE 88
VI   WASHINGTON, THE NEW CAPITAL 94

PART II
THE AMERICAN NATION-BUILDERS AND THEIR WORK

VII   PIONEERS OF AMERICA 107
VIII GEORGE WASHINGTON 124
IX   SCENES OF THE REVOLUTIONARY WAR 137
X   EMBLEMS OF THE NEW REPUBLIC AND STATES . . 146
XI   BENJAMIN FRANKLIN AND HIS PRECEPTS 158
XII   NAVAL HEROES OF THE WAR OF 1812 172
XIII GENERAL LAFAYETTE'S VISIT TO AMERICA . . . 192
XIV   OPENING OF THE ERIE CANAL 213
XV   INTRODUCTION OF NEW MODES OF TRAVEL . . . 225

APPENDICES

I   THE WHITE HOUSE COLLECTION OF
        PRESIDENTIAL CHINA 245
II   CHECKING LIST OF AMERICAN VIEWS FOUND
        UPON ENGLISH OLD POTTERY . . . 267
III THE WILLOW PATTERN AND OTHER IMPORTANT
        BLUE-CHINA SERIES 287
IV   LIST OF BRITISH POTTERS EMPLOYING
        IDENTIFIABLE MARKS ON WARES MADE
        FOR THE AMERICAN MARKET 293

LAKE GEORGE. (*Wood*)

ALPHABETICAL LIST OF ILLUSTRATIONS

FACING
PAGE

Albany (Wood) 14
Albany, Dutch Church (Stevenson) 6
Albany, Rensselaer Island (maker unknown) 15
Allegheny, Penitentiary (Clews) . . . . . *Introduction*
Arms, of Connecticut (Mayer) 152
Arms, of Delaware (Mayer) 150
Arms, of Georgia (Mayer 149
Arms, of Maryland (Mayer) 149
Arms, of Massachusetts (Mayer) 151
Arms, of New Jersey (Mayer) 146
Arms, of New York (Mayer) 152
Arms, of North Carolina (Mayer) 148
Arms, of Pennsylvania (Mayer) 146
Arms, of Rhode Island (Mayer) 148
Arms, of South Carolina (Mayer) 153
Arms, of Virginia (Mayer) 153

Bainbridge, Commodore (bust portrait) 177
Baker's Falls, Hudson R. (Clews) . . . . *Introduction*
Baltimore (Godwin) 88
Baltimore (Unknown maker) 90
Baltimore, Almshouse (unknown maker) 91
Baltimore & Ohio R. R., so called (cup and saucer) . . 229
Baltimore & Ohio R. R. (Wood) 233
Baltimore & Ohio R. R. Inclined Plane (Wood) . . . 233
Baltimore, Battle Monument (Jackson) 92
Baltimore, Exchange (unknown maker) 92
Baltimore, Hospital (unknown maker) 91
Baltimore, University of Maryland (unknown maker) . . 90
Boston, Almshouse (R. Stevenson) 38
Boston, Athenæum (Ridgway) 39
Boston, Common, State House, Dwellings (Stubbs) . . . 26
Boston from Chelsea Heights (C. C.) 24
Boston, Fusileers of, (Liverpool pitcher) 142
Boston, Hancock House (Jackson) 30
Boston, Hospital (R. Stevenson) 34

ALPHABETICAL LIST OF ILLUSTRATIONS

FACING
PAGE

Boston, Insane Hospital (Ridgway) 35
Boston, Lawrence Mansion (R. S.) 27
Boston, Mitchell & Freeman's China & Glass Warehouse
    (Adams) 35
Boston, Nahant (Stubbs) 39
Boston, Octagon Church (Ridgway) 34
Boston, State House (chaise) (Rogers) 30
Boston, St. Paul's Church (Ridgway) 27
Buffalo, Erie Canal at (R. S.) 213
Bunker Hill, Battle of (R. Stevenson) 138
Bunker Hill Monument (Jackson) 139

Cadmus (Wood) 196
Catskills, Pine Orchard House (Wood) . . . *Introduction*
"Chancellor Livingston," steamboat (Wood) 236
"Chief Justice Marshall," steamboat of "Troy Line" (Wood) 232
Clinton, Jefferson, Washington, portraits, (Stevenson)
    (vegetable dish) 214
Columbia College (R. S. W.) 53
Columbus, Landing of, cavalry view (Adams) 112
Columbus, Landing of, Indian shooting wild goose, (Adams) 113
Columbus, Landing of, two caravels (Adams) 113
Columbus, Landing of, (Wedgwood pitcher) 118
Conway, N. H., View near (Adams) . . . . *Introduction*

Decatur, Commodore Stephen (bust portrait) 179
Detroit, Michigan (unknown maker) . . . . *Introduction*
Don Quixote's Attack on the Windmill (Clews) . . . 287
Dr. Syntax Starting out upon his First Tour (Clews) . . 287

Emblems of Success of Revolutionary Arms (Liverpool
    pitcher) 131
"Enterprise" & "Boxer" (Liverpool pitcher) 183
Erie Canal, at Albany (Wood) 218
Erie Canal, at Albany (Liverpool pitcher) 222
Erie Canal, at Little Falls (Wood) 218
Erie Canal, at Little Falls, horses on tow-path (Jackson) . 222
Erie Canal, at Rochester, Aqueduct Bridge (Wood) . . . 215
Erie Canal, at Rochester, Aqueduct Bridge (vegetable dish)
    (Stevenson) 215
Erie Canal, DeWitt Clinton Eulogy (unknown maker) . . 219
Erie Canal, Utica Inscription (unknown maker) . . . 219
"Escape of the Mouse," Wilkie (Clews) 287

ALPHABETICAL LIST OF ILLUSTRATIONS

FACING
PAGE

Fort Hamilton, New York (Godwin) 43
Franklin, Bennington Toby 166
Franklin, Benjamin, Fur-cap portrait (from "Anglo-American Pottery") 162
Franklin, Benjamin, "Maxims"—"Constant dropping wears away stones" 167
Franklin, Benjamin, "Handle your tools without mittens, etc." 167
Franklin, Benjamin, "He that by the plough would thrive, etc." 166
Franklin, Benjamin, "He who lives upon Hope will die fasting" 167
Franklin, Benjamin, "Keep thy shop & thy shop will keep thee" 167
Franklin, Benjamin, "Not to oversee workmen is to leave them, etc." 167
Franklin, Benjamin, "Three removes are as bad as a fire, etc." 167
Franklin, Benjamin, "Morals"—"Flowers that never fade" —"Good Humor" 162
Franklin, Benjamin, "Many a little makes a mickle" . . . 163
Franklin, Benjamin, "No Gains without Pains" 163
Franklin, Benjamin, "Poor Richard's Way to Wealth," Maxims: "Now I have a sheep & a cow, etc." . . . 168
Franklin, Benjamin, "What maintains one vice would bring up two children, etc." 168
Franklin, Benjamin, "Success to the plow, etc.". . . . 169
Franklin, Benjamin, "Handle your tools without gloves, etc." 169
"Fulton" steamboat 228
Fulton's Steamboat passing West Point (Leeds teapot) . . 236

Gilpin's Mills (Wood) 139
" Guerrière" bound for Russia (Liverpool pitcher) . . . 178

Hartford, Deaf & Dumb Institute (Ridgway) 203
Harvard College, Buildings (E. W. & S.) 31
Harvard College, Campus and Halls (E. W. & S.) . . . 25
Harvard College, University Hall (R. S. W.) In the author's collection 22
Harvard College, University Hall, Built 1815 (R. S. W. or R. S. & W.) 31
Hoboken, N. J., Stevens Mansion (Stubbs) 228
Hudson, View on the (Clews) 16
Hull, Commodore (bust portrait) 182

ALPHABETICAL LIST OF ILLUSTRATIONS

FACING
PAGE

Jefferson, Lafayette, Clinton, portraits in Vegetable dish
(Stevenson) 214
Juniata, Headwaters of (Adams) 11

Lafayette, as he appeared in 1824 (Erie Canal) (Stevenson) 196
Lafayette, at the Tomb of Franklin (Wood) 203
Lafayette, at the Tomb of Washington (Wood) 197
Lafayette, crowned at Yorktown (luster pitcher) 208
Lafayette, Landing of, at Castle Garden (Clews) 202
Lafayette, "The Nation's Guest" (portrait pitcher) . . . 208
La Grange, Lafayette's Home in France (E. W. & S.) . . 192
La Grange, East View (E. W. & S.) 197
Lake George (Wood) . . . . *Introduction*
Lexington, Kentucky, Transylvania University (Wood)
Introduction
Little Falls at Luzerne, Hudson River (Clews) . *Introduction*
Log Cabin (Ridgway) 10
Louis XVI and Franklin, Treaty Statuette (From "China
Collecting in America," by Alice Morse Earle; copy-
right, 1892, by Charles Scribner's Sons) 158
Louisville, Ky., Marine Hospital (Wood) . . . *Introduction*

Macdonough's Victory on Lake Champlain (Liverpool
pitcher) 187
Madison, War President (Liverpool portrait) 179
Marks on pottery 271
Mohawk & Hudson River R. R. (C. C.) 240
Montmorenci, Falls of (Wood) 7

New Haven, Yale College and State House (unknown maker) 10
"New Style" travel (English pitcher) 237
New York, Almshouse (Ridgway) 67
New York, Battery Walk (Wood) 47
New York, City Hall (Ridgway) 66
New York, City Hotel (Stevenson) 62
New York, Church in Murray St. (A. Stevenson) . . . 63
New York, Commons, American Museum (Stevenson) . . 66
New York. Esplanade (R. S.) 59
New York, Flagstaff Pavilion (R. S.) 58
New York, Fort Clinton (Wood) 58
New York from Brooklyn Heights (A. Stevenson) . . . 46
New York from Weehawk (A. Stevenson) 52

ALPHABETICAL LIST OF ILLUSTRATIONS

FACING
PAGE

New York, Merchant's Exchange, Ruins of (unknown maker) 43
New York, Park Theater (R. S. W.) 53
New York, St. Patrick's Cathedral (unknown maker) . . 63
New York, St. Paul's Chapel (Stevenson) 62
Niagara Falls (Adams) 17
Niagara Falls (Wood) 19
Niagara Falls, Table Rock (Wood) 15

"Old Style" Travel (English pitcher) 237

Penn's Treaty with Indians (T. G.) 119
Penn's Treaty with Indians (platter scene) (T. G.) . . . 119
Perry, Commodore, "Hero of the Lake" (portrait pitcher from "Anglo-American Pottery") 177
Perry, Memorial, Temple of Fame (Stevenson) (from "Anglo-American Pottery") 188
Perry's Victory on Lake Erie (Liverpool pitcher) . . . 172
Philadelphia, Bank of the United States (Stubbs) . . . 75
Philadelphia, Dam & Waterworks (side-wheel steamboat) . 75
Philadelphia, Dam & Waterworks (stern-wheel steamboat) . 229
Philadelphia, "Faire Mount" (Stubbs) 74
Philadelphia, Library (Ridgway) 78
Philadelphia, Mendenhall Ferry (Stubbs) 85
Philadelphia, Pennsylvania Hospital (Ridgway) 71
Philadelphia, Staughton's Church (Ridgway) 74
Philadelphia, Upper Ferry Bridge (Stubbs) 79
Philadelphia, United States Hotel (Tams) 84
Philadelphia, Waterworks Pumping Station (Jackson) . . 78
Pike, General (bust portrait) 182
Pilgrims, Landing of, pitcher (Wood) 107
Pilgrims, Landing of, plate (Wood) 107
Pittsburgh, "Pennsylvania" steamboat (Clews) 225
Pittsburgh, Pa. Primitive craft (Clews) . . . *Introduction*
Pittsfield, Winter View of (Clews) 18
Preble, Commodore, Attacking Tripoli (Liverpool pitcher) . 186
Presidential China, George Washington 248
Presidential China, John Adams 248
Presidential China, Thomas Jefferson 249
Presidential China, James Madison 249
Presidential China, James Monroe 250
Presidential China, John Quincy Adams 250
Presidential China, Andrew Jackson 251

ALPHABETICAL LIST OF ILLUSTRATIONS

FACING
PAGE

Presidential China, John Tyler 252
Presidential China, James K. Polk 252
Presidential China, Franklin Pierce 253
Presidential China, Abraham Lincoln 253
Presidential China, Ulysses S. Grant 256
Presidential China, Rutherford B. Hayes 256
Presidential China, James A. Garfield 257
Presidential China, Chester A. Arthur 257
Presidential China, Grover Cleveland 264
Presidential China, Benjamin Harrison 264
Presidential China, William McKinley 265
Presidential China, Theodore Roosevelt 245

Quebec (unknown maker) 6

Sailor Pitcher: "May they ever be United" 176
Sailor Pitcher: "The Sailor's Return" 176
Sailor Pitcher: "The True Blooded Yankee" 178
Seal of the United States (front of pitcher) 127
Seal of the United States, adaptation of 154
Seal of the United States, adaptation of, "America" . . 154
Shannondale Springs, Va. (Jackson) . . . . *Introduction*
"States" design (Clews) 94
Stonington, Conn., "Defense of" (Liverpool pitcher) . . . 186

Troy, Hudson river (Clews) 11

"Union Line," steamboat (Wood) 232

Washington, D. C., Capitol (Ridgway) . . . *Frontispiece*
Washington, D. C., early view of Capitol (Wood) . . . 99
Washington, D. C., Plan of city (Liverpool pitcher) . . 98
Washington, D. C., President's House (Jackson) . . 98
Washington, D. C., site of (unknown maker) 99
Washington, Lafayette, Jefferson, Clinton (Dutch Church at
    Albany, cover) (Stevenson) 6
Washington, George, "Map" portrait pitcher 3
Washington, George, portrait on Erie Canal dish . . . 134
Washington, George (scroll in hand) 130
Washington, George, Stuart portrait 126
Washington, George, portrait festooned with names of 15
    states 126
Washington, George, portrait, "Honor the Brave, etc." . . 130

ALPHABETICAL LIST OF ILLUSTRATIONS

FACING
PAGE

Washington, George, Portrait on Monument 131
Washington, George, "Washington in Glory; America in
    Tears" 127
Washington, George, on lawn at Mount Vernon 134
Washington, Martha, "States" plate 124
"Wasp & Frolic" (Liverpool pitcher) 183
West Point Military School (Adams) 137
Willow Pattern 286

Yorktown, Surrender at (luster pitcher) 138

PINE ORCHARD HOUSE IN THE CATSKILLS
(*Enoch Wood*)

PENITENTIARY AT ALLEGHENY, NEAR PITTSBURGH, PA.
(*Clews*, "Picturesque Views")

A NOTE TO THE READER

This book does not undertake to cover with thoroughness the entire field of blue china, for interest in the collecting of pottery, like to that in the gathering together of other groups of objects, is at the present time, with rare exceptions, many-sided and highly specialized. Each collector has his particular viewpoint, his own choice of objects of the chase. One person, for example, may select his specimens with an eye to a display of the work peculiar to several countries; another may confine his fancy to the output of one nation alone; still another may make pastes, glazes, or decorative motifs, his study; while perhaps the largest number will, like Charles Lamb and Horace Walpole, yield to the fascinating lure for the simple reason that "china's the passion of their souls," and will secure whatever pieces opportunity brings to hand.

The author of the present volume has confined her interest not only to "Blue China," as the title suggests, but to the particular wares known to collectors as Staffordshire historical pottery. And this interest has been further specialized upon the history and topography of America. For, in the process of forming a collection, the fact was discovered that this group of English pottery is not only a valuable record of the American country and cities as they appeared a century ago, but it is at the same time a surprisingly complete history of the first three centuries of our national life. Supplementing

these annals, there is presented in this volume an illustrated chapter describing the tableware which was used
from the earliest times in the Executive Mansion at
Washington, by our presidents and their families, together with a brief story of the Mansion itself. And,
for the benefit of the collector, the Checking List of
American Views compiled by Dr. Edwin Atlee Barber,
together with a short explanation of the Staffordshire
potters' marks, is included.

There are, in addition, outside of the historical views
which make up the main body of this volume, other important groups of prints that are of concern to the general collector of Staffordshire wares, for example, the
Dr. Syntax, the Don Quixote, the Sir David Wilkie, and
the ever-interesting Willow Pattern, series. For those
whose collections may embrace specimens of these designs, a third Supplementary Chapter will be found, devoted to a short exposition of their stories. Another
large and attractive group of prints of which mention
should be made, as it claims the attention of certain
American collectors, is that portraying Scriptural subjects. Specimens of these illustrations were put out by
nearly all of the prominent Staffordshire potters of the
period under consideration, and Dr. Barber enumerates
more than 60 titles of this class. The borders vary
with the potter, and the colors range from the familiar
deep blue through the paler shades of the later Staffordshire period.

Still other fields remain for the American collector of
old Staffordshire. One of them includes views of countries other than the United States and Canada, for at

the same time that English artists were sent to these shores for sketches, many beautiful views of English castles, cathedrals, and other important buildings in their own island, were adopted by the potters.   Foreign fields were likewise visited for decorative material— Italy, France, India, even the "Gold Coast of Africa," contributing to the demand.   Masonic emblems or current political cartoons as decorations make an appeal to some collectors, old-copper- and silver-luster tea-sets form charming displays, while Liverpool pitchers and Toby-jugs, or the quaint mantel-ornaments of Staffordshire manufacture, such as dogs, bears, cows, peasant-figures, flower-festooned cottages, etc., etc., have a distinct charm and fascination for the old-china lover.

ADA WALKER CAMEHL.

PITTSBURGH, PA.
Primitive Craft on River
(*Clews*, "Picturesque Views")

SHANNONDALE SPRINGS, VIRGINIA
(*Jackson*)

PART I

THE COUNTRY AND THE CITIES OF EARLY AMERICA

WASHINGTON AND FRANKLIN EXAMINING A MAP OF
THE UNITED STATES
("Map" Pitcher)

THE BLUE-CHINA BOOK

CHAPTER I

A TOUR OF THE LAND

"I CAN never tire my eyes in looking at such lovely vegetation, so different from ours . . . the herbage like April in Andalusia . . . the trees are as unlike ours as night from day, as are the fruits, the herbs, the stones, and everything, . . . and I feel the most unhappy man in the world not to know them. The mountains and islands seem to be second to none in the world; . . . there is much gold, the Indians wear it as bracelets on the arms, on the legs, in the ears and nose, and round the neck, . . . flocks of parrots conceal the sun." These are among the expressions with which Columbus sought to make known to the Spanish sovereigns the beauty, the richness, and the strangeness of the land he had taken possession of in their name. Americus Vespucius, who visited the new world a few years later than Columbus, and whose name by strange chance remained with it, noted its "altogether delightful" climate, its many hills, lakes, rivers and forests, as well as the various species of wild animals and the numerous parrots with which it abounded, together with the gold which the natives told him was so abundant it was little esteemed. "In short," he concludes his narrative, "if there is an earthly paradise in the world, without doubt it must be not far from this place."

True to these conceptions of primitive America, which long continued to color the imaginations of Europeans, are the fanciful scenes (illustrated in a later chapter) wherewith the Staffordshire potters sought to picture pioneer incidents of American history. In them, unfamiliar trees and shrubs are introduced, together with Indians gowned in paint and feathers and adorned with golden ornaments, against backgrounds of imaginary forest or mountain scenery. Parrots appear in a border device, another border presenting flowers and animals supposed to be native to the little known wilderness regions.

With the passing of the years and the increase of ocean travel, a truer and somewhat more extended knowledge of the new world became diffused throughout the countries of Europe. Many people, for one cause or another of discontent, abandoned their homes in order to adventure others in America; until the seventeenth century saw the Atlantic seacoast from Canada to Florida dotted with Old-World settlements. French adventurers and missionaries came into the region of the

Saint Lawrence River; English Puritans settled the
shores of Massachusetts Bay; traders from Holland
made homes upon Manhattan Island; English planters
sought the fertile hillsides of Virginia; and Spain sent
her knights to Florida in quest of the Fountain of
Eternal Youth.

Land companies sprang up in Europe, whose business
it was to exploit their broad, and oft-times vague, American acres, and to direct to them departing groups of emi-
grants. But even after the political independence of the
new country had been achieved, ignorance of the conditions there to be met with continued widespread. A
curious French volume of the year 1803, entitled, "The
Pros and Cons, or Advice for Those who Intend to go to
the United States of America, Followed by a description of Kentucky and Genesee, two of the most important settlements of the New World," was written, the
author states, to aid intending settlers, "all of whom lack
definite directions." "The United States of America,"
he begins, "are not yet entirely cultivated, centuries will
probably roll away before they will be." He then proceeds to divide the territory into three regions. The
first, nearest to the cities and the coast, is best cultivated, "with farms so close together that it seems a continuous village"; the second, as one goes into the interior,
is less cultivated, with villages small and far apart, "a
saw mill and a flour mill and a few houses there form-

ing an important settlement." To the west of these regions he recounts a third—a wilderness of forest and stream recently inhabited by savage tribes who have "now departed to the Great Lakes and the immense River of Mississippi," beyond which the author's knowledge, or imagination, does not venture to stray. He recites the advantages of the many rivers—the Hudson, carrying the products of New York State to the seaboard; the Delaware, bearing its "multitude of vessels" laden with the wealth of Pennsylvania to the cities at its mouth; the Ohio, entering the Mississippi with the produce of Kentucky to exchange for "the piastres of the Spaniards" at New Orleans. The "Endless Mountains" (Alleghany range), he states, divide the United States into two natural parts and are its backbone, even as the Apennines are of Italy. The East is more populous, and the West is where the new settlements are located—one of these settlements being toward the south, "at the rear of Virginia," and called Kentucky; the other, toward the north, "at the rear of Pennsylvania," and known as the Genesee country (then controlled by the Holland Land Company). The cession of Louisiana to France by Spain, he declares, has much alarmed the United States by threatening to cut off the navigation of the Ohio River. He closes his interesting volume with a *Salve* to the great rivers and lakes of the New World, and the hope for those who betake themselves

CITY OF QUEBEC
(*Unknown Maker*)

DUTCH CHURCH AT ALBANY,
1715–1806

MEDALLION HEADS ON
COVER IN COMMEMORA-
TION OF ERIE CANAL

(*Stevenson*)

FALLS OF MONTMORENCI, NEAR QUEBEC
(*Wood*)

thither, "May they leave in Europe their vices and their misery and carry with them only their virtues."

Maps of the United States were outlined for the further convenience of prospective settlers, and as this was the period when English potters were utilizing American subjects for decoration, one of them was printed upon a set of Liverpool pitchers. The design presents an oval framing the section of the world then known as the new Republic of the United States. The Atlantic coast, though heavily lined, is uncertain in detail, and names of cities and towns are thickly printed against it. The northernmost region is Canada, bounded by the chain of the Great Lakes. A number of States are designated, and the indefinite region to the west stretching from Canada on the north to the Gulf of Mexico in the south is marked "Louisiana." "Liberty," of course, is present, in the form of her contemporary European prototype—a female figure holding aloft a pointed cap. She is here represented calling the attention of George Washington to the map, the first President standing by her side with the inevitable scroll, presumably the Declaration of Independence, in his hand; while Fame floats above them upon a cloud, bearing a wreath marked "Washington," and trumpeting his glory to the world. Benjamin Franklin, who assisted in the achievement of independence and who, like Washington, was a well-known figure in Europe, is seated upon the opposite side of the map, an open book in his hand and History, personified as a woman, behind his chair. A detail of historic interest is the pine-tree flag displaying upon its starry field the newly chosen Seal of the Republic, both flag and seal being described in a later chapter.

So thoroughly did the early nineteenth-century artists perform their task of securing sketches of American scenery for reproduction upon Staffordshire pottery, that it is quite possible by means of the decorations (a small number only of which are presented in this and the preceding chapter) to enable the student of our early history to make a fairly complete tour of the land, and to look upon it as it appeared a century ago. Starting at the northernmost extremity of the country as it is portrayed upon the map pitcher, the city of Quebec is first displayed upon a plate, seated, as at the present day, upon her mighty citadel of rock, the original Lower Town of her French founder, Champlain, huddled at the cliff's base and washed by the broad Saint Lawrence River. A yellow jug of Liverpool manufacture pictures an imaginary death-scene of the British General Wolfe who, in the year 1759, having successfully scaled the rock, expired upon the Plains of Abraham at the moment of the victory of his troops over the French—the battle which gave Quebec into the hands of the English. One artist went out to the far-famed falls of Montmorenci, a few miles above Quebec, and in his sketch one looks upon the imposing cataract as it appeared before its volume had been reduced, by mechanical use, to the trickling stream which meets the eye of the visitor of to-day.

Passing southward, the mountain ranges, country roadways, and log houses of primitive New Hampshire, Vermont and Massachusetts, are displayed in a variety of sketches; a fort in Rhode Island is pictured; while a separate chapter records the appearance of the city of Boston. Examining the beautiful Pittsfield platter-scene, the beholder pauses to learn its story. In Revolutionary times, it is recorded, a primitive Meeting House stood upon the site of the white church facing the Common, whose pastor was the Reverend Thomas Allen, an ardent patriot who had served as chaplain to the American army under Washington. Upon the Sabbath morning following his return to Pittsfield (so the story goes), Parson Allen entered his pulpit, clad in Continental uniform concealed beneath his gown. He began his sermon, but his zeal for his country's cause becoming so overpowering he soon threw aside his robe and displayed himself to his people in army uniform. He stepped down from his pulpit and led the men of the congregation to the Common in front of the church, and under the elm tree he formed them into the first detachment of Berkshire Minutemen. The elm became therefrom one of the historic trees of America; "from

Greylock to Monument Mountain," the saying ran, there being no inanimate thing "so revered and venerable." The tree may be seen in the illustration as it appeared about the year 1825, after a fence had been built around it to preserve it from destruction as a hitching post for horses. In 1861, it was felled by a lightning stroke and its sound wood was made into souvenirs; at the present time, in the center of the beautiful, elm-shaded park of the city of Pittsfield, a sun-dial erected by the Daughters of the American Revolution marks the historic spot where the old elm stood. To the right of the white church, which is the First Congregational edifice, the illustration presents the old Town Hall, and at its left the First Baptist Church, with the Berkshire Hotel by its side.

A view of the town square of New Haven, Connecticut, printed in the lighter colors of a later period of Staffordshire potting, exhibits Yale College, together with the Connecticut State House. In contrast to the interest displayed by the old-time artists in the halls of Harvard which resulted in numerous pottery souvenirs, Yale College, though second only to the Boston institution in age, appears in few decorations only, the work of less important potters.

The Hudson River affords a delightful imaginary excursion possible to be made by means of the many illustrations of its beauties which exist upon pottery,

YALE BUILDINGS—STATE HOUSE, NEW HAVEN
(*Unknown Maker*)

LOG CABIN
W. H. Harrison Campaign
(*J. Ridgway*)

HEADWATERS OF THE JUNIATA RIVER, PA.
(*W. Adams & Sons*)

TROY ON THE HUDSON
(*Clews*, "Picturesque Views")

delightful by reason of the scenery and historical associations, as well as for the presence, rare in our land, of the legendary folk who people its banks. One English potter, James Clews, decorated a set of plates in various colors with views copied from water color sketches of Hudson River scenery painted by W. G. Wall and reproduced in England in a volume called "The Hudson River Portfolio." Upon the back of each plate, printed in a scroll, is the legend, "Picturesque Views of the Hudson River." The border of the series, a spray of rose branches with parrots perched upon them, is one of the most graceful to be found. It is of interest to know that in the year 1836, some time after these plates were printed, James Clews came to the United States and engaged in potting in Indiana, but being unsuccessful he remained but a short time and returned to end his days in England. Enoch Wood also printed a series of Hudson River views in deep blue color, with his famous sea-shell border.

Setting out from New York, the illustrations of which another chapter presents, the first view in the Hudson River series is of West Point. High on a plateau above the river and crowned with lofty mountain peaks, may be seen the small group of buildings which was the nucleus of the present Military Academy, founded in 1802. Newburgh is portrayed as a small village on the river bank, appearing no doubt as it did on the evening when General Lafayette stepped ashore on his famous visit in 1824, and was driven through its muddy, torch-lighted streets to the Orange Hotel where impatient guests awaited his tardy arrival. One may possibly discover in the picture the balcony upon which the French General presented himself in order to quell the tumult of the crowds below.

The traveler presently enters the enchanted region of the Catskills, the legendary abode of the ancient squaw whose duty it is forever to open the doors of day and night, to hang up new moons in the sky, and to cut the old ones into stars. In these oft-pictured wilderness heights dwells Manitou, the great Indian Spirit, who in the form of a bear was wont to lead the redmen a chase through the forests—and hark! Is not the vague rumbling sound reverberating through the valleys the echo of the ninepins of Hendrick Hudson and his somber crew? A famous inn situated high in the mountains, Pine Orchard House, gleams white against the dusky pines, as one continues up the river, and here and there along the banks picturesque mills and villages and mountain passes are, by means of the illustrations, opened to his view.

Albany, the oldest city in the Union, boasts a state Capitol, fine churches, and a harbor filled with busy shipping; one decoration shows a passage to the city from the islands made in a ferry boat called a "horse's back," carrying both animals and men. Albany at the period of the imaginary tour has a population of about 16,000 people, and is one of the most important commercial cities in the United States, all western produce entering by way of the newly-built Erie Canal, and shipped thence to eastern ports, twenty-four steamboats plying the river between Albany and New York. A covered vegetable dish, whose medallion portraits of the four men whom the English potters commonly associated with the Erie Canal place it among the memorials of that enterprise, presents upon the surface of its interior the Dutch church of Albany, one of the seven churches of the country to be perpetuated in pottery decoration. The original edifice was erected in the year 1652, a second in 1655, around which the walls of the third structure, here shown, were carried up and enclosed without disturbing the old edifice. This illustration is of importance as presenting one of the earliest types of church building in America, its square proportions and its pyramidal roof topped with a belfry contrasting with the rectangular bodies and tall slender spires which characterize many of the later models. This structure resembles in its outlines the "Old Ship Meeting House," a co-temporary which still stands at Hingham, Massachusetts. The interior of the Albany church was gayly painted and ornamented, with a pulpit of polished Dutch oak. Low galleries, to which the

13

men were relegated, lined three sides of the interior, and a bell rope hung down in the center aisle which when not in use was wound round a post set in the center for the purpose. Rich stained glass windows displayed the arms of eminent Dutch families, members of whom were accustomed to bring hot bricks or portable stoves to keep their feet warm during the long winter service, the men sitting with hats on their heads and their hands in muffs. Deacons went around with collection bags on the end of long poles, to which little bells were attached, their tinkling arousing any sleepers and preventing drowsiness from being an excuse for failure to contribute. The structure was demolished in 1806, much of the material being put into the Second Dutch Reformed Church.

When in the year 1824, Lafayette looked upon the town of Troy with its 8,000 inhabitants, appearing much as it is pictured upon the plate, he exclaimed in astonishment, "What! Has this city risen from the earth by enchantment!" For here it was that he, in Revolutionary times, with difficulty could find a cup of milk and a bit of Indian bread at the two or three humble cabins which then composed the settlement. The northernmost of the Hudson River series of sketches presents the village of Luzerne, among the Adirondacks near the river's source, while, continuing northward,

CITY OF ALBANY
(*Wood*)

TABLE ROCK, NIAGARA FALLS
(*Wood*)

PRIMITIVE FERRY AT ALBANY
RENSSELAER ISLAND
(*Unknown Maker*)

A TOUR OF THE LAND

Lake George may be seen—a shining mirror framed in wooded hills.

Several charming bits of New Jersey and Pennsylvania river and mountain scenery may be seen upon specimens of old pottery. The Falls of Passaic, on a sugar bowl, were famous for their beauty a century ago; very lovely, too, is the view of the headwaters of the Juniata River, the stream which flows so peacefully through southern Pennsylvania. In the distance rise the rugged peaks of the "Endless Mountains," in the foreground may be seen the trees and flowers native to the region—and, may not the tourist with bundle slung over shoulder, crossing the rustic bridge, be the very traveler from England who, struck with the charm of the spot, set down his burden for awhile and added this scene to his sketch book? Pittsburgh is presented as a row of low buildings bordering the banks at the confluence of the Monongahela and Allegheny rivers, with two primitive vessels sailing past the town. In the nearby village of Allegheny is the Penitentiary, an imposing structure for so early a date. When Lafayette visited Pittsburgh, about the time these pictures were made, it had a population of 8,000 and the French party were much interested in examining the manufacturing plants for which Pittsburgh was already famous. Among the objects presented to Lafayette were some mirrors made in this city which he declared equal to any produced in France. Continuing southward, Virginia landscapes of rolling hills and substantial plantation homes are spread out to view, while the attractions of the cities of Baltimore and Washington are set forth in separate chapters.

Before the days of railroads, few tourists made the long and difficult and oft-times dangerous journey into the sparsely settled regions of the far South and West, sections now known as the States of North Carolina, South Carolina, Georgia, Louisiana, Michigan, Kentucky, and the valleys of the Ohio and Mississippi rivers; for this reason, a less number of pictured views of these localities are to be found. The cities of Richmond, Charleston, Savannah, New Orleans, Columbus, and Sandusky are exhibited in the old-china records by one or two views each. Detroit, no doubt, appears here as it did during the exciting period of the War of 1812, when the city was one of the disputed battle-grounds upon the western frontier. Its houses, as may be noted, faced the river, and, for the purpose of mutual protection, they were set close together in well ordered rows, their farm lands, like the tails of Bo-Peep's sheep, "behind them." The several examples of sailing craft pictured in Detroit harbor, one of them a newly invented stern-wheeler, are also of interest. Louisville, Kentucky, offers to view a substantial stone structure—the

VIEW ON THE HUDSON
(*Clews*, "Picturesque Views")

NIAGARA FALLS
(*W. Adams & Sons*)

A TOUR OF THE LAND

Marine Hospital, a government home for those who sailed the inland rivers and lakes; while Lexington, in the same State, boasts Transylvania University, erected in 1783, the first institution for learning west of the Alleghanies, from whose halls, the French author already quoted gravely asserts, a printing press sent out each week a gazette "to even the most distant farms with all the news of both the Old and the New World."

Beyond the Mississippi lies, at the period of this imaginary tour, the unknown—a region of vast extent and vague knowledge, called Louisiana, a region of mystery wherein fancy pictured limitless plains crossed by rushing floods and peopled by savage Indian tribes. The geographers of the day taught that the Mississippi separated Louisiana "from the United States and West Florida" on the east, its western boundary being New Mexico and "a ridge of mountains generally denominated the Shining Mountains, which divide the western waters of the Mississippi from those that flow into the Pacific Ocean." Not until the discovery of California gold in 1849, and the consequent tide of humanity toward it, was the region of the literally shining mountains opened to the general knowledge of the world.

The imaginary Tour of Colonial America, conducted by means of contemporary pottery, comes to an end at the most celebrated spot upon the continent—Niagara Falls. To look upon the "great Cataract of Niagara" was the ambition of every early European traveler to America, and for centuries the journey thither was the world's "grand tour." First reports of this wonderful fall of water came from the Indians who, in the early part of the seventeenth century, told Champlain and the Huron missionaries of a great body of water which "fell from a rock higher than the tallest pine trees." A few years later, French officers stationed at Fort Niagara made sketches of the Falls and carried them to Europe, together with tales of the grandeur of the spectacle hidden in the wilds of this new country. Eager tourists, fired by the accounts, came over to see the wonder, walking all the way from Boston or New York, or driving over almost impassable roads. Each gazer upon the spectacle felt called upon to record his impressions, and many and varied are the emotions chronicled; to some, the sight is an "ode" or a "rhapsody"; for others, its influence depresses the spirits. One tourist is disappointed because he is not, as he expected, met by a "vision of foam and fury and dizzy cliffs, and the ocean tumbling down out of the sky." A practical English captain, whose mind was probably filled with the new ideas of steam-power, longed to carry the Falls to Italy, pour their volume into the crater of Vesuvius, and thus "create the largest steam boiler that ever entered into the imagination of man!" Lafayette, as he looked upon the cataract, re-

PITTSFIELD, MASS.
Historic Elm
(*Clews*)

NIAGARA FALLS, FROM AMERICAN SIDE

(*Wood*)

gretted that their distance from his estate in France prevented his buying them.

Many tourists ventured out upon the broad flat rock which overhung the Horseshoe Fall, the celebrated Table Rock, the sketch being of special interest as the rock no longer stands. Table Rock was an excellent point from which to view the Falls, from it one being also able to gaze down into the brilliant green flood directly underneath him. At noonday, on June 25, 1850, the great Rock fell. The driver of an omnibus driving out upon the rock to wash his vehicle, had unhitched his horses and was at work, when of a sudden he heard the rock upon which he was standing give a loud cracking sound. No sooner had he led his horses to the land than the huge mass went down, carrying his empty omnibus with it into the gulf below.

Niagara Falls has been called the most pictured subject in the world, and the Niagara of Art equals in interest and variety the literary expressions it inspired. The first Niagara picture was drawn as early as 1697, from a description of it given by Father Hennepin, a French missionary who accompanied La Salle upon his expedition into the Niagara region. In this picture the English artist in imagination looks down upon the Falls and sees the river bordered with mountains all the way to Lake Erie. Three falls of water appear, Goat Island is but a slender pillar of rock, and from the banks and the island rise curious tropical trees. This old copper plate engraving was for many years the only Niagara picture, and from it the untraveled world gained its knowledge of the wonder. The Hennepin picture was many times copied, and each succeeding artist, who had never seen the Falls, added touches according to his fancy—a colony of busy beavers in the foreground gnawing down trees, or a band of redmen chasing bison across the stream below the Falls. A richer imagination put in Elijah emerging in a chariot of fire from the clouds above the cataract. Occasionally three distinct falls of water are found in an old print, the sharp bend in the Horseshoe Fall being difficult for the unskilled artist to depict. Not until nearly a century later than Father Hennepin's picture did the world possess, in drawings from the original, a more exact Niagara.

The Niagara of the early sketches is the Niagara of the Staffordshire potters, two of whose views are presented. In the first picture one seems to be looking upon the rushing flood from a point on the American side above the Falls. Three distinct cascades are visible, the familiar expanse of Goat Island has shrunk to a tree-crowned rock, and—can it be? Yes, there stand the pioneer Niagara Falls bridal couple!—the first of the long series of newly wed whose descendants still haunt the witching scenes about this mighty cataract. The bridegroom is pointing with his walking stick into the chasm, evidently explaining the mysteries of the swirling torrent to the wondering mind of his bride, who stands meekly by his side arrayed in shawl and poke bonnet—glass of early nineteenth century fashion! The second view of the Niagara spectacle is more fanciful than the first, and is no doubt a composition made from old prints by one who had never seen the original. In this scene the eye is carried up the gorge to the curve of the Horseshoe Fall; Goat Island and the American Fall are quite insignificant; and peculiar semi-tropical trees and foliage conceal from view the rugged banks with which our eyes are familiar.

CHAPTER II

IT has been said that in order to understand America of the present one must know Boston of the Fathers, and by what more delightful means may one acquire a knowledge of early Boston than from a study of the pictured china handed down from the Fathers themselves? For, upon the blue plates and platters, tea-pots and cream jugs which once graced the tables of our New England forefathers, the greater part of the early city is spread out to view—the harbor; the streets and the Common; the State House and the Court House in which the Fathers made the laws; several of the mansions in which they dwelt, and two of the churches in which they worshiped; the warehouses of commerce; the Hospital and Almshouse for retreat in illness and poverty, and the pleasure resort of leisure hours; finally, the Library and College which bred and fostered that leadership in letters upon which the citizens of Boston long justly plumed themselves.

Boston was settled by some of the earliest homemakers to come to the American shores. About the year 1634, John Winthrop being Governor of Massachusetts Col-

RARE VIEW OF UNIVERSITY HALL, HARVARD COLLEGE
(*R. S. W.*)
(In the collection of the Author)

POTTER'S MARK ON BACK WITH WRONG
TITLE

ony, the settlers upon the shores of the Bay purchased of William Blackstone, the hermit who lived on the sunny slope of one of the three hills which bordered the Bay, his estate "lying within the said Neck called Boston," every inhabitant agreeing to pay six shillings, "none less and some more." This sum was collected and paid to Mr. Blackstone, "to his full satisfaction for his whole right, reserving only about six acres on the point commonly called Blackstone's Point, on part whereof his then dwelling house stood." Two views present Boston harbor as it appeared nearly two centuries after the original purchase, sketches made from the heights of Dorchester and Chelsea. In them may be seen the Bay and shores in a very primitive condition. In the Chelsea view is the bridge which connected that township with the main city, spanning "the River that renders their attendance on Town-Meetings very difficult," as the preamble of the Act of Separation of Chelsea from Boston in the year 1737 reads, adding, "and whereas they have a long time since erected a Meeting House in that District." Sailing craft rest upon the water, and in the distance may be dimly discerned the three hills (now but a memory) which gave the settlement its original name, Tri-Mountain, an echo of which lingers still in "Tremont" Street. Above the summit of the center hill, named Beacon, soars the dome of the new State House, while the spires of numerous churches tower above the housetops. A group of early Bostonians occupy the foreground of the picture, gowned in the fashion of the early nineteenth century, a style of dress which prevails in all of the old-china prints.

Early Boston fringed the harbor, the western limit of the city until after the Revolution being the foot of the Common on the margin of the Back Bay; Boylston Street was "Frog Pond" well into the nineteenth century; and, until after the Revolutionary War, the western reach of Beacon Hill was but a place of pasture for cows, whereon the barberry and the wild rose grew at will. In early nineteenth-century years, Boston numbered between fifty and eighty thousand inhabitants and was a city eminently English in character and appearance, although after independence had been declared an attempt had been made to efface the hated British stamp by changing the names of some of the streets—King and Queen, for instance, to State and Court. But symbols over shop doors still reflected London, taverns bore the signs of famous London inns, and even to this day some obscure court or alley may be found clinging to its first London-flavored name.

Unique among the features of American cities is Boston Common, a spacious park in the heart of the business and shopping district. The Common was a portion of the estate purchased of William Blackstone, laid out for use, old chronicles record, as "a training field and the

BOSTON FROM CHELSEA HEIGHTS, 1848

(*C.C.*)

HARVARD CAMPUS AND HALLS
(*E. W. & S.*)

feeding of cattle." The chronicle also states that all persons admitted to inhabit Boston were "to have equal rights of Commonage, others not unless they inherit it." It was further ordered that but seventy "milch kine" might be kept on the Common, but that "Elder Oliver's horse may go there," and that a fine be imposed for any cow or horse except the seventy "if found upon ye Neck." A delightful letter written by an English visitor to Boston in the year 1740 gives a picture not only of the Common, but also of the habits and customs of early Bostonians. He says: "For their domestic amusement, every afternoon after drinking tea, the gentlemen and ladies walk the Mall, and from thence adjourn to one another's houses to spend the evening—those that are not disposed to attend the evening lectures, which they may do, if they please, six nights in seven the year round. What they call the Mall is a walk on a fine green Common adjoining to the southwest side of the Town. It is near half a mile over, with two rows of young trees planted opposite to each other, with a fine footway between in imitation of St. James's Park; and part of the bay of the sea which encircles the Town, taking its course along the northwest side of the Common—by which it is bounded on the one side, and by the country on the other—forms a beautiful canal in view of the walk."

Upon the Common, in Colonial times, the British troops set up camps and reviewed, the uneven surface of the ground where they dug their cellars and pitched their tents being still visible at the time the present sketch of the Common was made, probably about the year 1820. Upon the Common, for two hundred and fifty years, the famous Liberty Elm stood, from whose limbs, old records say, witches were tortured, Quakers hung, and, in Revolutionary times, the effigy of a hated Britsh officer sometimes dangled. Upon the Common, on the eve of April 16, 1775, the British troops assembled before marching upon Lexington and Concord; here, upon June 17 of the same year, the redcoats gathered before setting out to quell the rebellion at Bunker Hill; and later, upon this same ground, the Revolution ended and independence declared, the British army paraded under General Howe before leaving the city forever.

The "feeding of cattle" upon the Common continued long after Boston became a populous city, and as late as the year 1830 (when laws were enacted to put an end to the practice) the tinkling of cow bells and the lowing of cattle, as the animals made their way to and from the pasture ground, were pleasant and homely sounds to be heard about its hills and dales. The illustration presents several of the early Boston cows contentedly dozing in the shade of the trees, the winding paths which they have worn being, it is claimed, the original tracings of certain streets—a saying which reached the ears of the English potters and inspired the memorial of a Liverpool pitcher

BOSTON COMMON—STATE HOUSE AND DWELLINGS

(*Stubbs*)

ST. PAUL'S CHURCH, BOSTON
(*Ridgway*)

LAWRENCE MANSION, BOSTON
Near Corner Park St. and Beacon St., Facing Common—
Spire of Park St. Church Rises above Roof
(*Ralph Stevenson*)

inscribed, "Success to the Crooked but Interesting Town of Boston."

A number of interesting details of the Common and its neighborhood as it appeared a century ago may be studied in the platter decoration—the fence which was put up in 1820 to inclose Beacon Mall; the tree-bordered Mall itself along which equestrians are pictured as passing; and the newly erected mansions facing the Common upon Park and Beacon streets. Park Street had been laid out in 1802 as a dignified approach to the new State House, the street itself as well as the mansions which lined it being designed by Bulfinch, the architect of the State House and the greatest early exponent of the classic revival in American architecture. Beacon Street was originally known as "the lane which led to the Almshouse," the public home for the poor being situated upon the corner of the present Park and Beacon streets. By the side of the Almshouse stood the Bridewell and the Workhouse, and where Park Street Church stands was the city granary. These buildings had all been removed at the time the present sketch was made, the homes of Boston's Fathers occupying their sites. The house immediately at the right of the State House in the illustration was the home of Joseph Coolidge, the tall one below it, at the corner of Park and Beacon streets, being the Thomas Amory mansion which was built on the site of the old gambrel-roofed Almshouse. In later years the

Amory house was divided into four dwellings, the Hon. George Ticknor home being the part which faced the Common; in 1825 the entire mansion was rented for the use of General Lafayette and his suite. The last house at the right was for many years the home of Governor Christopher Gore, and below this stood the dwelling of Josiah Quincy, Jr. At the extreme left of the platter sketch may be seen the home of the Hon. John Phillips, father of Wendell Phillips and first mayor of Boston. By its side stands the home of Dr. John Joy, and, overtopping this, the Thomas Perkins mansion. At the left of the State House may be seen the Hancock mansion, a separate picture of which is also presented, but this view is of peculiar interest as showing the wooden wing which was added for the purpose of furnishing a more spacious apartment for the balls and receptions for which the mansion became famous.

Several of these old time Bostonians lie to-day in the burial plot in the Common before their doors.

With the passing of the years, Romance has also added its touch to the old Common, many a courtship having been carried on while strolling through its shady paths—"Whom does Arabella walk with now?" was in olden times a significant question in circles of gossiping friends or in anxious deliberations of family counsels. To-day, at the entrance to the Long Mall which starts at Beacon Street Mall and runs across the Common's length to Tre-

mont and Boylston streets, one may read the sign "Oliver
Wendell Holmes Path," a title given it from the following pretty story of the Autocrat's proposal to the schoolmistress: "We called it the long path and were fond
of it. I felt very weak indeed (though of a tolerably
robust habit) as we came opposite the head of this path
on that morning. I think I tried to speak twice without
making myself distinctly audible. At last I got out the
question, 'Will you take the long path with me?' 'Certainly,' said the schoolmistress, 'with much pleasure.'
'Think,' I said, 'before you answer; if you take the long
path with me now, I shall interpret it that we are to part
no more!' The schoolmistress stepped back with a sudden movement, as if an arrow had struck her. One of
the long granite blocks used as seats was hard by, 'Pray,
sit down,' I said. 'No, no,' she answered softly, 'I will
walk the *long path* with you.' " Reduced to-day to about
fifty acres, the old Common is regarded with something
akin to reverence by the older generation of Bostonians,
and, although from time to time encroachments have
been made upon its territory, public opinion may be
counted upon to rise in indignation at any suggestion of
radical interference with its quiet and dignified acres.

The most important building facing the Common is
the State House, once a favorite subject for the decoration of Staffordshire dinner-sets, and later, as Dr.
Holmes declared, the "hub of the entire solar system."

The State House was designed by Bulfinch on classic lines and in a style of elegance heretofore unknown in the city, its columned façade and gilded dome always distinguishing it and ranging it even at the present day among the splendid buildings of the United States. The State House was erected upon a portion of Governor Hancock's pasture lot, purchased in 1795, upon the Fourth of July of the same year, Samuel Adams laying the corner-stone and dedicating the pile forever to the "cause of liberty and the rights of man." Until quite recent years, the summit of Beacon Hill ran up behind the State House and was about even with the base of the dome; the hill has since been graded down about 80 feet and the material used for filling in the low lands of Back Bay. The gilded dome was long visible far out in the harbor and was a glorified descendant of that tiny beacon which, in primitive times, hung from a pole upon this spot and, like its prototype in the little Boston town of Old England, guided incoming mariners to port. After having been several times enlarged, Boston State House is perhaps Boston's most interesting structure, sheltering numerous relics of its historic past.

Facing Beacon Street, "the sunny street that holds the sifted few," as Dr. Holmes dubbed the aristocratic thoroughfare, for many years stood the Hancock mansion, a dwelling which acquired such wide-spread fame that it was made the subject of a separate design for china deco-

HANCOCK HOUSE, BOSTON
(*Jackson*)

BOSTON STATE HOUSE
Chaise in Foreground
(*Rogers*)

UNIVERSITY HALL, HARVARD COLLEGE
BUILT 1815
(*R. S. W. or R. S. & W.*)

HARVARD COLLEGE BUILDINGS
(*E. W. & S*)

ration.   Built in the year 1737 by Thomas Hancock, to
this home came Dorothy Quincy as the bride of his
nephew, Governor John Hancock, and here for many
years she reigned as first lady of the State.   The house
was a substantial structure, the dormer windows giving
a broad view of the city and of the harbor.   A low
stone wall protected the grounds from the street, and
guests passed through the gate up the paved walk and
the stone steps into the broad entrance hall.   At the
right of the hall was the drawing room furnished in
bird's-eye maple covered with rich damask, and beyond was the spacious dining room in which Governor Hancock gave his famous banquets—one of
them being a breakfast to the French Admiral d'Estaing at the time his ship was anchored in the harbor.
Gossip whispers that the French Admiral brought along
so many of his officers and men to the breakfast that
Mistress Dorothy's wits were hard pressed to find food
enough to go around, and she was obliged to send the
cooks out to borrow cakes of her friends and to milk the
cows on the Common.   At the left of the hall was the
family drawing room, its walls covered with crimson
paper, from it an exit leading to a formal garden.   The
Hancock House was pillaged by British soldiers at the
time of Lexington fight, when orders came from England
to hang the "Proscribed Patriots," John Hancock and
his friend Samuel Adams—orders which failed of exe-

31

cution, however, but which inspired the decoration of a set of Liverpool pitchers (described in another chapter), as well as the following lines of a British rhymster:

> As for their King, John Hancock,
> And Adams, if they're taken,
> Their heads for signs shall hang up high
> Upon that Hill called Beacon.

The Lawrence mansion, a view of which with the top of the spire of Park Street church visible above its roof is here presented, was a near neighbor of the celebrated Amory mansion on Park Street. It was occupied by the Hon. Abbott Lawrence, of the firm of distinguished merchants "A. & A. Lawrence," who in 1849 was minister of the United States to the Court of St. James. The house is now, on the authority of an old Bostonian, No. 8 Park Street, the home of the Union Club.

The Suffolk County Court House, a view of which is one of the interesting souvenirs of the Boston of the Fathers to be found printed upon tableware in the rich deep blues of Staffordshire manufacture, was erected in the year 1810 from a design by the architect Bulfinch. It was an interesting structure, with an octagonal center flanked by two wings. Until the year 1862, the building served as City Hall as well as Court House, in that year having been demolished to make room for a City Hall of more modern construction.

Among the church edifices of early Boston pictured

upon pottery, one searches in vain for the historic Old South and Old North which played such active parts in driving the English from America, the artists for some reason having overlooked them in their quest for American views. King's Chapel, the "perfectly felicitous" Park Street church, and Christ church are also missing, two church buildings only having been reproduced for china decoration—Saint Paul's and the New South or Octagon Church. Saint Paul's church, now the Episcopal Cathedral, is to-day, like its namesake in New York, hemmed about with tall modern structures which serve to dwarf its modest proportions. Saint Paul's dates from the year 1819, it being the fourth Episcopal church to be built in Boston. The congregation of the old church, wishing a new and impressive edifice, erected this handsome Grecian-like temple of stone which Phillips Brooks pronounced "a triumph of architectural beauty and of fitness for the church's service." The architects were Alexander Parris and Solomon Willard, the last named being also the architect of the Bunker Hill Monument which is presented in another chapter. In their design they gave full expression to the Revival of Greek thought which at the time was beginning to make itself felt in the architecture of the country, Willard himself carving the Ionic capitals. The original plan called for a bas-relief in the pediment somewhat after the idea of the pediment sculptures of the Parthenon, representing Paul preaching at Athens; but the funds proved insufficient, and the temporary stone was destined to become a permanent fixture.   Underneath the church were several tombs, one of which being for a time the resting place of the body of General Warren who fell at Bunker Hill.

The series of old china illustrations now conducts the historian of early Boston to Church Green in Summer Street, a plot of ground in the south end of the city, the original petition for a grant of which for the purpose of erecting a church thereon declaring, that it was "by its situation and name no doubt intended by our forefathers for that purpose."   The original edifice was erected in 1717, Mr. Wadsworth of the Old South and Dr. Cotton Mather of the Old North preaching the dedicatory sermons.   The church was called the New South Meeting House to distinguish it from the Old South, and was considered the handsomest edifice in Boston.   The representation here given is of the structure rebuilt in 1814, its octagonal form a marked departure from the customary at that period, whence it received its popular name, "Octagon Church," printed upon the back of the pieces of pottery which illustrate it.   The design was one of Bulfinch's and the material was granite, a tall slender spire and a portico supported by Doric columns being characteristic features.   At the time the Octagon Church was built an uninterrupted view of the harbor

OCTAGON CHURCH, OR NEW SOUTH CHURCH,
BOSTON

(*Ridgway*)

BOSTON HOSPITAL

(Massachusetts General Hospital)

(*Ralph Stevenson*)

INSANE HOSPITAL, BOSTON
(*Ridgway*)

MITCHELL AND FREEMAN'S CHINA AND GLASS
WAREHOUSE—CHATHAM ST., BOSTON
(*Wm. Adams*)

might have been had from its door, but sixty years later the city had reached such proportions that the edifice was demolished and its site occupied by business blocks. A curious style of carriage, with postilion in attendance, is an interesting detail of the composition, while in the background appear the homes of two of Boston's Fathers, Nathaniel Goddard and James H. Foster.

A view of the Massachusetts General Hospital was naturally selected by the English artists in search of decoration for their pottery, for it was one of Boston's most imposing foundations, its architect being the famous Charles Bulfinch. The Hospital building was erected in the year 1821, was 168 feet long and 54 feet wide, built of granite and adorned with an Ionic columned portico; the large wings were added in 1846. It is on record that within these walls ether was first used in a surgical operation of magnitude. The foundation was the recipient of large endowments, among them the notable bequest of John McLean, which made possible the purchase of other buildings for the use of insane patients, one of these buildings, known as the McLean Hospital, being the subject of a separate illustration.

The Insane Hospital was originally the home of Joseph Barrell, a wealthy merchant, and was also designed by Bulfinch. The estate, which was noted for its beautiful gardens, was purchased in 1818 for the Massachusetts General Hospital Corporation, at which time the wings were added and other changes made in order to fit it for a home for the insane.

Of especial interest to the collector of Staffordshire pottery is the specimen entitled, Mitchell & Freeman's China and Glass Warehouse, Chatham St., Boston, Massachusetts. Here is pictured a building which stood from 1828–32, a commodious warehouse of the early type situated not far from the wharf. Within its walls no doubt some of the historic blue pottery was received and stored upon its arrival from England, to be distributed later on among the homes of our New England ancestors. At the curb may be observed several boxes or bales, and workmen about to carry them into the building, and upon the opposite side of the street stands another large block of warehouses. Looking down the street in the direction of the harbor, one may see evidences of the extensive foreign and coast trade in which Boston for many years took the lead over other American cities. The tall masts and spars of brigs and schooners, the view dating from a period before steamboats were in common use, bespeak one of the sources of the city's pride a century and less ago—its waterfront stretching from north to south, indented and built up with spacious docks and numerous wharves than which no port on the Atlantic could boast of better, and flanked with fine warehouses. For many years a wealth of commerce was carried on between Boston and the principal ports of Europe, Asia, Africa, South America, the West Indies and the West Coast.

The city Almshouse originally stood in Park Street at the corner of Beacon, as has already been stated. This building was burned, and in the year 1800 the "New Almshouse" was erected at the river bank near the site of the old Lowell depot, where it stood, as it appears in the illustration, until 1825, when the ground was needed for the laying out of new streets. The structure was quite ornate, being fashioned of brick, 270 feet long, with commodious wings, arched windows and an ornamental pediment; on either gable stood a carved figure of ancient origin.

In the picture of the Athenæum building one looks upon the meeting place of an association of Boston Fathers of literary taste, who about the year 1810 established a small library and reading room. In twelve years the library had grown to ten thousand volumes, and the association removed to the larger quarters of this house. The collection of books made by the Athenæum society was the nucleus of the magnificent Boston Public Library of to-day, one of the most notable institutions of which the United States can boast. In the present Athenæum building, is preserved a plate like the one here shown, accompanied with the following explanatory note: "This building stood in Pearl Street and one half was given by Mr. James Perkins, the other half bought of Mr. Cochran in 1822, and the whole occupied by the Athenæum until 1849."

Did the Boston Fathers of the struggling, stormy years of Republic-building find time to yield to the allurements of the beautiful seashores which lay so near their door? That they did so is proven by two views of the still popular resort of Nahant with which at least two Staffordshire potters decorated sets of blue tableware. In the view here reproduced, the famous inn at Nahant occupies the center of the sketch, with the rugged rocks in the foreground presenting much the same appearance that they do at the present day. The inn was built of stone, surrounded with wooden verandas and had 100 rooms; it was the first hotel to be erected at that point. Shooting and fishing and dining upon sea foods were, a century ago, the same as to-day, the attractions of Nahant, the well-to-do inhabitants of Boston driving out in their stylish turnouts, one of which, a cabriolet with horses tandem, is presented in the picture; poorer folk patronized the little steamer called the *Eagle,* which may be discerned in the distance, and which once a day plied to and fro between the city and Nahant.

In the strange, wilderness country of America, the sight of the imposing Halls of Harvard College must have aroused in the minds of the foreign artists an interest second only to that inspired by the natural beauties of the Niagara cataract. And too, the sight must

38

BOSTON ALMSHOUSE
(Ralph Stevenson)

BOSTON ATHENÆUM
(*Ridgway*)

NAHANT HOTEL, BOSTON
(*Stubbs*)

have bespoken to them the quality of those pioneer settlers who, before every other consideration, planned so well for the instruction of youth. Nearly a dozen different views of Harvard were secured and reproduced in various colors, some sketches presenting the entire campus surrounded with its famous Halls, others one Hall alone.

The first settlers of New England, at a time before adequate provision had been made for food, shelter or civil government, recognized the importance of higher education and began at once the founding of a University. In 1636, the Governor of the Colony pledged £400 for the undertaking; the following year, the site was chosen at Newtown, the name of the suburb soon afterwards being changed to Cambridge, not only to tell whence the settlers came, but, as has been aptly said, in order to indicate "the high destiny to which they intended the institution should aspire." In 1638, John Harvard with his gift of about £800, together with his library of 320 volumes, toward the endowment of the college, made the project a certainty—the foundation, in gratitude, receiving his name. The avowed object of Harvard was the training of young men for the ministry, one of the first rules for students enjoining that they "lay Christ in the bottom as the only foundation of all sound knowledge and learning"—a rule in perfect accord with the principles which led the Puritans to

America. Next to religious training was placed the classical, for those days marked the beginning of the period in this country, now almost disappeared, in which a person without a classical training "might be ashamed to count himself a scholar." In 1642 and succeeding years, the following conditions for admission to Harvard were in force: "Whoever shall be able to read Cicero or any other such like classical authors at sight and make and speak true Latin in verse and prose, suo ut aiunt Marte, and decline perfectly the paradigms of nouns and verbs in the Greek tongue: Let him then and not before be capable of admission into the college." It is not to be wondered, therefore, that as early as 1719, a Londoner making the grand tour of America recorded in a book of his impressions of the country the following lines concerning Boston: "It appears that Humanity and the Knowledge of Letters flourish more here than in all the other English Plantations put together; for in the City of New York there is but one Bookseller's Shop, and in the Plantations of Virginia, Maryland, Carolina, Barbadoes, and the Islands, none at all."

At the present time, after the lapse of over three centuries, it is interesting to read the regulations governing the conduct of freshmen toward the members of that first college community in America. A freshman was not allowed to wear his hat in the college yard, "unless it rains, hails or snows, provided he be on foot and have not both hands full"; he must not have it on in a senior's chamber, or in his own, if a senior be there; he must go on errands for seniors, graduates or under graduates. All students were admonished to honor their parents, the magistrates, tutors, elders, by being silent in their presence except when called upon to speak; to salute them with a bow and stand uncovered. They were also forbidden to speak upon the college grounds in any language but Latin, and must not, until invested with the first degree, be addressed by the surname. Imagination fails to picture any marked display of exuberance of spirits under the restraint of the Latin tongue!

Flogging was an authorized mode of punishment in earliest times, the president in the beginning personally attending to it; later on, it was administered by the prison-keeper at Cambridge in the college library, in the presence of all who cared to be present. Prayer was offered by the president, after which the prison-keeper "attended to the performance of his part of the work;" the "solemn exercise" then closed with prayer, after which the chastised was required to sit alone uncovered at meals as long as the president and fellows should order. In the years succeeding, plum cake, dancing, swearing, punch, flip, lying, stealing, playing at sleeping at public worship or prayers, and similar irregularities crept in and caused such trouble that a committee reported the college "in a weak and declining state;" whereupon a more rigid set of rules came in force, in keeping with the changing conditions of society.

Harvard was from the first of its inception so generously sustained with gifts and endowments that at the time the drawings for pottery decoration were executed the College boasted an imposing array of Halls, some of them the gifts of or memorials to individuals—Harvard, University, Hollis, Holworthy, Stoughton, etc.— in striking contrast to the lone building which, until the year 1857, was the home of Columbia in New York. An interesting view of old University Hall is in the author's collection—a six-inch plate printed in deep rich blue and framed in the acorn and oak leaf border of the Stevenson potteries. The mark upon the back of the plate, within a flowered scroll, is incorrectly printed, "Scudder's Museum." (*See Frontispiece to this chapter.*)

FORT HAMILTON, NEW YORK
(*Godwin*)

RUINS OF MERCHANTS' EXCHANGE
(*Unknown Maker*)

CHAPTER III

A S one makes his way at the present time from the Battery through the rambling, canyon-like and crowded streets of lower New York, his mind filled with visions of the city of the Past, he searches almost in vain for a sight of its most ancient landmarks. Where, in the confusion of sight and sound, was located the inclosure within which stood the "mighty and impregnable fort," sheltering under its protecting walls the neat brick-fronted and tiled-roofed homes, set in luxuriant cabbage gardens, of the Dutch settlers of New Amsterdam? Where were their "bouweries," or farms, "sloping down to the river," which left the old Dutch name an inheritance to the Present? Where was the Bowling Green, and where stood Peter Stuyvesant's wall, with its gate through which the cows of the burghers went daily to pasture upon the Commons,—and, where was the famous Commons? Strolling up Broadway, one looks about for the more pretentious structures— churches, taverns, theaters and municipal buildings— erected by the English occupants under whom the city

43

became New York; and his search is rewarded by a glimpse now and then of an historic structure hidden away in a corner of the valley-like thoroughfares or crouching modestly in the shadow of some towering modern pile.

Next to Boston, New York was the most important city of early America, and the English artists naturally were at pains to secure sketches of its most imposing structures, views of its streets, its harbor, and of the life of its people. A study of these prints as reproduced upon pottery reveals to us, therefore, a very comprehensive idea of the topography and the customs of the old city.

The harbor itself as one views its shores to-day from Battery Point is little changed since the time, over three centuries ago, when Hendrick Hudson turned the prow of the *Half Moon* into its unknown waters, little doubting that it was the much-looked-for passage to China; or when, about one hundred years ago, the sketches of the spot upon which, the Dutch navigator said, "the eye might revel forever in ever-new and never-ending beauties" were printed upon the blue platters entitled, "New York from Brooklyn Heights" and "New York from Weehawk"—the platters which to-day bring the almost fabulous prices. Nowhere can there be found a more interesting commentary upon the growth of the city during the past century than is presented by the first two illustrations, one a view from Brooklyn and the other from the shores of New Jersey. In place of the massed group of towers whose outlines call forcibly to mind the silhouettes of the towered cities of mediæval Italy, together with the vast and varied shipping of the world, which at the present time meets the gaze of one approaching New York from the sea, here may be seen a collection of low buildings loosely filling the point of Manhattan Island, with about a dozen church spires rising from the level of the roofs. Several varieties of vessels, all sailing craft, are upon the waters of the bay; a windmill, no doubt a relic of Dutch times, appears in the view from Brooklyn Heights; while, looking from the Jersey shore, the distant Narrows may be discerned, the rolling shores of Long Island, and, nearer still, a fair-sized island intended perhaps for Staten Island. In the left foreground of the view from "Weehawk," as the name is printed upon the back of the platter, a Dutch homestead is pictured, with sloping-roofed farm buildings snugly nestled within the shelter of a grove of tall pine trees, a circular driveway bordered with a neat fence leading to them through the grounds. We are indebted for these interesting views of old New York to W. G. Wall, Esq., the Irish artist, who came to the United States in the year 1818, set up his easel in these sightly places, painted what he saw and sent his sketches to the Stevenson potteries in Co-

THE BLUE-CHINA BOOK

bridge, Staffordshire, for reproduction. The same border of roses and scrolls encircles the two views, but the blue in which they are printed is less intense and more transparent than the blue of the Enoch Wood potteries. At the time of his visit to New York, Wall also executed views of Fort Gansevoort, Columbia College and City Hall; the "Troy from Mt. Ida," which is presented in a previous chapter, as well as the imaginative "Temple of Fame" in honor of Commodore Perry, reproduced in a later chapter, being likewise from his hand.

Bordering upon the harbor at the foot of the settlement which comprised New York in Colonial times was an open piece of ground known as The Battery, two excellent views of which are presented. The Battery, as its military name suggests, was originally the outworks to Fort Manhattan, known later under Dutch rule as Fort Amsterdam (the English destroying it in 1789), which Peter Stuyvesant erected to protect the seaboard at the point of the island—formidable mud batteries solidly faced, "after the manner of Dutch ovens common in his day, with clam shells." As time went on, the bulwarks became overrun with a carpet of grass and the embankment shaded with spreading trees. Here the old burghers in times of peace would repair of an afternoon to smoke their pipes under the branches, while for the young men and maidens the embankment became a favo-

VIEW OF NEW YORK FROM BROOKLYN HEIGHTS
From a Painting by W. G. Wall
(A. Stevenson)

BATTERY WALK—FORT CLINTON

(*Wood*)

rite haunt for moonlight strolls; and so, from a place of war-like defense, the Battery Walk became renowned as a rendezvous for the delights of peace—the fashionable promenade, or "Esplanade," whereon of a Sunday afternoon the Dutch housewives and the English matrons were wont to walk up and down in the shade of the trees, enjoy the seabreeze and flaunt their bravest finery for all their world to admire. In the illustrations, several of the old-time ladies and gentlemen may be seen strolling along the paths, sitting upon the benches or stopping to chat with their neighbors, the ladies in large poke bonnets, pointed shawls and narrow, high-waisted skirts, with tiny sun-shades in their hands; while their escorts appear every whit as fine as they, arrayed in long full-skirted coats, broad brimmed hats and white trousers, sporting slender walking sticks—a valuable record of the topography, the customs and the fashions of Colonial New York. Plying the waters of the harbor many pleasure boats may be seen, in the distance Governor's Island is faintly outlined, and, nearer by, is Fort Clinton, connected with the mainland by a foot-bridge. The strollers upon the Esplanade were accustomed to repair to the nearby ornamental structure built around the historic flagstaff, where luncheon and music were to be found, the view of the Flagstaff Pavilion which is here given being, it has been said, the only existing record of that popular resort which until the time Fort Clinton was turned into Castle Garden was the sole amusement place thereabout.

Castle Garden, in recent years the landing place of immigrants and at the present time a municipal Aquarium, was a favorite subject for china decoration, a number of Staffordshire potters making use of it. Originally as Castle Clinton erected in 1807 upon an outlying rock, the structure was a fort for the defense of the English town and was reached from the Battery, as the illustrations show, by a bridge three hundred yards long—a space filled in later on and made a portion of Battery Walk. In the year 1824, the building was leased to private individuals and transformed into an in-door garden, with its name changed to Castle Garden. Its floor was elaborately laid out as a garden, with pieces of statuary to ornament its walks, and a stage was erected at the north end, where concerts were given at intervals, refreshments being meanwhile sold to the audience. Six thousand people easily found room for recreation within its walls, and upon various occasions as many as ten thousand were in the garden at one time. Here was held the famous Fête in honor of General Lafayette when he was the guest of the nation, a description of which may be found in a subsequent chapter. A few years later, the place became more distinctly a play-house, and, later still, the home of Grand Opera in America where such operas as

"Ernani," "Norma" and "La Sonnambula" were sung—
the crowning occasion, however, being the appearance in
four concerts, in the year 1850, of Jenny Lind, under the
management of P. T. Barnum.   Castle Garden's career
as a theater ended in 1855, when the building was turned
into a depot for immigrants.   At the present time, the
elaborate display of marine life within its walls makes
of the old fort and theater a fascinating and valuable
educational center.

Leaving the Battery, one shortly finds himself in
Bowling Green, the little park which still clings to the
name the Dutch gave it when they appropriated this
plot of ground in the midst of their settlement for their
favorite game.   The small, fountain centered spot, set
to-day like a tiny pool at the foot of the cliff-like buildings which surround it, was long the center of both
Holland's New Amsterdam and England's young New
York—the village green where maypoles were erected
and fairs were held; where the market place stood, the
parade ground, the shambles; and where was smoked
the Indian pipe of peace.   Upon this spot the doughty
Governor Stuyvesant surrendered his sword to the English officers; later on, bonfires were kindled in Bowling
Green when the hated Stamp Act was repealed, the
grateful people erecting here an equestrian statue of
King George the Third—only to pull it down as soon as
independence was declared.   At the same time, the

angry populace tore away the iron crowns which decorated the fence around the green, traces of their work of destruction still being visible as the fence itself survives to the present time. The first post-office, whence the mounted post for Boston set out, stood on Bowling Green, and the Executive Mansion after Washington's first inaugural, the building later on, when the national capital had been removed to Washington, being used as the Governor's House, before the state capital was removed to Albany. The fountain was placed in Bowling Green at the time Croton water was brought into New York, the mansions of the fashionable folk of the city still lining its sides. In recent years steamship business took possession of the place, and to-day history-crowded Bowling Green is known only as the terminus of the surface railway on Broadway.

Here begins Broadway, beloved of all New Yorkers, "the greatest street in the world." At the present time, as the searcher for memorials of the historic Past joins its hurrying throng, in imagination there comes to him, amid the confusing sounds of tramping feet and of strident street-car bells, a faint echo of "Sweep, ho! Sweep, ho! From the bottom to the top! Without a ladder or a rope! Sweep, ho! Sweep, ho! Sweep!"— the cry of the chimney sweeps familiar here but little over a century ago. In those same days, thousands of hogs roamed Broadway, the only garbage collectors the city knew! Sidewalks came in 1790, the first ones being of brick and set unevenly. Benjamin Franklin used to say that he could always tell a New Yorker upon the smooth pavements of Philadelphia by his shuffling gate, "like a parrot upon a mahogany table"; twenty-five years later, however, visitors to New York remarked upon the city's "neat houses and fine pavements."

At the corner of Broadway and Wall Street the searcher pauses, for at this point cluster many memories of old New York, several of which are called to mind by the illustrations. Facing Wall Street near the spot where Trinity Church now stands, in Dutch times there opened upon Broadway the "Land Poort," one of the gates to the picket-wall which Governor Stuyvesant built across the island above the settlement in order to shut out the Indians from the north and to protect his people from a dreaded attack of the English who were established in Massachusetts. The wall stretched along the course of Wall Street, which received its name therefrom, and through the Land Poort the cattle of the Dutch citizens passed each morning, the village herdsman going the rounds of the streets blowing a horn, at which the settlers turned their cattle out from their yards, and forming them into a common herd and driving them up to the pasture called the Commons, or Fields; in the evening, the herdsman drove the cattle back to the gate, through which they made their own

THE BLUE-CHINA BOOK

way home. The paths through the bushes which the cattle established in their daily rounds became in the course of time lined with houses—the origin, it is recorded, of the rambling and picturesque turns and labyrinths which distinguish certain streets of lower New York to this day.

A few steps from the corner of Broadway, facing Wall Street, the first Federal Building or City Hall stood in Colonial times, from the balcony of which George Washington took oath as first president of the United States. Several popular inns were within a short walk of this corner, one of them, Fraunce's Tavern, still remaining at Broad and Pearl streets, its rooms thronged with memories of New York's early days. The visitor mounts the low steps to the Colonial door, thoughts of Washington filling his mind, for this inn was his headquarters in Revolutionary days, and in 1783, after peace had been declared, in its assembly hall he bade farewell to the officers of the Continental army. One sounds the old-time knocker upon the door, when lo! is it a spirit of the Past who, clad in powdered wig, full-skirted coat, knee-breeches and buckled shoes, attends? Some Colonial officer, mayhap, stepped out from audience with his chief? He politely leads the visitor to the assembly hall above and ushers him within its door. The inscriptions upon the memorial tablets over the mantels first claim attention; then, in fancy, he

52

NEW YORK FROM WEEHAWK

From the Painting by W. G. Wall

The $1,225.00 platter owned by Mr. George Kellogg, of Amsterdam, N. Y.

COLUMBIA COLLEGE
(*R. S. W.*)

PARK THEATER
(*R. S. W.*)

turns and looks upon the long table spread, the officers one by one taking leave of their beloved General; at last, the mind's eye follows from the window the little group as it winds its way through the streets to the waiting vessel at the dock. . . . A luncheon partaken in the room below, in company with the spirits of the Past and the pleasure seekers of Today, concludes the visit.

Above Wall Street, upon Broadway between Thomas and Cedar streets, stood what was in its day the most famous inn in America—the City Hotel, erected in the year 1792. The illustration shows it to have been a plain structure, five stories high, a veritable sky-scraper of its time, old chronicles proudly stating that the City Hotel was visible as far away as the shores of Brooklyn and New Jersey. The City Hotel contained 78 rooms, and, until the Astor House was erected in 1836, it was New York's best-known hostelry, famed far and wide not only for the splendor of its accommodations and its entertainments but also for the importance of its guests. During the period of the War of 1812, five hundred gentlemen sat down in its long dining hall to a dinner in honor of the gallant and successful naval Commodores Hull, Decatur and Jones. On Saturday eve, February 11, 1815, Henry Carroll, a secretary to the American envoys, alighted before the door of the City Hotel, bringing from Europe such joyful news that all Broadway became quickly illumined and men with lighted candles in their hands marched up and down the street—the news of the signing of the Treaty of Ghent, that compact the keeping of which for one hundred years the contracting parties a few months ago celebrated with keen satisfaction. In the year 1824, a banner stretched above the door of the City Hotel announced that the inn was the home of General Lafayette while he was the city's guest; some years later, Charles Dickens was tendered a banquet at the City Hotel, Washington Irving being master of the brilliant toasts. But those history-making days were also primitive times, for behold in the illustration the load of wood in the street waiting to be sawed and stored away, New York having at that time no coal. And upon the sidewalk may be noted one of the many pumps which stood at intervals along Broadway—the chief source of city water until the year 1842, when Croton water was introduced. The spire of Old Trinity, as it appeared in 1788 before the present structure was erected, is visible in the distance. The portraits of Washington and Lafayette appear at the top of the design, with a view of the aqueduct bridge of the Erie Canal at the bottom, this piece of china having probably been made in honor of the famous visit of the "Nation's Guest."

Of the numerous church edifices whose spires may be seen in the view of New York from the Brooklyn and New Jersey shores, three only are pictured upon pottery

OLD NEW YORK

—Saint Paul's Chapel, the Murray Street church and the Roman Catholic Cathedral. It is to be regretted that no sketch of Old Trinity, the mother church of New York, found its way to England for use as pottery decoration. Saint Paul's Chapel, the oldest of the chapels of Trinity parish and second only in historical importance to the mother church, stands to-day, as the illustration pictures it, with its back turned to Broadway at the corner of Vesey Street, which was as far uptown as Broadway extended when St. Paul's was built, all traffic turning off there to the Boston Post Road, now as of old keeping guard over its quiet God's acre (which when this sketch was made sloped to the river), and appearing each year a little more bowed and ancient in contrast with the tall structures which arise around it; for Saint Paul's, whose corner stone was laid in 1756, is of greater age than any other public building in New York. As the sketch pictures, the architecture of Saint Paul's is simple and impressive, an excellent example of church design of a century and a half ago, with its rectangular body, columned portal and exquisite spire which calls to mind one of Sir Christopher Wren's conceptions. The spacious interior of the Chapel is of interest, both for its architectural beauties and for the hints it gives of the taste and ideas of splendor which belonged to the men of the past. At the time New York was the country's capital, President Washington attended service at Saint Paul's, and his square pew marked with the Arms of the United States is still shown to visitors; upon the opposite side of the nave, designated by the Arms of New York state, is the pew of New York State's first governor, George Clinton. An urn in the portico contains the body of the young and brave General Richard Montgomery, a former parishioner, who in the first year of the Revolution lost his life before Quebec. The memorial, an elaborate one of bronze, was authorized by Congress and purchased in France by Benjamin Franklin, being brought over in an American privateer which was captured by a British gunboat, before it could be safely placed. The dwelling house at the right of the Chapel, as the sketch presents it, was the residence of Major Walter Rutherford, which later on became a store, and was finally demolished by J. J. Astor to make way for his famous hotel.

The edifice known as the Murray Street church, erected in 1812, stood on Murray Street facing Columbia College, and, from the circumstance that its pastor, Dr. Mason, was a man of extreme popularity, it was also called Dr. Mason's Church. It was built of red sandstone, with a steeple 200 feet high, and in place of the portico usually to be found in specimens of Colonial church architecture, this example presents a pilaster-decorated façade. Not only was Dr. Mason a pulpit orator of world-wide reputation, he was as well a lecturer in Columbia and a man of influence in the city's activities.

St. Patrick's Cathedral in Mott Street was consecrated in 1815, and was the largest building erected in New York for religious purposes. Of so-called Gothic architecture, it was 120 feet long, 80 feet deep and its walls rose 70 feet. Its roof was of peculiar construction, rising sharply nearly 100 feet. The front of the edifice was of brownstone, with niches for statues.

To City Hall Park, in Colonial years a spacious piece of ground upon which stood the Bridewell, the Almshouse and the Debtors' Prison, the quest next leads the seeker for memorials of New York's early days, the potter's art having preserved pictures of six buildings erected upon the Commons. He is here in the very pasture ground of the favored cows of the Dutch settlers, for this small park, at the present time closely hemmed in by lofty towers and alive with hurrying throngs of humanity, was the Commons, or Fields, a long distance above the Dutch settlement and far out of town in later English times. In the year 1732, after Bowling Green had been fenced in and business and fashion had begun to creep up Broadway, the citizens resorted to the Commons for their holiday merry-makings—Maypole dances, drills, bonfires and patriotic gatherings. Here also a gallows was erected.

The "Sons of Liberty" many times gathered in City Hall Park, and, upon the spot where the fountain now stands, General Washington and his staff assembled upon July 9, 1776, to listen to the reading of the Declaration of Independence, a tablet upon the wall of the City Hall preserving this memory.

The specimen of pottery known to collectors as the Scudder's Museum design is of extreme interest, for it presents an excellent view of the Colonial Commons, together with several of the original buildings which stood upon it. Upon the right hand side of the design may be seen the structure known in its early days by the names, The New Gaol, The Provost and The Debtors' Prison. The building was erected in 1757 as a suburban prison on the Boston Post Road, and during the period of the Revolution when the English occupied New York many patriots were confined within its walls. Later on, when punishment for debt was yet imprisonment, the building was used as a Debtors' Prison, continuing to serve in that capacity until the year 1840, when an Ionic-columned portico, together with other improvements, which made the building a replica of the Temple of Diana at Ephesus, were added to it and the structure became the Hall of Records, remaining such until within a few years when its walls were demolished to make way for the new Post Office. The building at the left of the illustration, designated in large letters upon the sign over the door as

FLAGSTAFF PAVILION AT THE BATTERY
(*R. S.*)

FORT CLINTON, LATER, CASTLE
GARDEN
(*Wood*)

THE ESPLANADE (NOW BATTERY PARK), NEW YORK

(R. S.)

AMERICAN MUSEUM, was erected and occupied first as a public Almshouse, until the time the city's poor were transferred to the new home built for them at Bellevue. Upon their departure, the "worn-out mansion of the poor in pocket" was given over to several learned societies, among them being Scudder's Museum and Dr. Griscom's Lecture Room. To this place then flocked the people to gaze in wonder upon the Scudder collection of shells from far-off seas, the strange reptiles confined in bottles and to laugh over the antics of the curious animals from South America and the Orient, which formed the exhibit. In the year 1842, P. T. Barnum purchased the Scudder collection of shells, bottled reptiles and caged animals and added to it a so-called Moral Lecture Room, in fact naught but a theater, where talks and plays were given—the modest building here pictured thus being the nucleus of what grew into fame as "Barnum's Greatest Show on Earth." Among other attractions here exhibited was the dwarf known upon the stage as General Tom Thumb, who made his appearance upon its boards before starting out to tour the country and charm the youth of a past generation with his tiny figure.

The glory of the old Commons, however, was the City Hall, erected to take the place of the out-grown building in Wall Street, four distinct views of which were sent to England for use upon pottery. Completed in the year 1812, the dignified structure deserved the praise of General Lafayette who, as he looked upon it twelve years later, inscribed in his note book, "the only building in New York worthy the attention of an artist." The City Hall is constructed of white marble, with the exception of the north side which was originally of stone, the prudent New Yorkers of the day deeming it beyond imagination that the city would grow beyond it and cause its back to be visible to the observer! Designed upon pure classic lines, the City Hall presents an interesting example of pretentious Colonial architecture, a joy forever to the beholder, be he student of the art of building or a weary laborer passing through the park. Indeed, a popular vote of but a decade ago placed the old City Hall of New York tenth in a list of the country's beautiful buildings. It is recorded that a recent mayor of New York once said that if a person happened to be in City Hall Park and glanced to the north, he would be made happier and better by the sight of the City Hall. As the years have gone by, City Hall has acquired the appearance of ancient European edifices, the white marble having taken on the same creamy, mellow tones so much admired in them. The beautiful circular stairway (which the designer of a century ago was warned could not last a week!) rises from the entrance hall to the rooms above, a suite of which, known as the Governor's Rooms, shelters many mementos of the country's historic past—the chairs which served in the first inaugural, Washington's desk dated 1789, tables, mirrors, and portraits of notable statesmen.

New York's first Almshouse, as has been stated, stood upon the Commons, the building later on being transferred to the American Museum. The original building was erected in the year 1796 from the proceeds of a lottery issued by the City Fathers, a common method in Colonial days of raising funds for public enterprises, and when, in 1816, the Almshouse was turned over to Dr. Scudder for his collection of curiosities, the new Almshouse which is the subject of the platter decoration was erected on the bank of the East River, near Bellevue; in 1848, the paupers were removed to their present quarters on Blackwell's Island, and the Almshouse became Bellevue Hospital. The structure presented was 325 feet in length and was flanked on either side with commodious wings—a large and imposing foundation for its day and one which naturally caught the eye of the English artists in their search for representative views. The same potter, by the way, as the rose and medallion border indicates, executed the design here presented of the City Hall, these two being part of the Ridgway series of American buildings designated as the "Beauties of America."

Framed in the same artistic acorn and oak leaf border which encircles, among others, views of the City

Hotel, Saint Paul's Chapel and Scudder's Museum (a border attributed to R. Stevenson & Williams of Cobridge, a firm which produced some of the best-drawn designs of American subjects), may also be found the Park Theater. This plain, plaster-covered, brick structure fronted the Boston Post Road, now Park Row, which crossed the fields upon the east side of the Commons. It was erected in the year 1798, and for over fifty years it was the most prominent playhouse of New York. Performances began upon its stage, one reads, at 6.30 in winter and an hour later in summer, the patrons having also the privilege of a coffee room and a "punch room." Many notable actors appeared in Park Theater, chiefly in Shakespearean rôles—Edmund Kean, Edwin Forrest, Booth, Wallack, Fanny Kemble, Tyrone Power among the number. The ballad "Home, Sweet Home" was first sung here, and, at the age of four, Joe Jefferson made his initial appearance upon its boards. Italian opera was sung for the first time in America in Park Theater, and there also Fanny Ellsler aroused the indignation of all the clergymen and church going people of New York with her imported dances. The building was twice burned, the last time in 1848. Just beyond the theater may be seen the homes of several well-known New York families, while in the distance rises the spire of the old Brick Church, the "meeting house" erected as an offshoot of

CITY HOTEL, NEW YORK
With View of Erie Canal Bridge at Little Falls, and
Portraits of Washington and Lafayette
(*Stevenson*)

SAINT PAUL'S CHAPEL, NEW YORK
(*Stevenson*)

CHURCH IN MURRAY STREET, OPPOSITE
COLUMBIA COLLEGE
(*A. Stevenson*)

ST. PATRICK'S CATHEDRAL, IN MOTT ST.
(*Unknown Maker*)

the First Presbyterian Church in Wall Street. Adjoining the theater may be noted an old tavern which was commonly frequented by the rural folk who came to town over the Boston Post Road. The fence which is a conspicuous part of the design enclosed the City Hall Park, its tall stone posts united with iron railings brought from England.

In contrast to the campus of Harvard College lined with its many Halls, which a study of old Boston has presented, the single and rather unpretentious building which sheltered Columbia College at the period of our research found but two potters to record its history— A. Stevenson and the firm R. S. W. Clews, who succeeded A. S., also reproduced his design. Unlike the first settlers of the Massachusetts coast, those who earlier came into the region of Manhattan, traded with the Indians and made permanent homes for themselves upon the island, did not concern themselves with projects for an educational institution—the city thus early in its career receiving the imprint of commercialism. Not until some time after the Dutch traders had yielded to the English, in the year 1702, was a proposition made for the acquisition by Trinity Church, for college purposes, of a parcel of outlying land known as "Queen's Farm," the proposers being actuated not so much by the need for religious instruction as were the founders of Harvard, although Columbia is indebted for its initiation to a religious institution, but, as they declared, believing that "New York is the Center of English America & a Proper Place for a Colledge." The land was acquired, but a period of forty years elapsed before the Colony authorized the raising of funds by means of lotteries, and not until the year 1754 was a charter by King George II of England for "a Colledge and other Buildings and Improvements, for the use and convenience of the same, which shall be called and known by the name of King's College, for the Instruction and Education of Youth in the Learned Languages, and Liberal Arts and Sciences." The following year Trinity Church conveyed to the governors of the college, "for & in consideration of the sum of ten shillings," all that "certain piece and parcell of ground situate, lying & being on the West side of the Broadway in the West Ward of the City of New York fronting easterly to Church street between Barclay street and Murray street four hundred and forty foot and from thence running westerly between and along the said Barclay street and Murray street to the North river." The express condition of the grant was that the President should be a communicant of the Church of England. Dr. Samuel Johnson was the first president of King's College, and in fact, when in 1754 the instruction of the first class of eight who had successfully passed the required entrance examination began, he was the entire faculty, meetings being held in the vestry room of the church.

Upon August 23, 1756, the corner stone of the new college, inscribed in Latin phrase, was laid, after which the company partook of a "very elegant Dinner" where Health and Prosperity to the College were drunk—all being conducted, an old chronicle records, "with the utmost Decency and Propriety." The original stone may be seen to-day embedded in the mantelpiece of the Trustees Room in the Library Building at Morningside Heights, removed there in 1897.

In 1760, the college building was so far advanced that the officers and students began to "Lodge and Diet" in it, and in June the Commencement Exercises were held in it, an "elegant Latin speech" by the president before a "large and polite" audience being a conspicuous part. In honor of King George II the building was surmounted with an iron crown. In 1773, King's College was described as being situated upon a dry and gravelly sod, about 150 yards from the bank of the Hudson River and commanding a prospect of the shores of New Jersey, Long Island, Staten Island, the Bay, Narrows, etc. That same year John Parke Curtis, stepson of General Washington, was a student at King's College and in a letter to his mother he gives the following interesting survey of his life: "It is now time to give you a short plan of my apartments and of my way of living. I have a large parlour with two studys or closets, each large enough to contain a bed, trunk and couple of chairs, one I sleep in and the other Joe (presumably his servant) calls his, my chamber and parlour are papered, with a cheap though very pretty paper, the other is painted; my furniture consists of six chairs, 2 tables, with a few paultry Pictures. I have an excellent bed, and in short everything very convenient and clever. I generally get up about six or a little after, dress myself and go to Chappel, by the time that prayers are over, Joe has me a little breakfast, to which I sit down very contentedly, & after eating heartily, I thank God and go to my Studys, with which I am employed till twelve, then I take a walk and return about one, dine with the Professors and after Dinner study till about six at which time the Bell always rings for Prayers, they being over College is broak up and then we take what amusement we please."

During the stirring political period of the Revolution, King's College naturally played an important rôle, its alumni being leaders in the patriotic movement and of signal service in bringing about the independence of the country; the building itself, however, during the English occupation of the city, was turned into barracks and hospital wards for the British soldiers. It was a member of the class of '65, the Hon. Robert R. Living-

VIEW OF THE COMMONS
Scudder's, or American Museum: the Original Almshouse
and the Debtor's Prison
(*Stevenson*)

CITY HALL, NEW YORK
(*Ridgway*)

NEW YORK ALMSHOUSE AT BELLEVUE; LATER, BELLEVUE HOSPITAL

(*Ridgway*)

ston, who administered the oath of office to, and proclaimed, George Washington President of the United States. It was a member of the class of '58, the Right Reverend Dr. Provoost, who at the close of the inaugural ceremony conducted the divine service in Saint Paul's Chapel. John Jay belonged the class of '64, Daniel D. Tompkins was an alumnus, as was Dr. Mason of the Murray Street Church. DeWitt Clinton was the first student enrolled under its new name, the name being changed by Act of State Legislature in 1784 to Columbia College. From that date to the year 1810, there was an average of 17 graduates a year, in 1817 the college numbering 135 students. In comparison with the rules governing the students of Harvard, the following Resolution setting forth the requirements of admission into Columbia in 1810 is of interest: "Resolved, That from and after the first Day of October, 1810, no student shall be admitted into the lowest Class of the College, unless he be accurately acquainted with the Grammar, including Prosody, of both the Greek and Latin Tongues; unless he be master of Cæsar's Commentaries; of Virgil's Æneid; of the Greek Testament; of Dalzel's Collectanea Minora; of the first four books of Xenophon's Cyropœdia, and the first Two Books of Homer's Iliad. He shall also be able to translate English into Grammatical Latin; and shall be versed in the first four Rules of Arithmetic, the Rule of Three direct and inverse, and decimal and vulgar fractions." Although no rule, like that at Harvard, requiring students to converse in Latin upon the campus, may be found at Columbia, one of the principles of discipline at this time was, "During the whole course of education the youthful faculties are to be kept upon the stretch!"

As time went on, the need for a more adequate college building became pressing, the old structure "presenting a spectacle mortifying to its friends"; and in 1817 it was decided to erect at each extremity of the old Hall "a block or wing of about 50 feet square facing the college green and projecting beyond the front of the old building, so as to be in line with the fronts of the houses on the north side of Park Place." Finished in 1820, this is the College building which the china plate presents, the Lombardy poplars in the foreground being also of interest, from the fact that they were introduced from Paris in the year 1791 by André Michaux. Columbia College remained in its original location until the year 1857, when it was removed to Madison Avenue and 49th Street, and thence in later years to its present site on Morningside Heights.

In the year 1835, toward the close of the period in which the English potters made use of American designs, a wide-spread conflagration devastated a large portion of the business section of New York, laying waste thirteen acres of property and causing a loss of seventeen millions of dollars. The fire extended from Coffee House Slip along South Street to Coënties Slip, thence to Broad Street, along William Street to Wall Street, burning down the entire south side of Wall Street with the exception of a few buildings, to the East River. The Merchants' Exchange in Wall Street, on the site of the present Custom House, considered next to the City Hall the handsomest building in the United States, was the last to yield to the flames. The disaster must have appealed to the artistic sense of some foreign artist, for three sketches printed in the duller tints characteristic of the output of those years are found in commemoration,—"The Burning of Merchants' Exchange," "The Burning of Coënties Slip" and "The Ruins of Merchants' Exchange." The design here presented is of the ruins of the Exchange. The three-storied white marble structure may be seen with its ornate façade alone intact; flames and smoke are still rising from the roof; while citizens are gathered in groups about the ruin, an armed sentinel pacing before it on guard. In the foreground, a safe and a package of papers rescued from the flames are deposited, guarded by a squad of the National Guard in odd-looking fur caps and uniforms. The Post Office occupied a portion of the basement at the time of the fire, and in the rotunda stood a beautiful marble statue of Alexander Hamilton, a victim to the falling walls. The border which frames these designs, whether wittingly or without intent, embodies both history and prophecy. Within the scrolls is the record, "Great Fire of City of New York"; alternate spaces inclose pictures of the fire implements of the day —engine, hat and trumpet; while in the remaining spaces, against a background of city buildings, appears the phœnix, fabled bird of self-reproduction, rising from the flames—a prophetic symbol of the great metropolis which, out of the ashes of the past, to-day rises almost supreme among the cities of the world.

PENNSYLVANIA HOSPITAL, PHILADELPHIA

(Ridgway)

CHAPTER IV

A S children resemble parents, so cities grow up in the likeness of their founders. The streets of Boston still follow the circuitous paths worn by the cows of the city's Fathers to the pastures on the Common, and the marked regard for learning manifested by the early establishment of Harvard College is conceded to the Boston of to-day; likewise, are New York's boasted Broadway and Wall Street, her extensive docks and shipping facilities, other than glorified Manhattan trading-posts of the Dutch and the English settlers. So, too, the city of Philadelphia, enveloped in an atmosphere of harmony and quiet, bears to the present day in the character of her buildings, her streets, and her citizens, the impress of the formative touch of her founders—Penn's peace-loving English Quakers, who dreamed of a city of Brotherly Love in the far-off "woods of Penn;" and Benjamin Franklin, whose sound teachings in the form of "week-day sermons" (which will be recited in a subsequent chapter), and whose example of industry and thrift, were its corner stones.

Philadelphia was later than either Boston or New

York in its inception, its site, before the city was definitely planned, having been settled by successive companies of the Dutch, the Swedes and the English. In the year 1655, Peter Stuyvesant, with half a dozen vessels and 700 men, came over from New Amsterdam to subdue the Swedes in the Delaware Valley; both Dutch and Swedes, however, being soon afterward, through the territorial rights of the Duke of York, brought under English rule. Several years later, King Charles II, in lieu of claims which Admiral Penn owned against the crown, granted to his son, William Penn, the tract of land 150 by 300 miles in size which lies west of the Delaware River, and which Penn wished to call "Sylvania," or Land of Woods, but the king added to it the name of Penn, in honor of his friend, the Admiral. Thereupon William Penn, in order to induce settlers to cross the sea, offered such generous terms of payment for land that several vessels soon set sail, bringing hundreds of colonizers. This was in the year 1681.

Unlike Boston and New York and the immortal Topsy, however, Philadelphia did not "just grow;" she was carefully planned, the site selected and the new city laid out with deliberate and painstaking forethought. "Of all the many places I have seen in the world," wrote William Penn after his first visit to his infant city, "I remember not one better seated; so that it seems to me to have been appointed for a town, whether we regard the two rivers, or the conveniency of the coves, docks, springs, the loftiness and soundness of the land and the air." And Philadelphia *is* delightfully seated—in a well-chosen, wooded plot of ground in the spacious angle made by the junction of the Delaware and Schuylkill rivers, the harbor well adapted for shipping, the rivers natural roads for trade with the interior as well as an outlet to the sea, and the "soundness" of her climate a perpetual joy. The interesting view of young Philadelphia which the potters utilized for decoration of plates clearly defines the junction of the two rivers, the point of high land between them being filled with a massed group of square-built houses, their roofs topped with a lofty steeple.

Philadelphia's streets, unlike those of its northern cotemporaries, did not take their course from the wanderings of favored cows nor from the chance routes of public post-roads; they run where Penn planned them to run—straight and parallel, two miles in length from river to river, and fifty feet wide, with a broad street twice that width through their midst. Crossing these streets at right angles are others of the same width, leaving in the center an open plot of ten acres for the public buildings, the original design giving old Philadelphia much the appearance of a checker board. Penn also directed the naming of Philadelphia's streets, those running north and south bearing numbers, while those which run east and west—Chestnut, Walnut, Spruce, Pine, Buttonwood, etc.—". . . still reëcho the names of the trees of the forest, as if they fain would appease the Dryads whose haunts they molested," and keep alive to the present time memories of the city's wooded infancy.

The original houses, a number of which still line the oldtime streets of the pioneer city, were erected with the same forethought that ordered the thoroughfares themselves, all of them being built of brick, chosen for its enduring quality, and after one design, three stories high with plain front to the street and a stoop— "brave brick houses" Penn called them, he himself bringing the London style of architecture into this wilderness of the West. Lafayette liked the old houses of Philadelphia, but with his usual keenness of observation and cultivation of taste, he remarked that their excessive regularity "might fatigue the eye." An interesting picture of the interior of one of the homes of early Philadelphia is afforded in a letter of Mrs. Benjamin Franklin to her husband in France written in the year 1765, in which she describes their new home just erected in Franklin Court. One learns from this letter facts not only of household economy, but also of imported luxuries of this early date. She says: "In the room downstairs is the sideboard, which is very handsome and plain, with two tables made to suit it and a dozen of chairs also. The chairs are plain horsehair, and look as well as Paduasoy, and are

"FAIRE MOUNT" PARK, PHILADELPHIA
(*Stubbs*)

STAUGHTON'S CHURCH, PHILADELPHIA
(*Ridgway*)

THE BANK OF THE U. S., PHILADELPHIA
(Stubbs)

SIDE-WHEEL STEAMBOAT—PHILADELPHIA
DAM AND WATERWORKS
(Unknown Maker)

admired by all. The little south room I have papered, as the walls were much soiled. In this room is a carpet I bought cheap for its goodness, and nearly new. In the parlour is a Scotch carpet which has much fault found with it. Your time-piece stands in one corner, which is, as I am told, all wrong—but I say, we shall have all these as they should be, when you come home. If you could meet with a Turkey carpet, I should like it; but if not, I shall be very easy, for as to these things, I have become quite indifferent at this time. In the north room, where we sit, we have a small Scotch carpet, the small bookcase, brother John's picture, and one of the King and Queen. In the room for our friends we have the Earl of Bute hung up, and a glass. May I desire you to remember drinking glasses, and a large tablecloth or two; also a pair of silver canisters. The room we call yours has in it a desk,—the harmonica made like a desk —a large chest with all the writings, the boxes of glasses for the electricity, and all your clothes. The Blue Room has the harmonica and the harpsichord, the gilt sconce, a card table, a set of tea china, the worked chairs and screen, a handsome stand for the tea kettle, and the ornamental china."

At the time Philadelphia was the Capital of the nation, a picture of the city's formal life is afforded by the account of President Washington's levees held every two weeks in his home. Upon entering, the visitor was presented to the President, who was clad in black velvet, his hair powdered and gathered behind in a large silk bag. Yellow gloves were on his hands, and he held a cocked hat with a black cockade in it, the edges adorned with a black feather. He wore knee and shoe buckles, and a long sword.

With the exception of the Penn's Treaty scenes, which will be presented in a later chapter, the Philadelphia which the potters have commemorated is that of Franklin and his time, and comprises views of the Public Library, Pennsylvania Hospital, Deaf and Dumb Asylum, United States Bank, Masonic Temple, United States Hotel, one church edifice, scenes in Fairmount Park, including the Dam and Waterworks, together with occasional glimpses of street life. There are also sketches made in the suburbs of the city—country estates, bridges over streams, a primitive ferry, etc. Unlike the result of their search for the notable buildings of Boston and New York, the quest of the old-time artists fails to exhibit a view of Philadelphia's historic State House, or Independence Hall, within whose walls so much of vital importance to the Colonies and the young Republic was enacted, and wherein is preserved the piece of parchment which declares that the American colonies are "absolved from all allegiance to the British crown." The Independence Bell which rang out the first message of

PHILADELPHIA OF PENN AND FRANKLIN

"Liberty throughout all the land, to all the inhabitants thereof," here likewise finds a permanent home.

Philadelphia owes her Public Library to Benjamin Franklin, the thousands of volumes which to-day fill the shelves of the building in Locust Street being the gradual outgrowth of three small cases of books which were assembled in Pewter Platter Alley by Franklin and his friends of the Junto Club. With characteristic forethought and wisdom, those gentlemen made a rule that the volumes might be read not only by any "civil gentleman" who cared to come there to do so, but also that they might be carried home "into the bosom of private families;" in this manner the system of circulating libraries had its inception. The citizens of Philadelphia contributed forty-five pounds to purchase new volumes for the library, the learned Board of Managers modestly sending the money to England without specifications as to choice, and receiving in return a good, though rather heavy, assortment. A more commodious apartment in the State House was then secured to house the books, and, after a time, Carpenters' Hall was leased, with a librarian in attendance twice a week. Here the volumes remained during the Revolutionary period, a solace to both the American and English officers. After independence was achieved, in the year 1789, the cornerstone of the first real home of the Philadelphia Library,

the building illustrated upon the plate, was laid in Fifth
Street, having been engraved with the following curious
lines:

Be it remembered
In honour of the Philadelphia youth,
(Then chiefly artificers)
That in MDCCXXXI
They cheerfully,
At the instance of Benjamin Franklin
One of their number,
Instituted the Philadelphia Library;
Which though small at first,
It became highly valuable and extensively useful;
And which the walls of this edifice
Are now destined to contain and preserve.

In a niche over the doorway, Franklin himself stood
guard—a curious statue, made in Italy of finest marble,
draped in a Roman toga. Together with the books, the
statue was removed in the year 1880 to the present Library Building in Locust Street, where it was given a
place of honor over the new portal, the old corner stone
also being preserved and reset in the new walls. A number of interesting relics of early Philadelphia find a home
in this building, among them a bookcase and desk used
by William Penn, and his clock, still keeping time; a
clock once owned by Franklin is also there.

In the year of Christ
MDCCLV,
George the Second happily reigning,
(For he sought the happiness of his people)

PHILADELPHIA WATERWORKS: THE PUMPING
STATION IN CITY

(*Jackson*)

PHILADELPHIA LIBRARY

(*Ridgway*)

UPPER FERRY BRIDGE OVER THE SCHUYLKILL RIVER, PA.

(*Stubbs*)

PHILADELPHIA OF PENN AND FRANKLIN

Philadelphia flourishing,
(For its inhabitants were public spirited)
This Building,
By the bounty of Government
And of many private persons,
Was piously founded
For the relief of the sick and miserable.
May the God of Mercies
Bless the undertaking.

These are the words of Benjamin Franklin which are engraved in the corner-stone of the Pennsylvania Hospital, an interesting view of which is presented in the platter illustration. The record of the "bounty of government and of private persons" which made possible this noble foundation is a pleasant one to read. In the year 1755, the citizens of Philadelphia in order to found the needed institution gave of their wealth, England as well contributing funds for the "relief of the sick and miserable." From London came also a gift to the Hospital, for medical work, of a human skeleton, a thing of such novel interest that admission was charged by the thrifty Friends to look upon it, a handsome sum being thereby added to the Hospital funds. Benjamin Franklin was a member of the first Board of Hospital Managers, later on, its president, and to his wisdom and judgment are due much of the success and prosperity of the institution. The building itself, which when erected was considered far out of town, was originally, as may be seen,

79

a simple and substantial Colonial structure set in the midst of spacious grounds, shaded with spreading trees. One of the trees is of special interest as being the outgrowth of a sapling taken from the famous Treaty Elm, after its fall in the year 1810 upon the bank of the Delaware River. The gentleman in the foreground, with severely bent back, is evidently about to seek relief from his infirmity within the institution.

A building of unusual beauty for the time is the old Philadelphia Bank, the Bank of the United States as it was at first known, founded in the early days of independence, when Philadelphia was the center of the national life of the infant republic. The Bank of the United States was the first building in the severe Quaker City to be lavishly adorned, a stately white marble portico with tall Corinthian columns and pilasters of the same order being the principal features of its front. This bank was the parent institution of the country, the main office from which branches extended to other parts of the Union. At the time the present sketch of it was executed, the bank was the property of Stephen Girard, a wealthy Philadelphia citizen, and its name had been changed to the Girard Bank. The old houses by the side of the bank, the oddly shaped wagon and the pile of wood upon the pavement are interesting details of this illustration.

The taverns of old Philadelphia, like those of contemporary cities, reflected in their names and signs something of the characteristic quality of their frequenters. The "Crooked Billet Inn" was a public house which stood on the wharf at Water Street, and had the distinction of being the first house entered in Philadelphia, in 1723, by the young Benjamin Franklin, upon his arrival in the city. The "Pewter Platter Inn," with its sign a large pewter platter, became so famous that it gave its name to the alley at the corner of which it stood, obliterating that of "Jones." The "Bull's Head Tavern," with its sign of a bull's head, was so named from the fact of a bull thrusting his head through a window, the proprietor remarking that the fact and the sign might draw trade. There was the "Indian Queen," the "St. George and the Dragon," the "Cross Keys," the "Blue Lion," and, last but not least interesting, "The Man Loaded with Mischief," the sign portraying a man carrying his wife upon his back, an inn which stood in Spruce Street. Sign-painting was originally included among the finer arts, and it is related of Benjamin West that he did not disdain to put his talent to this form of work, a tavern sign done by him being considered of extreme merit. It represented upon one side in bright colors a man sitting on a bale holding up a glass of liquor as if looking through it; the other side showed two brewer's porters carrying a cask of beer slung with can hooks to a pole, which was the way beer was then carried out.

THE BLUE-CHINA BOOK

One famous old Philadelphia inn is recorded in the pottery records, the United States Hotel, the excellent view of it being framed in an exquisite border of trees and foliage. This place is memorable for the fashionable "Assemblies" which at one time carried on their festivities within its walls. Old chronicles relate that as early as the year 1749, and continuing through the years when Philadelphia was the nation's capital, with the exception of the period of the Revolution, to quite recent years, the Assemblies were a prominent feature of the amusement season. Upon every Thursday evening throughout the winter, the fashionable folk gathered at the United States Hotel, arriving precisely at six o'clock. The ladies who came first had places assigned to them in the first set of the dance, later comers being distributed throughout the other sets, the cotillion, minuet, reels and the newly-introduced waltz being the forms of dancing then in vogue. Card games were also indulged in at these Assemblies, the two forms of amusement—dancing and card playing, being looked upon by the Quakers with kindlier eyes than performances at the theater. Supper was of the lightest order, chiefly being, we read, "something to drink," and by twelve o'clock the entire company were wending their way homeward through the quiet streets. Cards of admission to these functions, as well as the fashionable visiting cards of the day, were playing cards, no blank cards being brought to the colonies and nothing but playing cards imported for sale. The invitation, or the name and address, were written or printed upon the blank side of the card, the back presenting, as might chance, the effigy of the King of Hearts or the Queen of Clubs. The United States Hotel witnessed also scenes other than those of gayety. Upon a June morning of '75, a breathless messenger alighted before its door bringing the startling news that the first shot of war had been fired at Lexington; in the year '77, Lord Howe and his English soldiers being quartered upon the city of Philadelphia, and Washington and his army at Valley Forge, the weekly balls at the United States Hotel were a prominent feature of that "rollicking winter"; and upon an October morning of '81, another messenger arrived, bringing the word that Yorktown and Cornwallis had surrendered.

A sketch of but one of the many houses of worship of early Philadelphia was transferred to English pottery, that of Staughton's Church. The illustration exhibits a low built structure whose dome-shaped roof and thickly proportioned columns set between piers, in striking contrast to the tall spires and rectangular proportions which are the distinctive qualities of the early Boston and New York edifices, call to mind the Pantheon at Rome and present an excellent example of the classic influence which was beginning to make itself evident in American ecclesiastical architecture early in the nineteenth century. Staughton's church stood on Sampson Street, between 8th and 9th streets, and was erected in the year 1811, for the Rev. William Staughton, a Baptist clergyman of such strong personality that the edifice for many years retained his name. The rotunda was capable of seating 2500 people.

Fairmount Park, or Faire Mount, as it was originally called, is a picturesque tract of land bordering the Schuylkill River above the city, and has always been, as it is now, a favorite resort of Philadelphia citizens. William Penn fancied the locality, and had the intention of building himself a home there, writing in 1701 to a friend, "My eye is upon Faire Mount." The plate-decorations of Fairmount, one of them framed in the eagle and scroll border of the potter Stubbs and the others in the handsome wreath of mingled fruit and flowers, show a rolling expanse of country on the edge of the river, with two of the country homes of Philadelphians situated upon the opposite shore. The Schuylkill River at this point became the source of the city's supply of water. Philadelphia's first water supply came from the use of pumps, and not until after an epidemic of yellow fever, in 1793, was the project of the introduction of river water seriously broached, many of the citizens being reluctant to give up the ice-cold water from their wells for the tepid waters of the Schuylkill. Benjamin Franklin, the city's great and versatile benefactor,

UNITED STATES HOTEL, PHILADELPHIA
(*Tams*)

MENDENHALL FERRY ON THE SCHUYLKILL RIVER, ABOVE PHILADELPHIA

(*Stubbs*)

early foresaw the need of a fresh supply of water for the city and recommended the Wissahickon Creek, the volume of which was proved inadequate. In the year 1813, river-water was made available, and in the following year there were nearly 3000 dwellings receiving the water from the Schuylkill at Fairmount; and when, in 1818, a steam engine was set in operation at the plant, the number rapidly increased.

After the construction of the Dam and the Power House for pumping water into a reservoir, these were the chief attractions of Fairmount, making of it a popular resort, the "glory of Philadelphia, combining beauty of scenery, usefulness of purpose and magnitude of design." The Philadelphia Dam and Waterworks are the subject of two old china decorations, one view with a side-wheel steamboat upon the water being here given; the other view, with a stern-wheel vessel in the foreground, is presented in the chapter upon Early Modes of Travel. In both illustrations, the dam across the river, the artificial fall of water and the pump-house may be seen, the last named being a white stone structure in the Doric style of architecture, the wings occupied by the offices of the company. The Waterworks were much frequented by Philadelphians, who drove out to spend a Sunday afternoon, bringing the children to play upon the grassy slopes, and every stranger in the city felt his visit incomplete without an excursion to Fairmount on the Schuylkill to examine the far-heralded plant. Lafayette was deeply impressed with the machinery at Fairmount, which was explained to him, remarking in his polite French way that he looked upon the Philadelphia Waterworks as a model of the American Government, "in which are found at once simplicity, economy and power." The city receiving-fountain of the Fairmount Waterworks was situated in Center Square, and, as may be seen in the print, was an ornamental structure of marble, its circular, dome-shaped upper story giving it the popular appellation of "pepper-box."

A number of interesting views of the suburbs about Philadelphia served as decorations for rich blue dinner sets. Owing to its mild and delightful climate and the country-loving inclinations of its citizens, suburban life became more of a feature of Philadelphia than of either Boston or New York, and many of the surrounding hills were dotted with handsome country homes. Glimpses of some of these homes may be had in the background of several of the sketches which have been reproduced, and one or two separate estates form the subject of an entire decoration,—"Woodlands," for example, on the bank of the Schuylkill River, which was noted for its beautiful gardens. In Colonial times there were few bridges over the rivers, fording and ferrying being the usual modes of crossing. Pennsylvania, however, was an exception, and the bridges which were constructed over the many streams in the State became so numerous that Pennsylvania received the title of "the state of bridges." Several of these structures were very elaborate and expensive and enjoyed a fame beyond their immediate locality. Such was the "Upper Ferry Bridge" over the Schuylkill River, a view of which is afforded in the beautiful platter decoration. In this illustration may be seen one of the covered type of bridge which has now almost entirely disappeared from the country roads of America. It was erected in the year 1813, and was remarkable for its single arch of a span of 328 feet. At the right hand entrance to the bridge stands the once-famed Harding Tavern, while in the foreground may be seen an old-time covered Pennsylvania wagon drawn by six horses—both bridge and wagon being valuable records of early America.

Another country scene typical of suburban Philadelphia is that entitled, "Mendenhall Ferry," which illustrates a common mode of river-crossing in the early days —a rope ferry over the Schuylkill River a short distance above the city. The country homes of Joseph Sims and of Dr. Philip Syng Physick, the most celebrated surgeon of his time and known as "the father of American surgery," may be seen upon the hillsides in the background, while Mendenhall Inn, long a favorite resort of Philadelphians, occupies the left of the design.

CHAPTER V

L ESS than a dozen views of early Baltimore are preserved upon blue china. The first one here presented is a harbor scene known to collectors as the harbor of Baltimore, but it is of disputed authenticity and resembles in its minaret-like spires some city of the Orient rather than a settlement of the young American Republic. The second harbor sketch is more probably taken from the original scene. In it two flagstaffs rise from a small wharf in the foreground, from which banners float —one of them displaying an anchor, and the other, the letter B. The water front of the city may be seen, with sailing vessels and small steamboats passing to and fro, and rows of low regular buildings lining the streets that run down to the river. Here and there a church spire or a monument towers above the roof line, those "spires and grove of vessels" which Lafayette remarked when he visited Baltimore in the year 1824. The French guest considered Baltimore one of the handsomest cities in the Union, with its streets so broad and regular, but without the monotony of the streets of Philadelphia. He was impressed with the elegance and delicacy of manners of

VIEW OF THE CITY OF BALTIMORE

(*Godwin*)

EARLY BALTIMORE

Baltimore's citizens, naturally ascribing the fact to the influence of their French blood; likewise, he was impressed with the beautiful buildings of the city, many of which had been designed by French architects. At the time of Lafayette's visit, Baltimore numbered about sixty thousand inhabitants.

Baltimore is younger than the other cities of the United States which have already been considered. To be sure, fourteen years before the Pilgrim Fathers landed on the New England coast Captain John Smith had sailed up the Patapsco River and looked upon the site of the future city of Baltimore; and fifty-three years later, Lord Baltimore, who afterwards gave his name to the settlement, had come into the region; but not until the year 1730, was the city laid out. Originally, Baltimore consisted only of a group of plantations whose owners were engaged in tobacco raising for the English market—the Horn of Plenty and the full rigged vessel in Maryland's Coat of Arms (presented in a later chapter) symbolizing her agriculture and her commerce. For many years the taxes of Baltimore were paid in tobacco.

A sketch of Baltimore which was made in the year 1752 shows that the city then contained but twenty-five houses, four of them only being of brick. In the year 1756, there came to Baltimore from Nova Scotia that little band of French exiles of whom the poet Longfellow sings, "Friendless, homeless and hopeless, they wandered from city to city." Here many of them found a refuge and settled, a number of the old French names lingering in the present city. Of Colonial and early Republican Baltimore, Staffordshire pottery illustrations present the Court House, Exchange, Battle Monument, Hospital, Almshouse, University of Maryland and Masonic Hall, several of them framed in borders of unusual attractiveness. The Court House, which is not standing at the present time, a view of which could not be procured, was a large, square, dingy gray-stone pile built above a basement, with arches for openings, the structure resembling, an old citizen remarked, "a house perched upon a great stool." In the basement there stood during the strict Colonial years a whipping-post, stocks and pillory—instruments for the serving of the sentences imposed in the Hall of Justice above.

The view of the Baltimore Exchange is very rare. The Exchange was erected in the year 1820, and in the old times at a certain hour each day the merchants of Baltimore were accustomed to meet in its great Hall for the dispatch of business. The building excited much admiration in the early days, becoming famed as one of the handsomest establishments of its kind in the world. It faced as the illustration presents it, upon an open square, several shops or warehouses of old Baltimore being seen in its neighborhood,

BALTIMORE
(*Unknown Maker*)

UNIVERSITY OF MARYLAND, BALTIMORE
(*Unknown Maker*)

THE BALTIMORE HOSPITAL
(*Unknown Maker*)

THE BALTIMORE ALMSHOUSE
(*Unknown Maker*)

while a coach and pair typical of the period are driving by. Indeed, our gratitude goes out to the English artists not only for the exact and beautiful reproductions of the prominent buildings of Colonial America which they took pains to secure, but as well for the interesting and significant details of everyday life which they depicted. The border of fruits and flowers around this scene might have been copied, so close is the resemblance, from some old Flemish tapestry picturing an allegorical figure of Abundance.

From the fact that a large number of columns adorn its public squares, Baltimore is known as the "Monument City," Lafayette remarking a century ago upon the number of her monuments, adding that the most beautiful one of them, the Washington monument, a white marble column 200 feet tall surmounted by a statue of the first president, called to his mind the lofty column in the Place Vendôme in Paris. Of the Battle Monument, which was erected in memory of the soldiers of Baltimore who fell in the War of 1812, an old chronicle records that on the day the corner-stone was laid a long procession of citizens passed through the streets of the city to Monument Square, a feature of the procession being a funeral car surmounted with a model of the intended shaft drawn by six white horses, caparisoned and led by six men in military uniform. The corner-stone is inscribed, "On the 12th day of September, 1815, in the fortieth year of Independence, James Madison being President, the Monument is dedicated to the memory of the brave defenders of the city." The monument, as a study of the illustration discloses, is of a peculiar style of architecture. The square base twenty feet high is of Egyptian type, the four corners of the pedestal being ornamented with sculptured griffins, and a door with inscriptions and reliefs being a feature of each front. The column is in the form of a bundle of Roman fasces, upon the bands of which are inscribed the names of those whom it commemorates; the whole is surmounted by a female figure, the emblematical genius of the city.

An elderly resident of Baltimore records the fact that the first hospital building was located on Franklin Street, near Calverton, outside the city limits, and that this foundation remained the city hospital until the year 1851, when Baltimore removed the institution within the municipality; the original structure is the one here presented. The poor of Baltimore, before a special home for them had been provided, were supported by a tax of tobacco. From the years 1812 to 1866, they were lodged in the spacious institution situated in the outskirts of the city which the potter-historians discovered and made subject for decoration.

The University of Maryland was founded at a much later date than the colleges of the northern cities which have been considered, having been chartered in the year

THE BALTIMORE EXCHANGE
(*Unknown Maker*)

BATTLE MONUMENT ERECTED TO THE HEROES OF 1812
(*Jackson*)

1807. The rather indistinct view of the University building which is presented upon the cup is of a dome-covered structure with a many-columned façade. Baltimore was the pioneer city in steam railway enterprise, as a later chapter will explain. One of her citizens, Peter Cooper, invented the first type of locomotive to be tried on rails in this country, the "Tom Thumb." Pictures also of the earliest engines in use upon the Baltimore and Ohio railway, one of the first roads in the country and one of the first highways into the great uncultivated region west of Baltimore, will be found in another chapter.

CHAPTER VI

WASHINGTON, THE NEW CAPITAL

L IKE Philadelphia, Washington was carefully planned; unlike Philadelphia or any other city of the Union, Washington was built for a special purpose. The youthful Government of the United States was in need of a fitting home of its own, a city wherein its President and other officers of government might reside, and where Congress might meet and make the laws. The first President of the new Republic had taken the oath of office in New York, and for some time Congress had assembled in the State House in Philadelphia; but those cities, together with the others which the Union considered, were situated along the north Atlantic seacoast out of ready touch with the States of the South, and for the most part, they were centers of growing commercial activity, with interests inclining towards trade and therefore unsuited to the business of government.

Where should the future Capital be located? The discussion aroused bitter controversy, the Northern States not wishing it placed too far south, and the South fearing it might be situated too far north to be mindful of the interests of the growing States of its own section.

"STATES" DESIGN. (Clews)

Names of fifteen states—President's House—Washington Portrait

WASHINGTON, THE NEW CAPITAL

At last, as a compromise, a plot of ground on the bank of the Potomac River was settled upon as being "as near as possible to the center of wealth, of population and of territory," and President Washington was chosen to select the site and to arrange for the building of the future Capitol. He called to his aid Thomas Jefferson and James Madison, and together the three settled upon the attractive situation with which we are familiar, an interesting view of which is presented upon a plate—the V-shaped rolling plain lying between the junction of the Potomac and its eastern branch.

The next step was to plan the new city, and the proposed design became such a widely debated topic that a drawing of it was carried over seas to the English potteries, and may be found to-day upon a yellow jug of Liverpool. Washington chose for the task of planning the new city a French resident of this country, Major l'Enfant, who carefully examined the site from all points, and, realizing the fact that he was creating a capitol not alone for thirteen States and three millions of people, but for a future mighty republic, he studied the plans of several of the beautiful cities of Europe—Rome, Paris, London, Venice. Jefferson told him that in his opinion none equaled the design of Philadelphia, "old Babylon revived"; but l'Enfant considered the chess-board effect of Philadelphia's streets too monotonous, his idea embracing three or four wide avenues running obliquely across the city in order to introduce pleasing curves and angles, as well as to render communication more ready.

L'Enfant's design, substantially as it appears in the illustration, was the one finally adopted. This charmingly executed drawing, full of significant details, is worthy of careful attention. Two graceful figures of women stand under the spreading branches of a tree holding aloft a scroll unrolled to view, above which is inscribed, "Plan of the City of Washington." The figure at the left, matronly and commanding, with the British emblem upon a shield at her feet, is supposedly Britannia; the other figure, designated America by a nearby eagle-adorned standard, is gazing interestedly upon the circular spot in the center of the design, presumably the site of the future Capitol of the new Republic, to which her elder sister is pointing with her finger as if in the act of explanation—or, possibly, considering the source of the production, may it not be admonition? The Capitol-site is upon the summit of a hill, with the President's house one mile away, down a broad avenue, or mall. Running east and west across the design are the many parallel streets which were named for the letters of the alphabet, A, B, C, and so on; while running north and south, at right angles to them, laid out in the drawing in prospective blocks, are other streets numbered 1, 2, 3, etc. Radiating from the Capitol and from the Executive Mansion, start sixteen wide avenues, named for the sixteen States which comprised the Republic in the year 1800. The avenues, as may be seen, cut the checkerboard at every variety of angle and form the squares, triangles and circles which render so beautiful the Washington of to-day. In the background of the illustration several sailing vessels appear upon a placid expanse of sea, while the foreground shows a bit of the "mille fleurs" pattern so popular in early decorative art.

Originally, the grounds of the Capitol and of the President's House extended to the banks of the Potomac, the "States" design reproduced in another chapter as well as the view of the President's mansion here given indicating its lawn sloping to the river's edge. An equestrian statue of Washington as an historic column from which all distances on the continent were to be calculated, five fountains and a grand cascade were among the features of the original plan which either were omitted or altered. The new city unanimously received the name of the first President and of its founder, Washington.

In the year 1793 the Capitol and the President's House were begun, and for several years thereafter the growing city was but a huge workshop, when long lines of teams might have been seen hauling blocks of Virginia sandstone from the river-landing to the places where the new structures were rising. As soon as the walls of the Capitol were laid, sculptors and skilled artisans were summoned from Europe to chisel the ornaments upon them; finally, in the autumn of 1800, one wing was sufficiently completed for the use of Congress, and a "packet sloop" sailed up the river bearing to their new home the public records and furniture of the Government. At the same time, the President's House, though not completed, was put in the best order possible for the occupation of President Adams; in the meanwhile, George Washington, the founder, having passed away at Mount Vernon, before his eyes could look upon the government of his nation housed in the city he had planned.

Mrs. Adams was the first lady of the Executive Mansion, and her letters give us charming pictures of the young capital city, then numbering about three thousand inhabitants, and of the beginnings of its official life. On her way to her new home she drove from Baltimore; "woods are all you see from Baltimore until you reach the city—which is only so in name," she wrote to a friend. But, in spite of the slight progress it had made in the twelve years of its existence, Mrs. Adams calls Washington a beautiful spot, and adds, "The more I view it, the more I am delighted with it." Pennsylvania Avenue, which now sweeps so stately from the Capitol to the White House, was, in the year 1800, mostly a deep morass covered with alder bushes, fine buildings being few and far apart, the roads muddy and sidewalks al-

PLAN OF CITY OF WASHINGTON
(Liverpool Pitcher)

THE PRESIDENT'S HOUSE
Rebuilt after Being Burned—South Front
(*Jackson*)

EARLY VIEW OF THE CAPITOL FROM
THE PRESIDENT'S HOUSE
(*Wood*)

SITE OF THE CITY OF WASHINGTON
(*Unknown Maker*)

most unknown. It is not to be wondered that disgusted statesmen wrote home to their families that the new home of the Government was "A Wilderness City," "A City of Streets without Houses," "A City of Magnificent Distances," "A Mud Hole," etc.

Northern journals stirred up feeling against the Capital, reviling its lonely situation and its slow growth. "The national bantling, called the city of Washington," they said, "remains after ten years of expensive fostering a rickety infant unable to go alone." "There sits the President," they went on, "like a pelican in the wilderness, or a sparrow upon the housetop"; they attempted, however, without success, to have the "bantling" removed to Baltimore.

In August, 1814, before the city had been completed, the War of 1812 was nearing its close, and to Washington came the British soldiers to destroy—a deed of reprisal inspired and executed by remembrance of the destruction of the Government buildings of York, the capitol of Canada, by the soldiers of General Pike. A company of redcoats reached the Capitol about six o'clock in the evening, and for sport they fired volleys into the windows; they trooped into the Hall of the House of Representatives and held a mock session: "Shall this harbor of Yankee democracy be burned? All for it say 'Aye'!" was the question. There was no opposition. "Ayes" and cheers rang out, books and papers from the

Library of Congress, desks and chairs were heaped for fuel, and within half an hour the beautiful edifice was in ruins, the bare walls only remaining erect. On to the President's House the British soldiers went, hoping to find President Madison and his wife, whom they wished "to exhibit in England," but the doors were locked and the occupants, taking with them the document of the Declaration of Independence and a portrait of Washington, had fled. A torch was applied, and the mansion together with all its furnishings was burned; the Patent Office, the Post Office, a hotel and a few dwellings only escaped the general destruction of the city. "The world is speedily to be delivered of a Government founded on democratic rebellion" was the approving comment of a London journal upon the incident.

The sketches for the old-china illustrations of the Capitol and the President's House were made soon after the city was rebuilt, for, notwithstanding their work of demolition, the British were among the first to picture the glories of the restored capital city of the young Republic. No less than six potters used prints of the Capitol, the handsomest building in America at the time Staffordshire pottery was made—a distinction which in its present enlarged form, keeping pace with the Republic's growth and importance, it proudly holds to the present day—and in them it may be seen rebuilt and remodeled, more imposing than before its ruin by fire. But the work of restoration had been slow, the autumn of 1819 seeing the Sixteenth Congress in possession of the new wings only, the main portion being yet incomplete. In the year 1824, Lafayette found workmen still engaged upon the building. At the time of the distinguished Frenchman's visit the city had a population of thirteen thousand, but "it was not rare," he recorded, "to see a plough tracing a furrow along Pennsylvania Avenue." As late as the year 1842, Charles Dickens, after his visit to Washington, wrote that "its streets begin in nothing and lead nowhere."

The illustration of the Capitol which is here shown [1] is of unusual interest, being taken from a sketch made about the year 1830, and presenting but the kernel of the present structure, before the addition of dome and extended wings. In this view, the lines of the Capitol bear a resemblance to the City Hall in New York, its pilastered wings, columned entrance and approach of many steps exhibiting those characteristic details which make of the Capitol one of the best examples of the revival of classic influence in architecture, known in America as Colonial, to be found in the United States. In place of the proud group of structures which at the present time share with it the imposing hill-top site, the Capitol is here portrayed surrounded with a grassy lawn set with spreading trees, the large tree in the foreground no

[1] As the frontispiece.

doubt being intended for the Washington Elm which was planted by the first President. In the foreground, two equestrian figures gowned in the styles of the day are pictured as pointing with their riding whips to the great foundation. The Capitol dome, for which the present structure is justly famed, required eight years of labor to erect. As one approaches the city of Washington and looks upon the airy dome lightly soaring above the roof-tops of the city, the scene calls to mind distant views of Florence dominated by Brunelleschi's famous cathedral dome, or of St. Peter's seen from the Pincian Hill in Rome. But, proclaiming it a product and expression of another system of government, from its summit springs a colossal figure of Freedom, represented as a goddess, her feet resting upon a globe inscribed E PLURIBUS UNUM, the motto of the United States, her head bound with a circlet of stars, and crowned with eagles' plumes. The inner walls of the great dome, or Rotunda, are decorated with mural paintings which illustrate scenes of the pioneer history of America.

The President's House, as exhibited in the view upon the plate, presents the appearance it did soon after it was rebuilt about a century ago—"a very simple building, but in good taste," was Lafayette's comment as he viewed it. Here one sees a substantial structure of Virginia sandstone, designed after the approved Colonial style of the period, with a formally laid-out garden of walks and parterres at the entrance, or south front, which was originally planned as the main entrance—the growth of the city changing it later on to the north side. To cover the marks of the fire upon the blackened walls, white paint was used when the mansion was rebuilt—the fact which gave to it the popular, and later on the official, title of White House. At the present time, although enriched with the addition of a portico and a colonnade, the home of our Presidents is fittingly defined by the modest phrase of the observing Frenchman.

A visit to the capital city to-day is not complete without an ascent of Washington Monument, the imposing pile erected in memory of the founder of the city, the first President. Lining the interior as one ascends the shaft may be seen marble tablets set in the walls, each one engraved with the name of the donor—State or society which from all parts of the world contributed them as memorials to Washington. From the summit, one is able to comprehend the plan of the city, locating the Capitol and the White House, with the connecting, but still unfinished, Mall, and the Government buildings; tracing the parallel streets and intersecting avenues spread out to view as upon a map; noting also, in this city dedicated solely to the uses of the government of a great nation, the absence of all those signs of industry and of commerce which are such prominent features in the illustrations of the cities previously considered.

Finally, the gaze of the beholder wanders over the beautiful stretch of valley, down the broad sweep of the Potomac, until it rests upon Mount Vernon, the spot where, nestling in the dusky grove of cypresses, are the modest home and tomb of the city's and the nation's founder.

Washington is destined to lead in beauty all other American cities, and when l'Enfant's original plan shall one day be carried to completion, with its glorious Mall, lined on either side with suitable structures, sweeping majestically from the President's Mansion up the hill to the Capitol, as its characteristic feature, it will, as its founder and designer dreamed, vie in distinction with the renowned cities of the world.

PART II

THE AMERICAN NATION-BUILDERS AND THEIR WORK

THE LANDING OF THE FATHERS AT PLYMOUTH
(*Enoch Wood*)

LANDING OF THE PILGRIMS
(*Enoch Wood*)

CHAPTER VII

"IF you are fond of romance, read history,"—the counsel of the learned Frenchman applies with special force to the stories of America's pioneers, for the true record of their adventures surpasses in marvels the fanciful imaginings of the weavers of romance. Out of the long list of achievements of those adventurous spirits of many lands who, from motives of conquest, exploration or home-making, braved the perils of unknown seas and came to America, the English potters selected but three incidents to illustrate and reproduce upon the sets of tableware destined for this young Republic—the Landing of Christopher Columbus, the Landing of the Pilgrim Fathers, and the Treaty of William Penn with the Indians.

The first series of views, numbering nine or more from the pottery works of Adams in Tunstall, Staffordshire, are fanciful sketches of the Landing of Christopher Columbus in America. Printed in red, green, purple, or black, upon plates and platters, the designs portray a wilderness inlet, with two, sometimes three, caravels at anchor in the bay, and small boats coming from them to the shore. Columbus is represented upon the beach, together with one or more of his Spanish companions; and native redmen in picturesque costumes are in hiding behind clumps of trees and shrubs. Tents and dogs are also in evidence, and upon one plate, here presented, an Indian is shooting at a wild goose. The border of the series consists of a pattern of roses, alternating with scrolls framing tiny landscape scenes, wherein roam wild deer and moose—animals native to the Western Continent. The trees and foliage of the Columbus series are tropical—tall cocoanut palms with fruit among the leaves, broad-leaved banana plants and other growths of the southland which Columbus found; for the English potters, like Columbus, long imagined the entire length of the Western Hemisphere one stretch of tropic or Oriental wilderness.

Indeed, the beliefs of European peoples of the fifteenth century, in which Columbus lived, in regard to the earth seem at the present time extremely curious. The marvelous tales which Marco Polo and his father had brought to Europe a century before from their journey into the Far East, and the glitter of the diamonds, emeralds, rubies and pearls which fell from out their coats when the seams were opened at a famous dinner party in Venice, still dazzled the minds of men. To find a shorter and less dangerous route to that kingdom which Marco had discovered in Cathay, ruled over by a Tartar

Khan who dwelt in a palace roofed with plates of gold, was the dream of every seaman. Wise men were saying, as some of the ancient Greeks had done, that the earth was a sphere or a pear-shaped object rather than the flat surface they had been taught to believe it—why not, then, to the west instead of to the east, might lie the shore of India where dwelt the lordly Khan? Thus Columbus argued, and his final doubt was removed when a learned man of Florence sent him a globe and a chart, both plainly marked with the western route to the eastern shores "where the spices grow."

But when Columbus laid his plan of sailing westward in search of India before King Ferdinand and Queen Isabella, the learned company which they called together to question him declared that it would take three years of sailing to reach this far-off shore, and that the sailors would die of starvation before they came to it. "Is any one so foolish to believe," they asked, "that there are antipodes with their feet opposite to ours; people who walk with their heels upward and their heads hanging down? Where trees grow with their branches downwards, and where it rains, hails and snows upwards?" Several of them objected that should a ship at last succeed in reaching India, it would be impossible for it to climb up the rotundity of the globe and get back again.

Familiar to all is the story of the three caravels, how they were fitted out in the harbor of Palos in Spain, the

Queen selling her jewels to obtain the necessary funds
for the expedition, and how Columbus and his companions, after prayers were said for their safety, sailed out
amid the tears and cheers of their friends, into the unknown waste of sea.

At last the morning of October 12, in the year 1492,
dawns. Upon the plate the hero is pictured stepping
upon the far-off shore, the ten weeks of sailing into the
trackless West, of watching for signs of land, of cheer-
ing the disheartened spirits of his men at an end, his
dreams come true. Two of the Spanish caravels ride at
anchor in the harbor, a small boat filled with their men
approaching shore. This to them is a new country and
these are a strange people who greet them—Indians,
Columbus names them—upon whose naked bodies gleam
rude ornaments of gold, and who crouch in fear behind
the trees, bows and arrows in their hands ready for defense. Is not this a part of the kingdom of Kublai
Khan—perhaps the island of Cimpango (Japan) which
Marco told about? Columbus, as the illustrated platter
shows, comes ashore arrayed in scarlet clothes, the royal
ensign in his hands. Behind him follow his men, some
bearing crosses, others holding aloft the standard of the
enterprise—a green banner embroidered with crowns
and the letters F and Y, the initials of Spain's rulers
Fernando and Ysabel. Columbus kneels, kisses the
ground and draws his sword in the name of Spain, call-

ing the land in honor of their safe arrival, San Salvador
—now Watling's Island.

The Spaniards are no less objects of wonder to the
natives. Observe them in the picture peering from behind the palm trees at the marvelous beings who, as they
believe, have flown down from the sky in their winged
boats. They come out from their hiding places and
touch the beards and armor and dress of the Spaniards,
and they gladly exchange their golden ornaments for the
gay caps, beads and bells which are offered them. When
asked where the gold comes from, they point to the south
and say that a great king lives there who is so rich that
he is served in vessels of gold—surely, thinks Columbus,
the "Khan" of Marco's tales.

After building a rude fort and a few huts on the
nearby Island of Haiti, Columbus left a number of his
men to search the island for gold, while he himself sailed
back to Spain. Upon his arrival, he arranged a procession of American Indians bearing palm branches and
gayly colored parrots—Indians and palms and parrots
all brought by him from the new world he had discovered. The procession wound its way through the
crowded streets of Barcelona to Ferdinand and Isabella,
who were seated upon a throne in the open air, under a
canopy of gold brocade, and there Columbus related his
adventures.

It may be a surprise to find horses pictured in one

Columbus view, but Columbus tells us in his journal that upon his second voyage to the new land he brought Spanish horses, as well as other animals, in the little caravels. His men rode the horses into the interior of the island to visit the gold mines in the mountains, and the natives upon seeing them believed them a new kind of being, the horse and rider one animal, and great was their astonishment when the men dismounted. Of the subsequent adventures of Columbus in his later journeys to America the potter-historians have left no record, but the remainder of the tale, which the pictured dishes have given us an eager desire to learn, may be found in the delightful diary of his daily life in the Western Hemisphere which Columbus kept for Queen Isabella.

Although Columbus, by finding land to the west, had the good fortune to solve "the mystery of the age," to the end of his life he never knew that he had discovered a world. But another mystery, one which in his time puzzled the minds of scholars, Columbus believed he had cleared—the whereabouts of the Garden of Eden. Wise men had located the home of our first parents in various parts of Asia; Dante in his Divine Comedy had placed it upon a mountaintop in the midst of the southern ocean; Columbus, one day while coasting the northern shore of South America, was almost capsized by a swift flood of fresh water which poured out of the land and, as he said, "sweetened the sea." He believed that this

LANDING OF COLUMBUS—CAVALRY VIEW
(*Adams*)

LANDING OF COLUMBUS—TWO CARAVELS
(*Adams*)

COLUMBUS—INDIAN SHOOTING WILD GOOSE
(*Adams*)

flood, now known as the Orinoco River, descended from a great height of land which was the summit of the pear-shaped earth, and that this river had its origin in the Fountain which springs from the Tree of Life, in the midst of the Garden of Eden.

THE LANDING OF THE PILGRIMS

The second romance of pioneer America which is recorded in the pottery decorations is also a "Landing" scene, but, in place of a gayly clad hero joyfully claiming a new world for a royal crown, here is pictured a small band of English Pilgrims struggling in a stormy sea to draw their shallop upon the "rockbound coast" of New England.   Out at anchor in the bay rides the small, three-masted sailing vessel, the *Mayflower,* which after a cold, bleak voyage of 63 days has brought the company of 102 brave souls from the Old World to seek in this untried wilderness of the New, freedom to worship God, not according to the laws of a king, but in response to the dictates of their own consciences.

Upon leaving the harbor of Plymouth, in England, the Pilgrims wished to find homes near the Delaware River, but had been driven by storms far to the north, sighting first the land of Cape Cod, where they decided to embark.   Two days after reaching the site of their future homes, on November 11, 1620, the *Mayflower's* company, wishing to "combine together in one body and to submit to such government and governors as we should by common consent make and choose," signed a Compact in the cabin, pledging themselves faithfully to keep what laws should be made—the first Declaration of Independence in America and the herald of that freedom in matters of government which has made of this country a Promised Land. After five weeks of exploration, the *Mayflower* reached the shore of Plymouth, the excellent bay, the wooded hills and pleasant streams which they discovered deciding the party to land; a bowlder protected by an ornamental shelter to-day marks the spot upon which the Pilgrims first set foot in America.

In the illustration, may be seen John Alden, "the youngest of those who came in the *Mayflower*," stepping first upon the rock. The two Indians standing on shore, one of them with arms outstretched as if in welcome, are no doubt intended by the artist to represent Samoset and Squanto, who unexpectedly appeared at the new settlement and astonished the people by saying in the excellent English which they had learned from earlier comers: "Welcome, Englishmen! Welcome, Englishmen!" and who, after a treaty had been arranged between Miles Standish and the Indian tribes, proved of great service in teaching the Pilgrims the ways of life in the strange wilderness. Upon the rock, may be read, "Carver, Bradford, Winslow, Brewster and Standish,"—five of the most famous names of that little company who, as

William Bradford said, "agreed to walk together" in this new land. The border of the design comprises a sketch of the national eagle, together with scrolls encircling the later historic dates, "America Independent, July 4, 1776," and "Washington Born 1732, Died 1799."

John Carver was chosen the first Governor of the English colony, and before the first spring came round a row of low, thatched-roofed, log-houses lined one side of the street bordering the bay, the residence of the Governor inclosed in a square blockade upon the opposite side, and atop the neighboring hill a fort fortified for defense; a meeting-house and a store-house had also been built. But the first spring saw likewise the graves of over one-half the band who had come in the *Mayflower,* John Carver's among the number, the cold and privations of the wilderness being more than they were able to endure; but, "It is not with us as with men whom small things can discourage or small discontentments cause to wish themselves home again," Elder Brewster said, speaking for the entire company. To succeed Governor Carver, they selected for Governor William Bradford, who remained in that office for 37 years. As the months went by, however, other vessels brought to them from England new companions and fresh stores of provisions, and renewed courage was theirs to establish firmly their own and other colonies along the Massachusetts coast.

Two hundred years after the Landing of the Pilgrim

Fathers, in the year 1820, the specimens of tableware pictured in the illustrations were made in the pottery of Enoch Wood, in Staffordshire, being parts of dinner-sets which at that time were sent over to this country in large quantities as souvenirs of the many celebrations of the bi-centennial. Much dining and speech-making in honor of the historic Landing took place that year throughout the United States, the principal festivities being held in Plymouth, Massachusetts, the scene of the original incident. And the banquet, at which Daniel Webster made one of his most famous addresses, was served upon one of the souvenir dinner-sets, the guests, as they listened to the speaker's eloquent periods, looking down upon the pictured scene which was the theme of his inspiration.

We as a nation owe much to this little group of Puritan Fathers, which is so quaintly presented upon the old blue dishes—the deep Christian faith which they brought with them, the love of freedom, the respect for law—convictions which took firm root and flourished bravely in the fresh New England soil. And later on, from out that Massachusetts colony of noble men and women there sprang and grew to manhood those regiments of fearless and liberty-loving patriots who, in Revolutionary times, laid so strong and deep the foundations of the American Republic. With Daniel Webster upon that notable anniversary day, we would ask:

"Who would wish that his country's existence had other-wise begun?"

One Staffordshire potter, Thomas Green, who potted between the years 1847–59, at Fenton, England, seems to have made use of but a single episode of American history for the decoration of the ware which he shipped across the sea to his American patrons—the famous Treaty of Shackamaxon, which his compatriot, William Penn, concluded with the tribes of Indians who roamed the forests about his new settlement of Philadelphia. As many as a dozen variants of the "Penn's Treaty" scene have been found in recent years, printed upon plates in the colors of the later period of Staffordshire manufacture—red, black, brown, green, pink and light blue—the border of the series being a delicate pattern of small diamond-shaped figures arranged to imitate open-work.

The sketches used in the Thomas Green pottery, two of which are presented, are the product of the imagination of English draughtsmen, who held somewhat vague ideas as to the character of American scenery. The fact of the Treaty being held under an elm tree is a tradition so well established that dispute is futile, the spreading elm pictured in old prints upon the bank of the Delaware River taking its place in the galaxy of the

117

world's historic trees. Nevertheless, in these sketches
Penn and his companions are represented in Quaker
garb, the artist having omitted to designate the blue silk
sash with which, tradition says, Penn was girt about the
waist upon the occasion, standing under a tall cocoanut
palm tree conspicuously laden with fruit.   In the background Eastern pagodas may be seen, one of them sheltering a group of squatting squaws.   Upon one Treaty
plate, Penn himself may be found in the robe of an
oriental mandarin—palms, pagodas, and robe all proofs
of the prevalent English belief as late as but a century
ago in the tropical and oriental character of the world
which Columbus discovered, an idea difficult, it seems,
to efface from the European mind, which for so long
had been nourished upon the adventures of Marco Polo
and other eastern travelers who cherished the belief
of the western route to India.   Penn is represented holding the parchment Treaty in his hand, Indians in fanciful costumes, with beautiful head-dresses, are con-
versing with him, one of the braves extending his hand
as if about to receive the document.

Another "Treaty" scene, printed by an unknown potter upon a porcelain plate, is a reproduction of one of
Benjamin West's famous paintings of the historic incident.   Herein, a tall branching tree, supposedly the
elm, is represented as sheltering a small assemblage of
Indians and Quakers, while Penn stands in the center

LANDING OF COLUMBUS
(Blue and White Wedgwood Pitcher, in the
Dickins Collection, National Museum,
Washington, D. C.)

WILLIAM PENN'S TREATY WITH THE INDIANS
(*T. G.*)

PENN'S TREATY
(*T. G.*)

of the group pointing to the document, which is being examined by the braves in the foreground. The background presents a row of buildings. Benjamin West lived in Philadelphia sufficiently early in its history to have heard the direct tradition of the Treaty, and in one of his paintings of the subject he drew the portrait of his grandfather as one of the group of Friends attendant upon Penn, history recording the fact that he was present upon the occasion—a fact which, it is said, inspired West to become a painter of the subject. The English characters in West's paintings were all intended to be resemblances and were so far true to life that at least one old-time citizen of Philadelphia could name them all. Much to the regret of early Philadelphians, however, Penn neglected truth so far as to have omitted the river scenery; to have given a wrong impression of the form of the Treaty tree; and to have put into the background a range of houses "which were certainly never exactly found at Shackamaxon." But his critics declared the extenuating circumstances that the artist was in England at the time he executed the paintings, and therefore could have no picture of the scene before his eyes.

A careful study of all of the designs, however, displays neglect of the actual scene upon that historic occasion. Each artist has failed to put into his picture those crescent-shaped groups of redmen who, as Penn records, seated themselves in the open air by the river's side, in solemn audience upon that autumn day in the year 1682, "according to the mode of their ancestors, under a grove of shady trees, where the little birds on the boughs were warbling their sweet notes." In the front row, sat the chiefs of the tribes with their wise men beside them; behind these, in the form of another half moon, sat the middle aged men; and, in the same form, still farther back, the "young fry."

None spoke but the aged. One may picture to himself the solemn air with which Penn arose and presented to Tawenna, the Chief Sachem, the roll of parchment—that treaty "which was not sworn to and never broken." After the terms of the treaty had been explained by an interpreter, Penn admonished the Indians to preserve the parchment carefully for three generations, that their children might know what had passed between them just as if he had remained to repeat it.

Thereupon, the Chief Tawenna slowly rose and offered to Penn, in exchange for the parchment, a Belt of Peace, at the same time declaring with great solemnity that "all Penn's people and all the Indians shall be brothers of one father, joined together as with one heart, one head and one body; that all the paths shall be open free to both; that the doors of Christian houses and the wigwams of the Indians shall be open and the people shall make one another welcome; that they shall not believe false rumors of one another, but, when heard, they shall bury them in a bottomless pit; that no harm shall be done, one to another; that complaints of wrong doing shall be made by either side; and, finally, that both Christians and Indians shall acquaint their children with the league and chain of friendship, and that it shall always be made stronger and be kept bright and clean, without rust or spot, between our children and children's children, while the creeks and rivers run, and while the sun, moon and stars endure."

This famous Indian Belt of Peace is now in the possession of the Historical Society of Pennsylvania, as it was brought over from England in the year 1857 by a great-grandson of William Penn, and presented to the Society. The belt is woven of eighteen strings of wampum, or beads made from muscle shells which grow upon the shores of our Southern States. It is twenty-six inches long and nine inches wide, the color being white, which signifies that it is a Peace Belt. In the center, two figures made of violet beads are represented—one, an Indian, is grasping in friendship the hand of another man, a European, known by the fact that he has a hat on his head! The Indian belts were the customary public records of the tribes and were preserved by them in chests; they were taken out occasionally, and the words spoken again which were spoken at the time of their giving.

In this manner, as the old-china records call to mind, under the elm tree was cemented that friendship between the Pennsylvania pioneers and their savage neighbors, which made possible the growth and prosperity of Penn's City of Brotherly Love. For more than a century after the Treaty, the historic elm stood upon the river bank, always cared for in the midst of the busy scenes of the wharf. In the later years of his life, Benjamin West wrote of the tree: "This tree, which was held in the highest veneration by the original inhabitants of my native country, by the first settlers, and by their descendants, and to which I well remember, about the year 1755, when a boy, often resorting with my school fellows, was in some danger during the American War, when the British possessed the country, from parties sent out in search of wood for firing; but the late General Simcoe, who had the command of the district where it grew (from a regard for the character of William Penn, and the interest he took in the history connected with the tree), ordered a guard of British soldiers to protect it from the axe. This circumstance the General related to me, in answer to my inquiries, after his return to England."

Upon a Saturday night in March, in the year 1810, the elm was blown down in a storm, the root being wrenched and the trunk broken off. Upon the following day, many hundreds of people visited the spot to

look upon it.   The tree is described as having been re-
markably wide spread, but not lofty, its main branches
which inclined toward the river measuring 150 feet in
length, its girth 24 feet and its age, as counted by the
circles of annual growth, 283 years.   Many souvenirs
were made from the wood, chairs, desks, picture frames,
etc.   Its most fitting memorial, however, was a descendant of the tree itself, grown from a stripling, which
until the year 1841, flourished in the lawn of the Pennsylvania Hospital, no doubt one of the trees to be seen
in the illustration of that institution which has been
presented in a former chapter.   A marble monument has
since been erected near the site of the original elm, the inscription upon its four sides being, "Treaty Ground of
William Penn and the Indian Nations, 1682, Unbroken
Faith; William Penn, Born 1644, Died, 1718; Placed
by the Penn Society, A. D. 1827, to mark the site of the
Great Elm Tree; Pennsylvania Founded, 1681, by Deeds
of Peace."   A commemorative poem to the Treaty Elm,
written by a loyal Philadelphian of history-loving bent,
closes with these lines:

> Tho' Time has devoted our Tree to decay,
> The sage lessons it witness'd survive to our day,
> May our trustworthy statesmen, when call'd to the helm,
> Ne'er forget the wise Treaty held under our Elm.

CHAPTER VIII

SCARCELY a person in Europe or America a century and more ago was unfamiliar with the features of George Washington, or unacquainted with the principles and actions of his life. Therefore, in their efforts for trade put forth by appealing to the patriotic pride of the Americans, the potters could have selected no more popular subject of design than the beloved features of "Liberty's Favorite Son"; of him who in the hearts of loyal Americans, as a Liverpool pitcher affirms, was "A Man without Example, a Patriot without Reproach"; or, as an old punch-bowl declares, "First in War, First in Peace" and "First in Fame, First in Virtue."

The list of pieces of pottery and porcelain which exhibit the name or portrait of Washington is longer than that of ceramics bearing any other American design, and includes specimens both of the deep blue pottery of Staffordshire manufacture and of the black-printed yellow wares of Liverpool. Numerous prints of his face, some seemingly imaginary, others copies of well-known paintings, are reproduced; his home at Mount Vernon

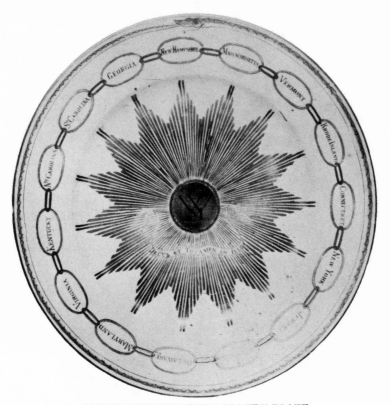

MARTHA WASHINGTON STATES' PLATE

is pictured; his monument; his tomb and funeral urn; the names of the States which he called into being are festooned with stars about his portrait; the dates of his birth and death are intertwined with symbols of his patriotic warfare and with emblems of the glorious reward hereafter, to which his deeds entitled him. Indeed, judging from the number and variety of Washington views, the English potters took pleasure in honoring the gallant and successful foe of their own Empire.

The first illustration is from the sugar bowl belonging to a deep blue tea-service, and presents Washington in Continental uniform standing upon the lawn of his estate at Mount Vernon, his favorite mount nearby held by a groom. Upon a similarly shaped tea-set of Staffordshire, Washington is presented upon the same lawn with an open scroll, doubtless the Declaration of Independence, in his hand, the columned veranda of the old mansion in the background of both sketches appearing the same as at the present day. The fact that the features of Washington accompany the portraits of Jefferson, Clinton and Lafayette upon specimens of ware made to commemorate the opening of the Erie Canal is judged by some persons proof that the potters held vague and oft-times incorrect notions of American affairs, another proof offered being "Boston" and "Tenasee" among the number of early States. But George Washington was the idol of young America, so it would seem but natural to link his memory with the others upon memorials of the nation's greatest enterprise.

Another Washington design which originated in the potteries of Staffordshire is known as the "States" pattern, and from the number of important circumstances it records this may be said, as was remarked of the first flag of Stars and Stripes, "to embody a whole national history." The eye is attracted first to the charming bit of landscape in the center, set in a graceful frame of scrolls, the beholder seeming to gaze out of a window upon the brilliantly illumined scene—a dignified mansion said to represent the President's House at Washington, with its well-kept lawn shaded by beautiful trees sloping, as in l'Enfant's original plan of the capital city, to the shore of the Potomac River. Two figures, a man and woman, stand upon the bank of a stream, and a small boat flying a very large flag rests upon the water. Supporting the frame upon the right hand side and gazing upon the scene it encircles, kneels a female figure crowned with a many-plumed head-dress and bearing aloft a Liberty cap, the word "Independence" appearing upon the platform beneath her. At the left stands blindfolded Justice, the decoration of the Order of the Cincinnati upon her skirt being in honor of George Washington, whose medallion portrait hangs suspended from her right hand. Flowers and fruits complete the design, and, enclosing all, a ribbon is festooned, each loop

GEORGE WASHINGTON, FESTOONED WITH
NAMES OF 15 STATES
(Liverpool Pitcher)

THE STUART PORTRAIT OF WASHINGTON

SEAL OF U. S. (FRONT)
(Liverpool Pitcher)

"WASHINGTON IN GLORY"—"AMERICA IN TEARS"
(Liverpool Pitcher)

of which bears the name of one of the fifteen States of the Union, Kentucky and Vermont having joined the sisterhood of the original thirteen at the time the device was made; fifteen stars mark the intervening spaces of the festoons.

An illustration from a Staffordshire specimen which is reproduced in the chapter upon Lafayette presents a fanciful Tomb marked "Washington," set in a brilliant sunset-lighted landscape, and before it, in an attitude of sorrow, reclines the figure of Washington's devoted French friend.

Numerous are the portraits and eulogies of our first President which the black-printed yellow pitchers and punch bowls of Liverpool manufacture exhibit, some of the portraits being fair likenesses, others with features "leaning all awry," and suggesting the queries: "What! did the Hand then of the Potter shake?" or, "Was there malice prepense in the heart of the fashioning artist?" At the same time, the flattering sentiment ascribed to Washington by the English potters at a period coincident with extreme international bitterness, and even open warfare, are astonishing revelations of British methods of securing trade with the colonies and the infant States. The Metropolitan Museum of Art in New York City contains a number of ceramic likenesses of Washington, by both artists and amateurs (one painted in China, with almond-shaped eyes, hair in oriental mode and mandarin coat!), the best known being copies of the Savage, Trumbull, Peale and Stuart portraits; the last named, the Stuart portrait with the lawn ruffles which is here reproduced, presenting the great American as we know him best and admire him most. An especially poor portrait is the next illustration, the face in profile, over which a cherub holds a wreath inclosing the word "Washington." Justice and Liberty are on either side, while Victory kneels before him offering the laurel branch. A ribbon scroll bears the names of fifteen States and shelters fifteen stars.

But—was it by reason of the secret, but suppressed, satisfaction they felt in the incident?—the designs which present Washington upon his monument or mounting to heaven upon a shaft of light, in the Apotheosis of Glory, borne aloft by winged seraphs and a choir of cherub angels, reveal the fancy of the potter-historians full and unrestrained. "Washington in Glory" we read at the top of one old pitcher, and at the bottom, "America in Tears"; a dignified delineation of the national hero, surmounted with a laurel wreath and urn, adorns the monument, with the dates of his birth and death beneath: "George Washington, Born February 22, 1732, Died December 17, 1799." Below the inscription is the Coat of Arms of the Washington family—a shield bearing five bars in chief three mullets—and the crossed swords of the dead warrior. The new Republic, represented by a female figure, leans in sorrow upon the base of the shaft, while an eagle, also typifying America, droops his wings and head in symbol of the mourning of a nation; abundant weeping willows, without which no memorial design of the early nineteenth century was complete, lighted with streaming rays of glory from on high, form the background for the monument. Upon the front of the pitcher, under the nose, is the design of the Seal of the United States, while upon the reverse, Ceres and Pomona stand at either side of a cannon upon which an American eagle perches in attitude of proclaiming to the world the successful achievement of Washington, inscribed as: "Peace, Plenty and Independence"; an early design of the national flag is an interesting detail of the background of this decoration.

Another monument pitcher gives a crude drawing of a shaft adorned with Washington's bust, the line, "Washington in Glory" above, and below, "America in Tears," accompanied by the historic dates, while a weeping figure and weeping willow again symbolize the nation's sorrow. Still other Washington pitchers record such eulogistic legends in honor of him and of the freedom he achieved as, "First in War, First in Peace, First in Fame, First in Victory," "He is in Glory, America in Tears," "His Excellency General Washington,"

"My love is fixed,
I cannot range;

I like my choice
Too well to change,"

"Patria," "May Columbia flourish," "E Pluribus Unum," the following lines to Liberty:

"O Liberty! thou goddess
Heavenly bright,
Profuse of bliss,
And pregnant with delight;"

also, the design of a harp in the hands of a soldier of the United States, who is standing before Liberty, presumably assuring her, as the legend states, that the instrument is "Tun'd to Freedom for our Country."

A number of pottery devices associate the memory of Washington with that of previous or contemporary historical incidents, a pitcher of especial interest, which is reproduced and described in a former chapter, bearing what is known as the "Map" design. This decoration, in addition to its valuable map of the United States, assembles, like the "States" patterns, several important historical records, for example—Washington and Franklin are examining the territory their judgment and deeds did so much to acquire; Liberty, the goddess of their inspiration, stands by Washington's side; while History, the muse who will record their acts, looks down upon Franklin, Fame sounding a trumpet on high and holding aloft a wreath inscribed, "Washington." A very clear representation of the pine-tree flag, one of

GEORGE WASHINGTON
Scroll in Hand
(*Wood*)

"HONOR THE BRAVE"—"THE UNION, IT
MUST AND SHALL BE PRESERVED"

(Pitcher in the Dickins Collection, National Museum,
Washington, D. C.)

EMBLEMS OF SUCCESS OF REVOLUTIONARY
ARMS
(Liverpool Pitcher)

WASHINGTON MONUMENT
(Liverpool Pitcher)

the earliest emblems of the Colonies (the significance of which is explained in a subsequent chapter) forms an especially valuable part of the Map device. Another Washington pitcher exhibits, on the reverse side, a female figure holding the American flag and facing two Indians, while in the background are several would-be portraits labeled, "Raleigh, Columbus, Franklin, Washington," together with the legend, "An Emblem of America."

A pitcher marked, "Proscribed Patriots," presents the portraits of Samuel Adams and John Hancock, the fiery Boston leaders of Revolutionary times, side by side in a medallion, surrounded with the following inscription, "In Memory of Washington and the Proscribed Patriots of America. Liberty, Virtue, Peace, Justice, and Equity to All Mankind." Below is the patriotic couplet,

Columbia's Sons Inspired by Freedom's Flame,
Live in the Annals of Immortal Fame.

Upon the upper part of the device may be read, "Sacred to the Memory of G. Washington, who Emancipated America from Slavery and Founded a Republic upon such Just and Equitable Principles that it will," etc. Upon another Liverpool jug, a soldier of the new nation is seen standing with his foot on the head of a British Lion, while below is his explanation of the unwonted attitude, "By Virtue and Valor we have freed our Country, extended our Commerce, and laid the foundation of a Great Empire"—strange words to put into the mouth of one's successful foe!

A large yellow punch bowl in possession of the Connecticut Historical Society exhibits Washington in full uniform upon a battlefield, mounted upon a spirited horse, with the accompanying inscription: "His Excellency General Washington, Marshal of France, and Commander in Chief of the North American Continental Forces." It is recorded that, in order to overcome a difficulty which arose over Washington's absolute control of the united French and patriot armies in America, the Count de Rochambeau being a lieutenant-general of France and therefore only to be commanded by the King or Maréchal de France, Washington was made a French Maréchal, the French officers at Yorktown addressing him as Monsieur le Maréchal. The reverse of the bowl has the fur-cap portrait of Benjamin Franklin which is shown in a later chapter, with the legend: "By virtue and valor we have freed our Country."

Our description of the Liverpool series of Washington designs closes with the "Apotheosis," in which the great American may be seen ascending to Heaven from his tomb, somewhat after the manner of the saved in early Italian frescoes of the Resurrection. Our first President is supported by Father Time, an angel holds his hand, at the same time pointing to rays of glory which mark the path to the upper regions, while charming winged cherubs, which would not have disgraced Raphael's hand, frame the top of the device; upon the tomb may be read, "Sacred to the Memory of Washington ob 17 December, A. D. 1799, ae 68." A fitting epitome of the fulsome praise accorded by the English potters to the memory of the great American is recorded in the oft-found expressions, "Peace and Prosperity to America," "America! Whose militia is better than standing armies," as well as in the alarming portent: "Deafness to the ear that will patiently hear, and dumbness to the tongue that will utter a calumny against the immortal Washington!"

In addition to tableware, a variety of busts, statuettes and medallions of Washington were produced both in England and in France, made of jasper and basalt, some of the last being exquisite works of art and intended for use as seals. Mirror knobs, or "Lookeing Glass Nobs," as ante-Revolutionary advertisements made mention of them, were much in evidence supporting the heavy mirrors in old-time Colonial homes, many of them being portrait heads of Washington in a cocked hat, or of Franklin with bald head and spectacles.

Several of the presidents who followed Washington likewise figure in a limited number of decorations turned out from the English potteries. "John Adams, President of the United States," is found under the portrait of Washington's successor in office. A "Proscribed Patriot" pitcher is described by Mrs. Earle in her delightful book, "China Collecting in America," as bearing, among others, the following inscription, descriptive of American policy at the close of the Revolution: "Peace, Commerce and Honest Friendship with all Nations, Entangling Alliance with none. Jefferson. Anno Domini 1804;" while upon another pitcher appear these stanzas to Jefferson:

> "Sound, Sound the trump of Fame,
> Let Jefferson's great name
> Ring through the world with loud applause
> As the firm friend of Freedom's cause.
> Let every clime to freedom dear
> Now listen with a joyfull ear.
> With honest pride and manly grace
> He fills the Presidential place.
>
> "The Constitution for his guide,
> And Truth and Justice by his side,
> When hope was sinking in dismay,
> When gloom obscured Columbia's day,
> He mourn'd his country's threaten'd fate
> And saved it ere it was too late."

Portraits of Jefferson also accompany those of Washington, Clinton and Lafayette upon the pottery designed to celebrate the completion of the Erie Canal. President Madison, the War President of 1812, appears upon one of a series of Liverpool pitchers illustrating that last armed conflict with Great Britain, while "Major Gen-

WASHINGTON ON ERIE CANAL DISH
(Other views of this specimen may be found in Chapter XIV)
(*Stevenson*)

GEORGE WASHINGTON ON THE LAWN IN FRONT OF
THE MANSION AT MOUNT VERNON
(*Unknown Maker*)

eral Andrew Jackson," who fought and won the final battle of the War of 1812, and later on became President of the United States, was not overlooked by the English artists, a globose pitcher preserving a print of his features. About the year 1840, John Tams, a potter at Longton, turned out two souvenir designs, one of them in honor of General W. H. Harrison, the other, of Henry Clay. Both are portraits, the first accompanied with symbols of warfare and the words, "Hero of the Thames, 1813;" the second, with the legend, "Star of the West." The log-cabin campaign of 1840, which placed the western hero in the presidential chair, likewise furnished decorations for the potters, a log cabin with its barrel of cider by the open door, and portraits of Harrison, being printed upon punch bowls and pitchers.

American industries were likewise noted and made subject for decoration, the Salem, Massachusetts Historical Society preserving a punch bowl of Liverpool make which bears the date 1800, together with two prints representing scenes of timber-rolling and ship-building, intended no doubt to commemorate the important Colonial industry of that town. Below the prints are the lines:

"Our mountains are covered with Imperial Oak
Whose Roots like our Liberties Ages have nourish'd;
But long ere our Nation submits to the Yoke
Not a Tree shall be left on the Field where it flourish'd.

"Should Invasion impend, Every Tree would Descend
From the Hilltops they shaded Our Shores to defend;
For Ne'er shall the Sons of Columbia be Slaves
While the Earth bears a plant, or the Sea rolles its waves."

Brave words! which imply not only knowledge of the spirit that imbued the colonists, but acquaintance as well with the physical conditions of the American wilderness.

George Washington was fond of having china in his home, and, after the close of the War, imported ware, much of it gifts to himself and his wife, took the place of pewter upon the table at Mount Vernon. The "Cincinnati" and other sets which he owned are described in Supplementary Chapter A of this volume.

A piece of the "Martha Washington States" set of china which was decorated for, and presented to, the wife of our first President is here presented. A number of pieces of this famous set are now in the National Museum of the Smithsonian Institution at Washington. Around the rim of the plate is a chain of fifteen links, each link inclosing the name of one of the first fifteen States. In the center is the interlaced monogram of Martha Washington—"M. W."—in a wreath of laurel and olive leaves, beneath it being a ribbon scroll upon which is inscribed in clearly traced letters, "Decus et tutamen ab illo." From the wreath spring rays of gold, and what at first glance appears to be a stripe around the extreme edge of the plate is in reality a gold serpent with its tail in its mouth—a symbol of eternity.

WEST POINT MILITARY SCHOOL
Scene of Arnold's Treason
(*Adams*)

CHAPTER IX

EXHIBITING the same curious lack of patriotism in their zeal for establishing commercial relations that inspired the reproduction of portraits of great Americans, the English potters made use of scenes of battle, surrender and memorial in that War of the Revolution which was of such fatal consequence to British arms. Bunker Hill, Quebec, Brooklyn Heights, Brandywine, the Treason at West Point, the Surrender at Yorktown—thrilling incidents the recital calls to mind! each one being either suggested or told in full upon the printed china.

Very clearly, from the brilliantly lighted and spirited scene upon the surface of the blue gravy-tray, may be read the familiar story of Bunker Hill. At the right rises Breed's Hill which the patriots determined to seize from the English, in the belief that their cannon once placed upon its summit would drive the English out of Boston. Upon the sides of the hill may be traced the breastworks and the rail fences banked with earth and brushwood which they hurriedly and quietly threw up in the silence of the night, fearful that some sound of pick or shovel might arouse the enemy watching in the ships of the nearby harbor. Upon the summit of the hill is the redoubt, and at its base, in three divisions, the "Thin Red Line of England" is seen marching under General Gage to attack the raw patriot troops—"country boys," General Gage derisively dubbed them—who upon this spot first measured strength with the trained militia of Great Britain:

> "Why, if our army had a mind to sup,
> They might have eat that schoolboy army up,"

being at the beginning of the struggle for independence the popular British notion of the American recruits. Certain of victory, gay in their white breeches, scarlet coats and cocked hats, carrying shining muskets, the British advanced upon that June day in '75, to face the schoolboy army lying concealed behind the redoubt, the haystacks, the fences and the stone wall, patiently waiting for them with such deadly fire that three attempts with overwhelming forces and ammunition were necessary to dislodge them. It was such a costly victory that General Gage in his report to the English Governor wrote: ". . . the rebels are not the despicable rabble too many have supposed them to be; and I find it owing to a military spirit encouraged among them for a few years past, joined with an uncommon degree

BATTLE OF BUNKER HILL
(*R. Stevenson*)

SURRENDER AT YORKTOWN
The reverse of this specimen is shown in Chapter XIII
(Copper Luster Pitcher)

BUNKER HILL MONUMENT
(*Jackson*)

GILPIN'S MILLS ON THE BRANDYWINE RIVER, NEAR
BATTLEFIELD
(*Wood*)

of zeal and enthusiasm, that they are otherwise." In the background of the illustration, beyond the hill, the vessels in the harbor may be faintly discerned, and the flames of burning Charlestown, and, farther away still, the spires and roof-tops of Boston—vessel-rigging, spires and roof-tops, we read, all crowded upon that day with anxious spectators of the opening tragedy of the War of the Revolution.

Although the scene of the Battle of Bunker Hill records a British victory, the illustration of Bunker Hill Monument, which 50 years later was erected upon the site of the battle, is a memorial of the final triumph of the patriot cause. General Lafayette, as a later chapter records, was present upon the occasion of the dedication of the monument, and, as one of the survivors of the War, he was the hero of the day. Upon Bunker Hill the patriots lost their brave leader, General Warren, and the autumn of the same year witnessed the death of another officer, General Montgomery, as he was making an attack upon Quebec, he and Arnold having heroically led a company of soldiers across the country and into Canada. Imaginary death and battle scenes in which these officers figure were printed as memorials upon Liverpool pitchers, one being inscribed, "The Death of Warren," and the other, "The Death of Montgomery." A large punch bowl in the Museum of Gloucester, Massachusetts, links their memories in the following lines,

THE BLUE-CHINA BOOK

"As he fills your rich glebs (glass)
The old peasant shall tell,
While his bosom with liberty glow,
How Warren expired,
How Montgomery fell,
And how Washington humbled your foe."

The view of New York City from Brooklyn Heights, which may be found illustrated in a previous chapter, calls to mind an important episode of the Revolutionary War which took place in the summer of 1776, a short time after the colonies had declared their independence of British rule. It was upon those wooded heights that Washington's army vainly attempted to oppose the entrance of the British forces under General Howe into New York City. In small vessels, such as those pictured floating in the harbor, Washington in the very face of the enemy took his army across the bay on a moonlight night, and entered the city just as Lord Howe and his troops were seen to occupy their former position on the heights of the Brooklyn side of the harbor. Then, northward to the heights of Harlem and farther still to the country about White Plains the patriot army marched, leaving the English officers and soldiers to settle themselves for a comfortable winter in New York.

The attractive country scene, white mill buildings and drooping trees mirrored in the quiet Brandywine stream —a design of Enoch Wood, known by the border of shells and mosses—was found not far from the spot

140

where, in the year 1777, was fought the historic battle which stained the still water with patriot blood. Washington's army was drawn up along the bank of the Brandywine engaged with a portion of the British forces, when of a sudden Howe and Cornwallis appeared upon the right flank, having led their main army far up stream, crossed it, and come down with such force upon Washington's army that Lord Howe's plans of spending another comfortable winter in America, this time in the city of Philadelphia, were assured; the gayety of the English officers that winter in the city contrasting strongly with the privations and sufferings of the patriot army at Valley Forge. The paper mill in the illustration stood on the farm of Gideon Gilpin, to whose home Lafayette was carried wounded from the field of Brandywine. It is recorded that in this mill the first machine to take the place of hand labor in the making of paper was introduced.

The same autumn the surrender of Burgoyne took place at Saratoga, a victory for the patriots which proved to be the decisive turning point in the war, as it brought France officially to the side of the colonies—an alliance commemorated in the field of ceramics by an exquisite porcelain statuette of Louis XVI and Benjamin Franklin, which is presented and described in the chapter upon Benjamin Franklin. After a disastrous defeat at Bemis Heights, General Burgoyne had retreated to Saratoga, where he was followed and surrounded by a superior army under General Gates, and, finding himself in a hostile and wilderness country far from his base of supplies, there remained nothing for him but surrender.

Then occurred the great Treason of the War, the attempt of its commanding officer, Benedict Arnold, to deliver to the enemy West Point, the key to the line of forts situated along the Hudson River, and thus to end forever the chances of independence for the colonies. The excellent view of the old fortress presents it as it appeared not many years after 1780, when Arnold had command—low stone buildings forming a line along the ridge of the mountain, taller hills rising beyond, and the Hudson flowing below. Upon the river bank may be distinguished the very spot where, in the darkness of a September night, Major André came ashore, met the traitor by appointment, and received from him the incriminating papers which later on were found upon him as he was attempting to pass to the English lines; their evidence sending the spy to his death, and Arnold to a more congenial home in England.

Again, one marvels at the nineteenth century English artists' lack of patriotic sensibility as he examines the evidence upon the jug of glowing luster which portrays the final scene of humiliation to British arms—the surrender of the sword of Charles, Earl Cornwallis, at Yorktown on October 19, 1781. This surrender, one of

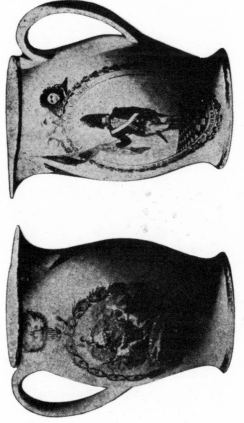

THE BOSTON FUSILIER

(Liverpool Pitcher)

the famous surrenders which History records, was an event of world importance, putting an end, by its disheartening effect upon English opinion, to the Revolutionary War and paving the way to peace. In his use of military tactics which resulted in the surrender, Washington is said to have equaled Napoleon in his famous Ulm campaign. Marching his army all the way from the Hudson River to Virginia—a distance of 400 miles —in twenty-eight days, Washington joined the army under General Lafayette which had recently suffered defeat at Cornwallis' hands, thus massing about twice the number of the enemy's forces who had gone into Yorktown. At once the patriot army surrounded the city, for three weeks laid siege to it, until at last, the looked-for reinforcements not being able to reach Cornwallis, the English surrendered—soldiers, seamen, cannon, muskets, ammunition, supplies and clothing, besides frigates and transports; the army, it is recorded marching out to the humiliating notes of the old English tune, "The World Turned Upside Down." In the illustration, two groups of officers appear face to face, Washington and Lafayette at the head of the patriots, Washington receiving the sword from the hand of General O'Hara, as Lord Cornwallis refused to be present and take his part in the scene of humiliation. Old records say that at the time of the surrender the band struck up "Yankee Doodle," so angering the British soldiers that, as they laid down their swords they broke them in pieces. The reverse of the jug, which is reproduced in another chapter, bears a medallion portrait of General Lafayette, crowned with laurel.

During the night following the eventful scene recorded upon the luster pitcher, a messenger rode out from the city of Yorktown bearing the stirring news of surrender. At sunrise, he reached the city of Philadelphia—and not many minutes thereafter, a German watchman on his rounds of the quiet streets might have been heard calling to the sleeping citizens: "Past three o'clock—and Lord Cornwallis is taken!"

With the assurance of independence came the establishment throughout the Union of a number of companies of militia, one of them, known as the Boston Fusileers, becoming of such widespread fame as to be noticed by the English potters, who printed a reproduction of one of its members upon a set of commemorative pitchers. There he stands arrayed in the uniform of his company, a flag of Massachusetts in his hand, while above his head is the motto, presumably of the Order, "Aut Vincere aut Mori"; below may be read the inscription, "Success to the Independent Fusileer, Incorporated July 4, 1789, America Forever." The reverse of the pitcher presents Liberty, Justice and Peace, and the motto, "United We Stand, Divided We Fall," together with other figures emblematic of Agriculture, Trade and

Commerce—the design as a whole typifying the happy results which were achieved by the long struggle for independence in the great War of the Revolution under the leadership of General Washington.

CHAPTER X

IN the decoration of a number of Staffordshire pieces, either in the border or as a detail of the design it frames, is the figure of an eagle. Oft-times a flag, bearing stars and stripes numbering either thirteen or fifteen, flutters from a vessel's mast, frames a hero's portrait or drapes his tomb; and a rare and valuable series of plates illustrate the Arms of the original thirteen States.

Emblems have always played an interesting part in the history of nations. It may be recalled how in ancient times the Roman legions marched to conquest under eagle-adorned banners, how wars were waged for the red and the white roses, and how the Turk fought always under the figure of the crescent. Familiar today, among the many devices of kingdoms and of empires, are the lilies of France, the lion and crosses of England, the eagles of Germany and of Austria. Many and varied, too, were the emblems which in the course of the centuries floated over the land of America. Previous illustrations have shown Columbus bringing the banner of Spain, and the Pilgrim Fathers the colors of

ARMS OF NEW JERSEY
(*Mayer*)

ARMS OF PENNSYLVANIA
(*Mayer*)

England; Canada long flew the lilies of France; and the old fort on Manhattan, before it spread to the breeze the Stars and Stripes, bore aloft first the Dutch and then the English ensign.

During the Colonial and Revolutionary periods, flags of various colors displaying devices other than the English emblem to which the colonists owed allegiance were made use of. The colors blue, red, and yellow and white were combined in patterns or stripes, the sketch of a pine tree together with the motto "Liberty" or the legend "An Appeal to Heaven" appeared upon several of the flags, while others bore the Liberty-tree in the center of the field and the words, "An Appeal to God." In one of the great historical mural paintings to be seen upon the Rotunda of the Capitol at Washington the Colonial troops are represented marching under a red flag emblazoned with a cross and a pine tree. Another Colonial flag is elsewhere pictured flying an anchor and the word "Hope," while still others, the words "Liberty and Union." Upon the "Map" Liverpool pitcher which is presented in a previous chapter may be seen a sketch of a pine tree flag. The most popular device, however, to be displayed upon Colonial flags was a rattlesnake coiled and ready to strike, together with the warning, "Don't Tread On Me," the rattles numbering thirteen, the number of the colonies, and, likewise typical of the colonies, each rattle distinct and at the same time joined to the others in defensive union. Upon one rattlesnake flag the tongue of the serpent was represented about to strike at the English emblems, the crosses of Saint George and Saint Andrew, while still another banner flaunted the challenge, "Liberty or Death."

Previous to the adoption of the Stars and Stripes by the new Republic, the emblems of the pine tree and the serpent were also intertwined upon flags flown by the vessels of the American navy—an act of such audacity that it brought forth from an English journal the following comment: "A strange flag has lately appeared in our seas, bearing a pine tree with the portraiture of a rattle snake coiled up at its roots, with these daring words, 'DON'T TREAD ON ME.' We learn that the vessels bearing this flag have a sort of commission from a society of people at Philadelphia calling themselves the Continental Congress." From the character of the devices chosen by the colonists to represent them, it is not difficult to conclude that the decision to secure for themselves the blessings of Liberty and Union were present in the popular mind long before the actual struggle for them was undertaken.

When the War of the Revolution was at last concluded and the American people no longer were required to display the hated British ensign, one of the foremost considerations of the new Republic was to choose fitting emblems with which to signal its entrance into the family

ARMS OF RHODE ISLAND
(*Mayer*)

ARMS OF NORTH CAROLINA
(*Mayer*)

ARMS OF MARYLAND
(*Mayer*)

ARMS OF GEORGIA
(*Mayer*)

of nations. And, as Staffordshire potters were at that period manufacturing tableware for the American market, the novel designs were naturally made use of for decoration. It is to be regretted that the emblems were not reproduced in the glowing hues of the originals, but in blue alone, the favorite color then in use.

> "O glorious flag! Red, white and blue
> Bright emblem of the pure and true;
> O glorious group of clustering stars!
> Ye lines of light, ye crimson bars!"

Such is the flag which, on June 14, 1777, the American Congress, in adopting the following Resolution: "Resolved, That the flag of the thirteen United States be thirteen stripes alternate red and white; that the union be thirteen stars, white in a blue field, representing a new constellation," voted should proclaim the United States of America.

Whence sprang the notion of the stars and stripes which so happily represent the Republic? One historian declares that the stripes were borrowed from the great-coats of the Continental soldiers, who, minus uniforms, made use of stripes to distinguish the different grades; others affirm that the Dutch flag, whose stripes symbolize their own union against foreign oppression, furnished the inspiration. A more popular belief is, however, that the Stars and Stripes were taken from the Coat of Arms of George Washington, he who gave to the colonies the freedom of which the emblem is now a symbol.

The flag of the United States, a patriotic statesman declared, is "a whole national history." In its thirteen stripes may be numbered the thirteen colonies; the colors red and white are tokens of that daring spirit and of that purity of motive which achieved the Union; and the stars, thirteen in number upon the original banner, uniform in shape and size, typify the likeness of the several States, and, grouped upon the blue canopy of heaven, they represent the strength and oneness of the young Republic. George Washington ordered the first flag made, taking a sketch of it to the little upholstery shop of Mrs. Ross in Philadelphia, where for many years "Betsey" Ross continued its manufacture.

The flag flying thirteen stars and thirteen stripes was in use until the year 1791, when Vermont and Kentucky joined the Union, and trouble arose. How were the new States to figure on the flag? A new Act of Congress was passed by which, "to keep the citizens of those states in good humor," as one statesman argued, two stars were added to those already on the field, and the stripes were increased to fifteen. The flag of fifteen stars and fifteen stripes may sometimes be found upon pieces of Staffordshire pottery, a few specimens (the "Martha Washington States plate" and the "States" platter, for example) naming the fifteen States of the Union, Vermont and

ARMS OF THE STATE OF DELAWARE

(*Mayer*)

ARMS OF MASSACHUSETTS
(*Mayer*)

Kentucky being among the number. After a few years, Tennessee, Ohio, Louisiana and Indiana came into the sisterhood of the States, and the subject of the flag came up anew. "We might go on adding and altering the flag for one hundred years to come," complained a weary statesman. It was at the time of this perplexity that the present flag, exhibiting thirteen stripes alternate red and white to represent the original thirteen colonies, one star to be added to the field upon the admission into the Union of each new State, was adopted. At the present time, the star spangled banner flings forty-eight stars to the breeze.

The new-born Republic required a national Seal as well as a flag, and tentative designs for the great Seal of the United States were submitted by Benjamin Franklin, John Adams and Thomas Jefferson. Franklin went to the Bible for his inspiration and proposed Moses lifting his wand and dividing the Red Sea, Pharaoh and his chariot being overwhelmed by the waters. Adams favored a classical subject—Hercules resting upon his club after his labors (no doubt of forming the Union) were ended. Jefferson suggested that the children of Israel in the Wilderness might aptly represent the new nation in the wilderness of the West, adding to his design the motto, "E Pluribus Unum." Chosen committees proposed Liberty (a female figure) with stars and stripes, warriors, etc. The Seal finally adopted by Congress, however—an American, or bald-headed eagle upon whose breast an escutcheon bearing the Stars and Stripes of the flag is displayed—is quite unlike any of the proffered suggestions. One of the eagle's talons holds an olive branch, while the other grasps a bundle composed of thirteen arrows, branch and arrows denoting peace and war. A scroll inscribed E Pluribus Unum, meaning one government of many parts or states, floats from the eagle's beak, and thirteen stars appear in the crest. No figures are pictured at the sides of the device in the position of supporters, it having been no doubt deemed out of place for a nation choosing to be represented by that powerful bird to require any support other than its own native strength.

Several adaptations of the design of the Seal of the United States may be found in the illustrations. It would appear that the English designers oft-times took liberties with the new emblem, for the American eagle may be found perched upon the shield with the arrows and motto underneath him, or, with the shield used as a background for the decoration; in one design, entitled simply "America," the national bird is figured erect upon a globe, the shield upon his breast, and the arrows and olive branch in his talons. His attitude, wings raised and beak open as if in angry dispute over his right to the portion of the globe he stands upon, may possibly be a sly joke of the English artist. A more exact copy of

ARMS OF CONNECTICUT

(*Mayer*)

ARMS OF NEW YORK

(*Mayer*)

ARMS OF SOUTH CAROLINA
(*Mayer*)

ARMS OF VIRGINIA
(*Mayer*)

the great Seal may be seen upon the front of a Liverpool jug in a previous chapter, displaying "Washington in Glory."

A series of decorations reproducing the Arms of the States were printed by T. Mayer of Stoke-upon-Trent, and, framed in an attractive border of trumpet-flower sprays, surviving specimens are among the most highly prized pieces of old Staffordshire. One device, the Arms of New Hampshire, has never been found, search in this country and in England thus far failing to bring a specimen to light. It is believed to have been printed along with the others, all pieces of it, however, having been destroyed. In the "Arms" devices the emblems of Justice and Independence and the colors red, white and blue were frequently made use of, the States evidently wishing to embody in their individual Seals emblems of the principles for which the entire nation stood. A number of the States likewise incorporated symbols of their own particular life and activities.

As early as the year 1647, the colony of Rhode Island provided that the "Seale of the Province shall be an ancker." Later on, the word HOPE was added, and the design encircled with a scroll, the color of the anchor and motto being blue, the scroll red and field white. The emblem was no doubt adopted as a symbol of the freedom, both civil and religious, in which the faith of the early settlers of Rhode Island, supported by the spirit of Hope, was so firmy anchored.

The first Seal of the colony of Maryland, still in use, bears the Arms of her founder, Lord Baltimore. The design which the potters made use of, however, is a copy of the seal which was adopted in the year 1794 and displayed for a period of twenty-three years only. In a blaze of light stands a female figure of Justice holding aloft the scales of her office in one hand, while the other grasps an olive branch. The horn of plenty at the base of the design symbolized the fertility of Maryland's soil, and the ship at sea her extensive commerce.

The device of the Seal of Georgia adopted in the year 1798, is composed of three columns typifying Wisdom, Justice and Moderation—virtues which support the arch of the Constitution and uphold the laws of the young Republic. By the side of one of the columns stands a man with drawn sword—mute proclamation that the army of Georgia is ever ready to defend the Constitution of the Union.

Connecticut adopted as her Seal three grapevines laden with fruit, upon a white field, together with the motto, *Qui transtulit sustinet*. The design was selected as a memorial of the three plantations of Hartford, Windsor and Weathersfield which formed the original colony, and, as the motto explains, it was a witness of the pious faith of the settlers of Connecticut in the divine

ADAPTATION OF THE SEAL OF THE UNITED STATES

ADAPTATION OF SEAL OF UNITED STATES
"America"
(*T. F. & Co.*)

assurance that "He who transplanted the vines was able also to sustain them."

North Carolina's emblems are the Goddess of Liberty and the Greek goddess of the harvest, Ceres—symbols of North Carolina's faithfulness to the Constitution and of the natural productiveness of her soil. Liberty bears a wand topped with a liberty cap, while in her lap lies the scroll of the Declaration of Independence. Standing by her side, Ceres holds in one hand three ears of corn and in the other a cornucopia, or horn of plenty, overflowing with the fruits and flowers in which the State abounds.

South Carolina also chose an emblem typical of her soil—a single palmetto tree. From its branches hang two shields and at its root are ten spears; if to their total the tree itself is added, the result is the number thirteen. An English oak tree, pictured with roots above ground and branches lopped, lies at the foot of the palmetto— the power of England broken by the vigor of the young republic, the lopped branches signifying that the American colonies have deserted the parent stalk.

Pennsylvania's Arms embody three of the State's activities: a sheaf of wheat for her agriculture, a plow for her husbandry and a ship for her commerce. Over all, forming the crest, a bald eagle grasps in his beak a streamer bearing the words, Virtue, Liberty and Independence; the supporters are two horses.

The Arms of New Jersey are three plows upon a white shield, Liberty and Ceres on either side as supporters and a horse's head the crest—Industry, Plenty and Independence.

New York, like Connecticut, went to her own beautiful landscape for a design, her Arms picturing the broad Hudson River flowing between level banks, two passing vessels, and, in the distance, the sun setting behind the Highlands. Above the shield is a globe surmounted with a heraldic eagle: Liberty stands on one side, her foot upon an overturned crown; while on the other side blinded Justice holds in either hand a sword and scales— tokens of deliverance from an oppressive royal yoke. Below the shield is *Excelsior*.

Massachusetts, possibly in memory of her first inhabitants, chose an Indian dressed in shirt and moccasins to represent her. At one side of the Indian's head is a star, one of the United States of America, and the crest is an arm grasping a sword. The motto, *Ense petit placidam sub libertate quietam,* is one of the following lines written two centuries ago by Algernon Sydney in an album of the Public Library of Copenhagen, Denmark:

> Manus haec inimica tyrannis,
> Ense petit placidam sub libertate quietam.

The English translation is:

> This hand, the rule of tyrants to oppose,
> Seeks with the sword fair freedom's soft repose.

EMBLEMS OF THE NEW REPUBLIC

The Arms of Delaware recite the homely story of her agriculture and her commerce—a blue shield divided by a white band into two equal parts, a cow occupying the lower division, a sheaf of wheat and a bundle of leaf tobacco the upper; a ship under full sail forms the crest. The supporters are a mariner and a hunter, beneath whose feet is the motto LIBERTY AND INDEPENDENCE.

Virtue, robed as an Amazon, a spear in one hand and a sword in the other, appears upon the Arms of Virginia. She stands upon the form of a prostrate man who may be said to represent Tyranny, a crown having fallen from his head, one hand still grasping a scourge and the other a broken chain. The motto, SIC SEMPER TYRANNIS, So shall perish all tyrants, upon a scroll at the foot of justice, gives voice to Virginia's patriotic sentiments.

CHAPTER XI

BENJAMIN FRANKLIN AND HIS PRECEPTS

IT is a happy fact that the memory of Benjamin Franklin, such a splendid type of the citizen of Young America and such a fond lover of blue china, is enshrined among our choicest ceramic treasures. His well-known placid and kindly face looks out upon us from many a jug and punch bowl, and his jolly rotund figure lives forever in medallions and statuettes of French and English porcelain.

"Your father's face is as well-known as that of the moon," wrote Franklin from France to his daughter in America, referring to the many prints and medallions of his face which appeared in Europe; and almost as familiar to each succeeding generation of school boys is the interesting record of the life of this early American. The story of how the Boston printer boy spent his leisure hours reading such books as Plutarch's Lives, the London Spectator and Xenophon's Memorable Things of Socrates, forming his literary style therefrom; how he ran away to Philadelphia, reaching that city with but one dollar in his pocket; and how, by his own industry, thrift and perseverance, he grew to be one of the greatest men

STATUETTE—LOUIS XVI. AND FRANKLIN
TREATY SCENE

(French Porcelain)

*(From " China Collecting in America," by Alice Morse Earle;
copyright, 1892, by Charles Scribner's Sons)*

in history, is, like the stories of Columbus, of the Pilgrim Fathers and of William Penn, one of the helpful romances of America's early years.

Franklin's home life in Philadelphia was plain and simple, and for many years he ate his breakfast of bread and milk out of an earthen porringer with a pewter spoon. "But mark," he says "how luxuries will enter families and make progress despite of principles; being called to breakfast one morning, I found it in a china bowl, with a spoon of silver! They had been bought for me without my knowledge by my wife, and had cost her the enormous sum of twenty-three shillings, for which she had no other excuse or apology to make but that she thought *her* husband deserved a silver spoon and china bowl as well as any of his neighbors. This was the first appearance of plate and china in our house, which afterward, in the course of years as our wealth increased, augmented gradually to several hundred pounds in value." In this manner Franklin was introduced to china tableware, the fondness for which grew with his years and with his wider opportunities for acquiring it.

We cannot dig deeply into the records of any civic or national institution of America without finding somewhere near the foundation the name of Benjamin Franklin. He was interested in all projects for the good of the colonies, his active mind putting into execution the best methods for improving every condition of affairs, therefore in examining the old-china chronicle of illustrations many phases of his work are revealed. The Philadelphia Library (as pictured in another chapter) was a small plain building, but within its walls was first sheltered the little collection of books which Franklin's literary club, the Junto, gathered for the use of its members, the collection expanding into a vast public Library. The Hospital Building (illustrated in the same chapter) which afterwards grew into the great Foundation of the Pennsylvania Hospital, affords another glimpse of Franklin's many-sided activities.

Franklin organized the fire company and the police force of Philadelphia, and the Academy he helped to found is now the University of Pennsylvania. Small affairs, as well as great, claimed his thoughtful attention—smoky fireplaces gave place to the Franklin stoves of our forefathers, farmers were instructed in the use of fertilizers, and sailors were taught the value of oil to still the troubled waves of the sea.

Franklin's famous discoveries that the frightful thunderbolt of the sky is but a huge electric spark, and that it can be drawn to earth and made the servant of man, became a favorite subject of china decoration. Plates picture the learned Doctor Franklin busily flying the immortal kite, which added to the sum of human wisdom by destroying forever the superstitious fear of lightning as a weapon in the hands of an angry God. Sometimes the portrait of Franklin is accompanied by this legend,

"Benjamin Franklin, Esq. LL. D. and F. R. S., the brave defender of the country against the oppression of taxation without representation—author of the greatest discovery in Natural Philosophy since those of Sir Isaac Newton, viz., that lightning is the same with electric fire."

Franklin medallions, printed with the motto in Latin: "He snatched fire from Heaven and the scepter from tyrants," were popular in France where they sold in large numbers. Franklin strove to supply not only the physical necessities of the colonists, but he also set himself the task of moral instructor, and his sermons, sent out in his Almanack under the guise of Poor Richard's sayings, entered thousands of homes where, with the exception of the Bible, it was often the only source of helpful influence. For twenty-five years the famous Almanack was printed, the value of its teachings being incalculable. Franklin's popular sayings naturally made their way across the sea to England, and the Staffordshire artists found in them fresh pictures for the decoration of their wares, stamping drinking mugs and small plates for children with colored pictures illustrating Franklin's "Morals," "Proverbs" and "Maxims."

"Poor Richard" gave practical advice for every condition of life, some of it humorous, some caustic, all, however, laden with a salutary lesson and an intent to do good to some person, and hidden beneath the wise saws we find Franklin's disgust for all shams, his censure of evil, his firm stand for honest ideals. Franklin collected the sayings of Poor Richard and printed them in narrative form, as if told by Father Abraham, another fictitious character, at an auction. The book was printed in England and later was translated into several languages, Poor Richard thereby becoming as well known a personage as Mr. Pickwick or Dr. Syntax. The story goes that at the time Franklin was envoy of the new Republic to the Court of France, Captain Paul Jones was in Paris, unsuccessfully trying to obtain a vessel from the French Court, and that one day while reading a French translation of Poor Richard's Almanack, he paused at the line, "If you would have your business done, go; if not, send"; without delay he went himself to Versailles and obtained an order for a ship. In gratitude he named the vessel *Le Bon Homme Richard,* which means "Poor Richard"—and his conquest of the *Serapis* is one of the historic tales of the sea.

In the illustrations may be found a number of Franklin's precepts which, set before children on their plates at table, had a share in forming the character of Young America. "Success to the Plow, the Fleece and the Pail; May the Landlord ever flourish, and the Tenant never fail" are homely sentiments illustrated by a milk-

FLOWERS THAT NEVER FADE
"Good Humour"

LIVERPOOL BOWL, WITH FUR CAP PORTRAIT OF
BENJAMIN FRANKLIN
*(From " Anglo-American Pottery"; by permission of Dr. Edwin A.
Barber)*

FRANKLIN'S MORALS
"Many a little makes a mickle."
(*Unknown Maker*)

"No Gains without Pains"
(*Unknown Maker*)

maid, a sheep and the implements of a farmer. Another illustration teaches a lesson of skillful labor, "Handle your tools without gloves; Remember the cat in gloves catches nothing." Again, a well dressed old lady is pictured speaking to her daughter, who stands near her with a bunch of flowers in her hand, offering this advice: "Good Humor is the greatest charm that children can possess; It makes them happy, and what's more, it gives them power to bless." This illustration is one of a series of pictured precepts entitled, "Flowers That Never Fade," and is an expression of one of Franklin's favorite theories, one which he himself was in the habit of practicing—that good humor is one of Nature's flowers of character most powerful in its influence upon men.

"Keep thy shop, and thy shop will keep thee," "Diligence is the mother of good luck," "He that riseth late must trot all day and scarce shall overtake his business at night," are a few of the saws with which Franklin strove to drive home the lesson of diligent attention to one's affairs. Franklin was a firm believer in improving each moment of the day, as the following proverbs make plain: "One To-day is worth two To-morrows," "Lost time is never found again," and the oft-quoted "Early to bed and early to rise makes a man healthy, wealthy and wise."

A brightly colored plate pictures within a border of

fruits and flowers a busy rural scene—a farmer planting a tree, a boy engaged at his task, and a vessel made ready to set sail—intended to illustrate the terse motto printed upon the back of the plate, "No Gains Without Pains." A familiar proverb of to-day, "Constant dropping wears away stones, and little strokes fell great oaks," belongs to this group. In a series of sayings classed under the title "Poor Richard's Way to Wealth," may be found these two: "What maintains one vice will bring up two children," and "It is easier to suppress the first desire than to satisfy all that follow." They are illustrated by pictures of two men in a tavern, one of them lazily smoking his pipe and the other raising a foaming glass of liquor to his lips. Upon the wall of the tavern is posted this warning: "Landlord, Caution, Pay To-day and Trust To-morrow," while in the background of the picture stand a neglected wife and her two forlorn children, the sad object lessons of evil habits. Another of the "Way to Wealth" series exhibits a portly prosperous farmer who has profited by Poor Richard's advice and grown wealthy, as his fat sheep and hog bear witness. His aristocratic neighbor approaches on horseback, lifts his hat and bows in respect, while below we read the caustic lines: "Now I have a sheep and a cow, Everybody bids me good-morrow." The design on the teapot, two farmers in a field, one plowing and the other sowing seed, illustrates the maxim: "He that by the plow would thrive, himself must either hold or drive."

In the year 1757, Franklin was sent to London to settle the disputes which had arisen in the colony of Pennsylvania over taxing of the estates of the Penn brothers, land which had been bequeathed to them by their father William Penn. While Franklin was in England, the process of transfer printing upon pottery was first practiced in the potteries of Liverpool, and, like all new things, it greatly interested him, and he tried to induce the potters to print a series of chimney tiles with his Poor Richard sayings, no doubt believing in this manner to bring his moral teachings more readily before the eyes and minds of the people of the colonies. But our forefathers were spared this novel method of preaching, as the English taste preferred livelier scenes upon their chimney pieces.

Franklin went again to London for the purpose of adjusting the measures of taxation, which England had imposed upon the American colonies, for ten years remaining there trying to prevent the enactment of those laws of the mother country—the Stamp Act, Duty on Tea and Boston Port Bill—which finally kindled into flame the smoldering fires of revolution. "Depend upon it," wrote Franklin in his practical way to a friend in America, "I took every step in my power to prevent the passing of the Stamp Act. . . . We might as well have hindered the sun's setting. That we could not do. But since it is down, my friend, and it may be long before it rises again, let us make as good a night of it as we can. We can still light candles. Frugality and industry will go a great way towards indemnifying us. Idleness and pride tax with a heavier hand than kings and parliaments. If we can get rid of the former, we may easily bear the latter."

As he was leaving England for his home in America, Franklin, in conversation with a friend, compared the British Empire to a beautiful china vase which if ever broken, could never be put together again. The first shot of the Battle of Lexington was fired while Franklin was on the sea, and it was as a conciliator in public affairs that he took his place in the troubled colonies—first, as a member of the Second Continental Congress, and later, as one of the committee to draft the Declaration of Independence. When it came his turn to sign the great document, Franklin, in response to Hancock's remark, "We must be unanimous, there must be no pulling different ways; we must all hang together," made the oft-quoted reply: "Yes, we must, indeed, all hang together, or, most assuredly, we shall all hang separately."

A beautiful French statuette of pure white porcelain illustrates the distinguished part which Franklin took in the affairs of the Revolution, in winning the recognition

FRANKLIN "BENNINGTON PITCHER"
"Toby" or "Cider Jug"

"He that by the Plough would thrive,
Himself must either hold or drive."

FRANKLIN'S MAXIMS

"He who lives upon Hope   "Handle your tools with-
    will die fasting."   out mittens," etc.

"Constant dropping wears   "Three removes are as bad as a fire.
    away stones,   A rolling stone gathers no moss. "
And little *strokes* fall great
oaks."

"Keep thy shop   " Not to oversee work-
    and thy shop   men is to leave them
    will keep thee."   your purse open."

of the countries of Europe for the young Republic. He crossed the sea for the third time, now as Ambassador of the infant Republic of the United States to the French Court of Louis XVI and the unfortunate Marie Antoinette. The statuette was designed to commemorate the treaty of the United States with France, made largely through Franklin's influence, after the news of the surrender of Burgoyne had opened the eyes of the world to the strength of the American cause.

We are told that upon the occasion of the formal recognition of the Treaty, Franklin intended to put off his plain dress and to appear before the King in Court costume, but the costume did not arrive in time, and the wig which the hairdresser brought refused to sit upon the Doctor's head. Franklin suggested that it might be too small. "Monsieur, it is impossible," cried the perruquier, and then dashing the wig to the floor, he exclaimed, "No, Monsieur, it is not the wig which is too small; it is your head which is too large." In the statuette, Franklin is modeled in his simple republican dress, a suit of striped silk which is now in the possession of the Historical Society of Massachusetts, with wigless head, in striking contrast to the King in his sumptuous royal garments. The face of Franklin is very fine, with much nobility and intelligence added to the benignancy and sweetness of expression with which his other portraits make us familiar. The attitudes of both King Louis and Franklin are full of dignity. Upon the scroll which the King holds out to his companion are inscribed in golden letters the words "Independence de l'Amérique," and "Liberté des Mers." Indeed, Franklin's plain large features, oft-times topped with the fur cap which he loved to wear, were almost always truthfully represented by the French and English potters, but his sober garb must have seemed to them scarce suited to one of his exalted station, for the gray garments are sometimes transformed in their kilns into yellow waistcoat, pink breeches and cocked hat; in one porcelain figure an ermine cape flows jauntily from his ample republican shoulders!

While in France at this time, Franklin enjoyed the greatest popularity with all classes of people. His "antique simplicity of dress and appearance" charmed the Court; his wide learning made him the intimate of scholars; shopkeepers ran to their doors to look upon this unique representative of a new people as he passed down the street. His picture was everywhere to be seen, porcelain medallions of his face being plentiful in Paris. "A variety of other medallions," writes Franklin at this time to his daughter, in the letter already quoted, "have been made since of various sizes; some to be set in the lids of snuff-boxes, and some so small as to be worn in rings; and the numbers sold are incredible. These, with the pictures and prints (of which copies upon copies are

POOR RICHARD'S "WAY TO WEALTH" SERIES
OF MAXIMS

"Now I have a Sheep and a Cow,
Everybody bids me good morrow."

"What maintains one Vice would bring up
two Children."
"It is easier to suppress the first desire
than to satisfy all that follow."

POOR RICHARD'S MAXIMS

" Success to the Plough, the Fleece, and the Pail, " etc.

" Handle your tools without gloves—Remember the
cat in gloves catches nothing."

spread everywhere) have made your father's face as well known as that of the moon, so that he durst not do anything that would oblige him to run away, as his phiz would discover him wherever he should venture to show it. It is said by learned etymologists that the name of doll for the image children play with is derived from the word idol. From the number of dolls now made of him he may be truly said, in that sense, to be idolized in this country."

Franklin's friendship with Lafayette began at the time of this sojourn in France, through the young French officer's application to him for a commission in the American army—a friendship not overlooked by the potters, for in consequence numerous Staffordshire tea, breakfast and dinner sets picture a man in foreign dress, supposed to represent Lafayette, seated before a tomb inscribed "Franklin." An illustration of one of these designs is shown in the chapter on Lafayette's Visit to America. The English potters also produced Franklin medallions and placques, Wedgwood designing a blue and white jasper medallion of Franklin for his series of "Illustrious Moderns."

Like George Washington, Franklin was fond of having blue china upon his table, and while he was in London he sent quantities of it home to his wife, at the same time writing her that letter which contains the oft-quoted lines: "I also forgot to mention among the china a large fine jug for beer to stand in the cooler. I fell in love with it at first sight; for I thought it looked like a fat jolly dame, clean and tidy, with a neat blue and white calico gown on, good-natured and lovely, and put me in mind of—somebody."

Not only did the potters of France and England immortalize Franklin in their clay, but his fame spread to the Orient, and the artists of China and Japan also pictured this strange representative of a new world. The result, no doubt intended for flattery, is for us an occasion for smiles, for they have made him one of their own almond-eyed selves and have transformed his familiar fur cap into a close crop of woolly curls! The early American potters of Bennington, Vermont, about the middle of the nineteenth century likewise fashioned in clay the figure of this great American, as the Franklin cider jug or toby in the rich browns of their manufacture bears witness.

The following amusing epitaph, composed by Franklin during his early life as a printer in Philadelphia, deserves a place in this story of his life:

The Body
of
Benjamin Franklin
Printer
(Like the cover of an old Book
Its contents torn out
And stript of its lettering and gilding)
Lies here, food for worms.

BENJAMIN FRANKLIN AND HIS PRECEPTS

But the work shall not be lost
For it will (as he believed)
Appear once more
In a new and more elegant edition
Revised and Corrected
by
The Author.

CHAPTER XII

NAVAL HEROES OF THE WAR OF 1812

A GROUP of pitchers, tall, yellow and melon-shaped, record in the illustrations on their sides stories of the heroes and engagements of the infant navy of the Republic. The Liverpool potters, when the new frigates of the United States began to visit their harbor, turned their attention to "Sailor Pitchers," decorating them with pictures of British and American sailor lads grasping hands in friendship, or with sketches of full-rigged vessels flying the American flag, and inscribing them with appropriate legends, such as: "May They Ever Be United," "The True Blooded Yankee," "Success to the Infant Navy of America," etc.; or, with jingles of which the following are typical:

> From Rocks and Sands
> And every ill,
> May God preserve
> The Sailor still.

> No more I'll roam,
> I'll stay at home,
> To sail no more
> From shore to shore;
> But with my wife
> Lead a happy, peaceful life.

FIRST VIEW OF COM. PERRY'S VICTORY

BATTLE OF LAKE ERIE
"Commodore Perry's Victory"

NAVAL HEROES OF THE WAR OF 1812

Lonely Jack, strolling the streets of Liverpool in search of a gift to carry home to sweetheart or wife in some far-away New England village, was pleased to find the attractive souvenirs and gave his hard-earned shillings for them. One such pitcher, carefully preserved since that time, is entitled "The Sailor's Return," and presents a young sailor husband come home from the sea, his happy wife beside him and their infant in his arms; the lines underneath the sketch doubtless are intended to voice his sentiments:

> I now the joys of life renew,
> From care and trouble free,
> And find a wife who's kind and true,
> To drive life's cares away.

Soon after the differences between France and the United States, which came to an issue in the year 1799, had been fought out in the southern seas, the English exploited on their pottery the congratulatory legend, "Success to the Infant Navy of America." A set of Liverpool pitchers is yet in existence which voice this sentiment in a spirited print of a naval engagement accompanied with the explanatory description: "L'Insurgente French Frigate of 44 guns and 411 men striking her Colours to the American Frigate Constitution, Commodore Truxton, of 40 guns, after an action of an hour and a half in which the former had 75 men killed

173

& wounded & the latter one killed & three wounded, Feb. 20th., 1799."

Commodore Truxton's capture of both *l'Insurgente* and *La Vengeance* was almost as keen a source of delight to Englishmen as it was to the people of the United States, the English Government in honor of the feat presenting the successful Commodore with many tokens of esteem, including a service of silver plate—an expression of generosity no doubt bitterly regretted in the years immediately following, when that same "Infant Navy" scored such brilliant "Success" turned against the British battle fleet.

The efforts of American sailors in ridding the high seas of the hated and feared African pirates who were levying tribute upon civilized countries next inspired the potters to print portraits of Commodores Bainbridge, Decatur and Preble. Looking upon their faces, what stirring scenes are called to mind: how, in the year 1800, Bainbridge, then a youth of 26, was sent by the United States Government with the vessel *George Washington* to carry the annual tribute money to the dey of Algiers; how, when he arrived, the dey forced him to play errand boy, hoist the Algerian flag at the main of the *George Washington* (which he promptly hauled down as soon as he had cleared the harbor) and sail to Constantinople with gifts for the sultan of Turkey, the overlord of the Barbary States. To his surprise, Captain Bainbridge was received by the Sultan with honor as a representative of a new nation, and was presented with a passport to insure respectful treatment in all the Sultan's domains. Armed with this powerful weapon, Bainbridge, upon his return to Algiers, refused to enter the harbor or to make a second voyage for the dey, and he so frightened the Algerian potentate into respect that he was even permitted to rescue and carry away some French exiles in the city—for which service he received the thanks of Napoleon.

Captain Bainbridge's second adventure among the Barbary Corsairs was more disastrous than the first. Before three years had gone by, he was again in the waters of the Mediterranean, this time as captain of the *Philadelphia,* one of a small squadron of American fighting vessels under command of Captain Preble of the flagship *Constitution.* In order to overawe the insolence of the pirates, Preble sent Bainbridge to blockade the harbor of Tripoli. Sighting a vessel of the enemy ahead, Bainbridge was giving chase in the shallow water near the coast, when suddenly his ship ran upon a hidden rock in twelve feet of water. All efforts were made to back the *Philadelphia* off the reef, even her guns being heaved overboard and her foremast cut away. These measures being of no avail, and the vessels of the enemy approaching, orders were given to bore holes in the ship's bottom, drown the magazine and destroy everything which would be of service to the pirates. Bainbridge and his men were taken prisoners and carried before the pasha, and for nineteen months they languished in the dungeons of Tripoli. Two days after the disaster the *Philadelphia* was floated by the pirates at high tide, her guns were raised and remounted, and she was towed, as good as ever, into the harbor of Tripoli—a prize of immense value.

Then followed the thrilling feat which will ever be associated with the names of Decatur and Preble. The daring scheme was proposed to fire the *Philadelphia* lying at her moorings in the harbor, and from among the many volunteers for the hazardous task, Commodore Preble selected Decatur. With a crew of picked men, a supply of combustibles and a Sicilian pilot who knew the waters of the harbor, Decatur boarded a ketch, a small vessel which had been captured from the pirates and renamed the *Intrepid*. They waited outside until evening, then quietly stole into the harbor; scarcely a man was to be seen on deck, for they wished to allay suspicion of being taken for a vessel of war, and to all appearance the little ketch was only a pirate ship making for port before nightfall. The watchword "Philadelphia" had been passed among them so they might be able to recognize one another should danger arise. A gentle breeze wafted them over the smooth water towards the huge bulk of the *Philadelphia* lying at her moorings and

176

SAILOR PITCHER
"May They Ever be United"

SAILOR PITCHER
"The Sailor's Return"

COMMODORE BAINBRIDGE PITCHER
(Liverpool Type)
(*From " Anglo-American Pottery"; by permission of Dr. Edwin A. Barber*)

COMMODORE PERRY
"Hero of the Lake"
(*From " Anglo-American Pottery"; by permission
of Dr. Edwin A. Barber*)

sharply outlined against the white walls of the city. The men aboard the *Philadelphia* spied the approaching vessel and called out to know her errand. The *Intrepid's* pilot, instructed by Decatur, answered that they had lost their anchors in a gale and wished to tie up to the frigate until morning. Permission was given, a rope passed, and the ketch made fast to the *Philadelphia*, when suddenly rang loud and clear over the water the cry, "Americanos!" They were discovered. Decatur and his men leaped aboard the frigate, struck down those who had not jumped overboard in their fright, scattered combustibles through the ship and kindled the flames, and in exactly twenty minutes from the time they boarded the *Philadelphia* they were again on the *Intrepid,* ropes cut and the men pulling for the open sea, three rousing cheers echoing through the harbor. But danger was not yet past: the enemy turned the guns of the battery in their direction, and the heated guns of the *Philadelphia* pointed their way—but no shot reached them as they sped to safety. With this deed, which Lord Nelson declared "the most bold and daring of the age," the infant navy of the United States made its bow to all the nations; and the gallantry of the young American seamen spread abroad the fame of the new republic across the sea.

A little later, Commodore Preble made a successful attack upon the city of Tripoli, the English in commemoration of his act bringing out a pitcher-design of ships attacking fortifications, with these descriptive lines: "Commodore Preble's Squadron Attacking the City of Tripoli Aug. 3, 1804. The American Squadron under Commodore Preble consisting of the *Constitution* 44 guns 2 Brigs & 3 Schooners 2 bombs & 4 Gunboats Attacking the City and Harbour of Tripoli Aug. 3, 1804, the city was defended by Batteries Mounting 115 Pieces of heavy Cannon & the Harbour was defended by 19 Gunboats 2 Brigs 2 Schooners 2 Gallies and a Xebeck. the city Received Great Damage Several of the Tripolitan Vessels were sunk 3 of their Gunboats taken & a Great Number of men Killed."

The navy, thus brilliantly introduced to the world, was enlarged by President Madison, acting upon the counsel of Captains Bainbridge and Stuart, who foresaw the need of an adequate naval defense if the Atlantic Ocean were not to become, as one journal declared, "the back dooryard of John Bull"; that parent, like many another, being loth to recognize the fact that his latest born had attained to manhood with its "inalienable rights" to be respected. A medallion portrait of President Madison, the "War President," is presented upon a tall yellow jug, encircled with thirteen wreaths, each wreath enclosing the name of one of the States of the Union. Upon a ribbon scroll above the portrait is the inscription, "James Madison President of the United States of America";

SAILOR PITCHER
"The True Blooded Yankee"

U. S. FRIGATE "GUERRIÈRE" BOUND
FOR RUSSIA
(Reverse of the "Defense of Stonington")

COMMODORE STEPHEN DECATUR

PRESIDENT MADISON—WAR PRESIDENT

the reverse bears the legend, "Independence and the Federal Union, 1815."

Continued British interference with American shipping, however, as well as the forcible impressment of American seamen into British service, finally led to open rupture with England, resulting in a declaration of war.

When after a few months the War of 1812, the actual "war of independence," as Benjamin Franklin had prophesied would come (the first being but a "war of revolution"), resolved itself into a series of spectacular sea-fights, the potter-historians of Liverpool found in illustrating them a new and a greater opportunity for trade, at the same time gratifying the pride of the American people; and the result was a large quantity of jugs and punch bowls bearing portraits of American Commodores, together with scenes of their engagements.

Who can look upon the forceful features of Captain Isaac Hull, framed in the emblems of his calling, without a thrill of pride as he calls to mind the brilliant opening of the great sea-drama of 100 years ago? The curtain rose upon the first important act on July 17, 1812; the scene was the open sea off the coast of our southern States; the action was a race rather than a battle. Hull, who had won honors in the Tripoli incident, sailed out from Chesapeake Bay in the frigate *Constitution,* and soon sighted a squadron of the enemy, who, when morning dawned, were seen to surround him. As fighting against such odds was out of the question, all that remained for Hull to do was to run for home—and the manner in which he ran made this act, without fighting or damage on either side, forever famous in the annals of the sea.

The ocean was so calm that no headway could be made with sails, so Hull began by kedging. He sent a small boat ahead for perhaps half a mile to drop a kedge anchor and carry the lines back to the ship, then the crew fastened the lines to the windlass and wound them up, pulling the vessel to the anchor. In this manner Hull gradually walked away from the enemy, much to their mystified surprise, until they caught sight of the "deus ex machina" and employed the same method. Hull promptly cut away some of the woodwork of his cabin, ran two twenty-pound guns out of his windows and mounted another gun as a stern chaser to keep the enemy at a proper distance. The unique spectacle is pictured before us—eleven vessels pursuing one, and all at the mercy of the wind, the star actor in all sea performances before the age of steam. For three days the chase continued; upon the evening of the second day a heavy squall came up and the *Constitution* furled all canvas; the enemy, sighting this maneuver, did the same. Then, under cover of the darkening storm, the *Constitution* quickly hoisted all sail and ran for home. When morning broke, the enemy was far astern and had given up the chase.

One month later, Hull again sailed out, this time from Boston, in search of adventure, and before long he came up with it in the form of an English frigate flaunting upon her mainsail in huge red letters the challenge:

> All who meet me have a care,
> I am England's Guerrière.

She proved to be one of the squadron which had recently chased Hull out of the southern seas; now she was alone and no time was lost in giving battle. For two hours the *Constitution* returned fire for fire in as fierce a sea duel as ever the ocean witnessed. At last, the boastful English flag was lowered and Hull lay by until the whitening dawn revealed the *Guerrière* a wreck, then her men were taken aboard Hull's vessel, fire was applied and she was blown to pieces. Captain Hull was the hero of the hour when he landed in Boston with his prisoners. He made a sort of triumphal progress to New York and Philadelphia, through villages decorated with banners and arches, gifts of snuff-boxes and swords being everywhere pressed upon him. Congress voted him a gold medal, a silver one to each of his officers and $50,000 to the crew. In this engagement the *Constitution* for the second time proved herself something more than the English journal's slighting description, "a bunch of pine boards under a bit of striped bunting," the same journal now voicing England's new-born fear that "this new enemy, unaccustomed to such triumphs, might be rendered insolent and confident by them."

That the confidence, at least, of the Republic was strengthened by success may plainly be understood by a study of the next pictured engagement—the duel between the American sloop-of-war *Wasp,* Captain Jones, and the English brig *Frolic,* which took place off Cape Hatteras on October 17, 1812. The fray continued close and furious for forty-three minutes, with the two vessels at last so close upon one another that the muzzles of two of the *Wasp's* guns were actually in the bow parts of the *Frolic,* her last discharge sweeping the English ship from stem to stern. Seeing no sign of submission from the enemy, a sailor of the *Wasp* leaped aboard the *Frolic* and to his amazement met no opposition—all were dead or wounded except the man at the wheel. The end of the engagement, however, was like the end of the fable—a British frigate suddenly hove in sight, made prize of both vessels and bore them off to Bermuda.

Upon the same day of the battle between the *Wasp* and the *Frolic,* Captain Decatur won a brilliant victory with the frigate *United States* over the British ship *Macedonian,* near the Azores Islands. On his return

COMMODORE HULL

GENERAL PIKE

THE "WASP" BOARDING "THE FROLIC"

BATTLE OF THE "ENTERPRISE" AND "BOXER"

to New York with his prize in tow, he, like Hull, was honored with a banquet, public rejoicings and a gold medal. "No one could suppose such an event could have taken place," was England's astounded comment, while at the same time a Liverpool potter printed on a jug, underneath a portrait of the successful Commodore, the following lines:

> "Then quickly met our nation's eyes
> The noblest sight in nature,
> A first-class frigate as a prize
> Brought back by brave Decatur."

And an American rhymster voiced the attitude of the American public thus:

> Let Britain no longer lay claim to the seas,
> For the trident of Neptune is ours, if we please,
> While Hull and Decatur and Jones are our boast,
> We dare their whole navy to come to our coast.

The following act in this drama, fast taking on the appearance of a melodrama, with eager spectators agaze over all Europe, took place off the coast of Brazil. It was the battle between the now veteran *Constitution,* this time in command of Captain Bainbridge, and the English frigate *Java.* The story of the *Constitution* and the *Guerrière* was repeated—after nearly two hours of fighting the wrecked *Java* was fired, while the American vessel received but slight injury. "Avast

Boys, She's Struck!" the words of Captain Bainbridge as he saw the enemy surrender are printed under his potrait upon a mug of Liverpool manufacture, together with this jaunty couplet:

> "On Brazil's Coast She ruled the roost
> When Bainbridge was her Captain."

Captain Bainbridge came in, after this victory, for his share of gold snuff-boxes and silver services, while the staunch ship *Constitution* (now preserved in the Boston dockyard for all to inspect) was newly christened *Old Ironsides*. The English papers then said that the situation called for "serious reflection," while they lamented that upwards of five hundred British vessels had been captured in seven months by Americans— "500 merchantmen and three frigates (ay and three sloops-of-war!)" are their words. That "Nucleus of trouble" which Lord Nelson had prophesied lay in the American fleet was developing rapidly for the mother country.

The naval scenery of the war now shifts from the ocean to the inland waterways lying between American territory and Canada, to secure control of which at this time was one of the chief concerns of the English. Many skirmishes took place along the wilderness shores of the Great Lakes, one of which is recalled by the portrait of General Pike, accompanied with his prophetic

words: "Be always ready to die for your country."
General Pike expired as he was about to enter, a victor,
into the city of York, now Toronto, at that time the capital city of Canada. The act of firing the Government
Buildings of that city by the American soldiers, against
General Pike's orders, was later on in the war avenged in
kind by the British burning the public buildings at Washington.

Command of Lake Erie was gained for the Americans
by that brilliant engagement, the recital of which will
forever stir the imagination of each succeeding generation of American school boys. "Perry's Victory on
Lake Erie," as they named the episode, was a favorite
subject for illustration by the English potters, sketches
of this first "fleet action" of the war decorating sets of
Staffordshire blue tableware as well as numerous yellow
pitchers of Liverpool.

Perry collected his boats at Put-in-Bay, and on the
evening before the battle, September 9, 1813, he gave his
orders to his officers, showing them a flag with "Don't
Give Up The Ship" in white letters upon it—the dying
words of Captain Lawrence in the battle between the
Chesapeake and the *Shannon* fought upon the sea near
Boston three months before, words and portrait of Captain Lawrence being also printed upon a commemorative
pitcher. "When this flag shall be hoisted at the main
yard of the Lawrence, it shall be your signal for going

into action," he told them.   At daylight the next morning the English squadron was sighted, and the engagement begun.

In the illustration may be seen the two lines of naval
ships drawn up in battle form, six on the British side and
nine under Commodore Perry—and, may not the tiny
boat passing from one vessel to another be the one in
which Perry, after his flagship *Lawrence* had been put
out of action, made his way through a storm of bullets
to the *Niagara,* on board of which he sailed through the
enemy's line and won the day?   "We have met the enemy
and they are ours; two ships, two brigs, one schooner
and one sloop"—the terse message of the gallant victor's
dispatch will never lose its power to thrill!   A deep blue
Staffordshire platter honors "The Hero of the Lake"
with a memorial design executed by W. G. Wall, who
came to New York in the year 1818 and sent this among
other paintings of American views, to English pottery
works for reproduction.   A fanciful structure with
gothic spires is shown, upon the summit of which Fame
is sounding a trumpet over an expanse of sea; at the left
of the design may be seen the abundant weeping willow
of conventional early nineteenth-century memorials.

Many minor sea engagements followed, that between
the *Enterprise* and *Boxer,* of which a spirited sketch is
shown, being among them.   This action took place off
the coast of Maine not far from the city of Portland,

(1) DEFENSE OF STONINGTON, CONNECTICUT
(2) A FRIGATE

COMMODORE PREBLE'S SQUADRON ATTACK-
ING THE CITY OF TRIPOLI, AUGUST 3,
1804. REVERSE—PORTRAIT OF COM-
MODORE PREBLE.

(Liverpool Pitcher, in Dickins Collection in
Washington, D. C.)

BATTLE OF LAKE CHAMPLAIN
Commodore Macdonough's Victory

and resulted in the death of both captains. The poet Longfellow, then a lad of seven years living in Portland, in later life recalled the scene in his poem, My Lost Youth:

> I remember the sea fight far away,
> How it thundered o'er the tide!
> And the dead captains as they lay
> In their graves, o'erlooking the tranquil bay
> Where they in battle died.
> And the sound of that mournful song
> Goes through me with a thrill:
> "A boy's will is the wind's will,
> And the thoughts of youth are long, long thoughts."

The charming view of the harbor of Stonington, Connecticut, framed in a waving steamer inscribed, "The Gallant Defense of Stonington, August 9, 1814. Stonington is Free whilst her Heroes have one Gun left," tells its own story. The little settlement of 100 houses situated upon an exposed neck of land was attacked, the ships of the enemy bombarding it with every kind of missile known to that war. The citizens of Stonington possessed plenty of courage, but only one gun, and when the enemy ceased firing on one side and sailed around to the other of the narrow peninsula, the patriots promptly dragged the lone six-pounder across the narrow strip of land and did such deadly execution with it that the disheartened enemy withdrew. The reverse of the pitcher (shown in another illustration) bears a print of a vessel under full sail, with the words beneath: "United States Frigate *Guerrière*, Commodore Macdonough bound to Russia July, 1818." It is recorded that a citizen of Stonington went to Russia on public service in the *Guerrière*, and while en route he stopped at Liverpool and ordered these pitchers, he himself making the drawing of the battle scene for the English engraver.

The china-history of the sea engagements of the War of 1812 closes with a sketch of the Battle of Lake Champlain. Like the Battle of Lake Erie, this too was a fleet action, and the tactics of Captain Macdonough which had much to do with deciding the final victory equaled in brilliancy and courage the dash of Perry through the enemy's line. Before taking command of the fleet on Lake Champlain, Captain Macdonough had seen considerable naval service, having been aboard the *Philadelphia* when she was captured by the pirates and towed into the harbor of Tripoli; and later, having served on board the *Enterprise* under Commodore Decatur. At sunrise on September 11, 1814, as the British squadron came in sight on Lake Champlain, Captain Macdonough called his officers about him upon the quarter deck, and together they prayed for wisdom and guidance in the task before them. The British vessels advanced to within a few yards, when a pet game cock on Macdonough's flagship flew upon a cannon and crowed

MEMORIAL OF COMMODORE PERRY
The Temple of Fame
(*Stevenson*)
(*From " Anglo-American Pottery"; by permission of Dr. Edwin A. Barber*)

lustily—a favorable omen, the sailors believed, as they cheered and rushed into the fray. In addition to commanding the fleet in this action, Macdonough worked like a common sailor at any task that came to hand, being also able to maneuver his flagship, the *Saratoga,* in such a way that it could be turned completely around, and, after deadly firing had disabled all the guns of his starboard side, to pour such a volley from his larboard battery that after two hours of desperate struggle the English hauled down their colors—and New York State was saved from invasion. When the English officers came to offer their swords to him, Captain Macdonough courteously said, "Gentlemen, your gallant conduct makes you worthy to wear your weapons. Return them to their scabbards."

Two interesting pitchers which aid in the recital of the story of the War of 1812 remain to be described. The first, of copper luster ware, shows a full-rigged vessel surrounded by a chain of elliptical links containing the names of Hull, Jones, Lawrence, Macdonough, Porter, Blakey, Beatry, Stuart, Washington, Perry, Rogers, Bainbridge, and Decatur, with two clasped hands holding the chain. Upon the other side, an American eagle with "E Pluribus Unum" is enclosed in a similar chain which links the names Brown, McComb, Ripley, Pike, Porter, Miller, Brainbridge, Izard, Van Rensselaer, Adair, Lewis, Gaines, Scott and Jardson—what a galaxy of events these groups of historic names summon to the mind!

The second pitcher was made by Enoch Wood & Son at their potteries in Burslem, Staffordshire, about the year 1824, and is immense in size for a pitcher, standing twenty inches high, with a body eighteen inches in diameter. This is known as the "Historical Pitcher of the War of 1812," the decorations portraying many incidents of that period. Upon either side of a secondary handle are portraits of Washington and Adams, while one side of the body bears portraits of Captain Jones of the *Macedonian,* Major-General Brown of the *Niagara* campaign, Commodore Bainbridge of the *Constitution,* and prints representing the *Constitution* escaping from the British fleet, Commodore Macdonough's victory on Lake Champlain, and an American eagle with the motto, E Pluribus Unum. Upon the reverse are portraits of Commodore Decatur, Commodore Perry and Captain Hull of the *Constitution;* below are represented the engagements between the *Chesapeake* and *Shannon* off Boston Harbor, June 1, 1813, Commodore Perry's Victory on Lake Erie, and the line from his message, "We have met the enemy and they are ours." This pitcher was made for an early citizen of Troy, New York, and was first publicly used at a reception given in that city in honor of General Lafayette upon the occasion of his visit in September, 1824.

NAVAL HEROES OF THE WAR OF 1812

The final battle of the War of 1812 was a land engagement fought at New Orleans, the United States forces
under command of General Jackson, who later on became
President. Before the battle was ended, peace with
Great Britain had been agreed upon, the Treaty being
signed at Ghent, Belgium, on December 24, 1814.
Upon December 26, an envoy set out for the United
States with a copy of the document, crossing the Atlantic
upon a British sloop of war. He arrived in New York
February 11, having been thirty-eight days upon the
voyage—and the tidings which he brought with him one
hundred years ago were a few months past the cause of
quiet, owing to the tragic circumstances of the other
contracting party to the treaty, but intense satisfaction
and congratulation. In the hearts of all Americans
echoes the sentiment which a century ago was inscribed
upon a Liverpool pitcher: "May they ever be united."

CHAPTER XIII

GENERAL LAFAYETTE'S VISIT TO AMERICA

NO event in the early history of the United States stirred such depths of popular affection as the famous visit of General Lafayette—for, was he not the friend of the first President, the adopted son of America, as well as, in many minds, the savior of the country? His life had been filled with stirring romance —the years of early manhood spent in defense of the freedom of the American colonies, in forwarding the cause of liberty in his own land and as a prisoner of state in the dungeons of Austria. Then, at the age of sixty-seven, after an absence of nearly half a century, upon the invitation of the young republic of the United States he crossed the ocean once more to look upon the land of his youthful affection.

From one limit of our territory to another he went, passing through each of the twenty-four States. He visited all of the principal cities; he was the guest of two presidents in the White House; he took part in three anniversaries of the Revolutionary War, in every place such crowds thronging to see him that few persons failed to catch a glimpse of his face.

LA GRANGE—LAFAYETTE'S HOME IN FRANCE

(*E. W. & S*)

GENERAL LAFAYETTE'S VISIT TO AMERICA

Many souvenirs in honor of Lafayette's visit made their appearance—the ladies wearing Lafayette buckles upon their slippers and his portrait upon their scarfs and their gloves; his features also appeared upon buttons and upon the material of which men's waistcoats were made. And, as blue china decorated with American views was then at the height of its popularity, numerous dinner and tea sets bearing the pictured story of his visit came to America from over the sea. "Welcome, Lafayette, the Nation's Guest and our Country's Glory" and "As Brave and Disinterested as Washington" were among the sentiments printed upon china with which the English potters honored their one-time foe. Lafayette's visit was coincident with the completion of the Erie Canal, therefore his portrait (as the following chapter relates) graced also the pottery produced in honor of that occasion.

The first illustration is of the *Cadmus,* the sailing vessel in which Lafayette, accompanied by his son George Washington Lafayette, and his secretary, came to America. This picture is of special value, for it preserves a sketch of an American merchantman, a type of vessel in common use upon the seas for many years after the colonies had become a republic. The *Cadmus* was placed at the disposal of General Lafayette and his party by its New York owners after the offer of President Monroe to send a Government vessel to fetch them had been refused. No other passengers were allowed on board, no cargo was shipped, nor would the owners accept any reward for their services, deeming the honor of conveying the distinguished guest a sufficient return. As it appears in the illustration, framed in an appropriate border of sea shells and mosses, the little vessel seems to float upon as calm and sunlit a sea as that which bore the hero to our shores.

After fifteen days' sail the *Cadmus* reached New York harbor, and, welcomed by the booming of cannon from Fort Lafayette, she put into port at Staten Island. It was Sabbath day, and, in compliance with the wishes of the citizens of New York, the guests were quietly received at the home of vice-President Daniel D. Tompkins on Staten Island. Upon the following morning the formal entry into the United States took place, and from the beautiful blue platter inscribed: "Landing of General Lafayette at Castle Garden, August 16, 1824," may be read the story of that famous landing scene. The old fort, or Castle Garden (other views of which may be found in a former chapter), is separated from the Battery by a bridge 300 feet long; the harbor is thronged with gayly trimmed vessels; the Battery guns are booming forth a welcome; and heralds are galloping excitedly to and fro. Three of the newly invented steamboats, "floating palaces," Lafayette called them, may be seen—the one in the center being the *Fulton,* and the large boat at the left the *Chancellor Livingston,* with the honored guest on board—the *Chancellor Livingston* at that time being considered the most beautiful and luxurious vessel in the world.   Following in the train of the steamboats, as the naval procession makes its way to the landing at the Battery, comes the *Cadmus* "borne in triumph rather than towed" by the new vessels.   Looking upon this scene, in fancy one hears the welcoming huzzas of two hundred thousand people as Lafayette steps upon the shore; strains of the French song, "Where can one better be than in the bosom of his family," fill the air; and listen, do you not catch the broken voice of the battle-scarred warrior of the Revolution as he grasps his hero's hand:—"I saw you in the heat of battle.   You were but a boy, but you were a serious and sedate lad."

To the City Hall (the beautiful building pictured in a former chapter), Lafayette's carriage is drawn, and the illustrious guest listens to the Mayor's speech of welcome, the popular sentiments of gratitude which he voices being later echoed throughout every State in the Union:

"Posterity will never forget the young and gallant Frenchman who consecrated his youth, his talents, his fortune and his exertions to their cause, who exposed his life, who shed his blood, that they might become free and happy.   They will recollect that you came to them in the darkest period of their struggle, that you linked your fortune with theirs when it seemed almost hopeless—that you shared in the dangers, privations and sufferings of that bitter struggle, nor quitted them for a moment till it was consummated in the glorious field of Yorktown. The people of the United States look up to you as one of their most honored parents."

In preceding chapters many of New York's buildings, streets and squares that met the eyes of the distinguished guests have been pictured, among them the City Hotel on Broadway, the famous hostelry in which they lodged; Saint Paul's Chapel, then out in the fields, in which Lafayette attended a concert of sacred music, remarking upon the beauty of the ladies of the audience; Columbia College, Scudder's Museum, the Hospital and Alms-house. The French guests went to see a play at the Park Theater, and such a tumult arose upon Lafayette's entrance that the actors were obliged to stop the per-formance and to sing verses bearing the refrains, "The Companion of Washington," "The Captive of Olmutz," "The Guest of the Nation."

At a banquet tendered by the French residents of New York to celebrate the 47th anniversary of the Battle of the Brandywine, Lafayette found the table carved in imitation of the Erie Canal, then nearing completion. For a distance of seventy feet, the length of the table, a slender stream of water found its way between banks lined with trees, under miniature bridges and through meadows dotted with tiny houses and cattle. The Grand

THE "CADMUS," IN WHICH LAFAYETTE
CAME TO AMERICA
(*Wood*)

LAFAYETTE AS HE APPEARED IN 1824
Erie Canal Series
(*Stevenson*)

LAFAYETTE MOURNING AT TOMB
OF WASHINGTON

(*Wood*)

LA GRANGE—EAST VIEW

(*Enoch Wood & Sons*)

Fête, for which the city had been preparing for many weeks, eclipsed all other entertainments. It took place in Castle Garden, the guests passing from the Battery over the long bridge, now laid with rich carpets, lined with evergreens and adorned with statues of Washington and Hamilton. From the center of the bridge rose a pyramid seventy-five feet high, illumined with colored lamps and crowned with a star blazing the name Lafayette. In the interior of the Hall stood thirteen columns, each one decorated with the Coat of Arms of one of the original thirteen States. Lafayette entered the vaulted building through a triumphal arch, and as he took his seat the familiar refrain, "Where can one better be than in the bosom of his family," filled the hall, up rolled the curtains which formed the sides, and a huge transparency of Lafayette's French château La Grange, entitled "Here is his Home," was flashed before him, to the accompaniment of rousing cheers.

Lafayette and his party, together with an escort of New York citizens, set out for a visit to Boston, traveling by coach, as it was several years before the days of railroads. At every village and hamlet in their five days' journey they were greeted with banquets, speeches, fireworks and processions; they passed under triumphal arches inscribed with the names of Lafayette and Washington, or with the dates of the Battles of the Brandywine and Yorktown; torch-bearing horsemen escorted them from village to village; and their passage was lighted with bonfires kindled on the hilltops and cheered with bugle calls echoing through the valleys. The approach to Boston was lined for two miles with militia, among the escort being a company of sixty boys drawing a cannon, which, in their eagerness to salute the guest, they stopped now and then and fired. Upon Boston Common, Lafayette made his way through a long double line of boys and girls from the public schools, each one decorated with a Lafayette ribbon; a little girl stepped forward and was raised to the General's carriage, she placed a crown of evergreen upon his head, embraced him and called him "Father."

The Boston which greeted General Lafayette has already been studied in illustrations—the State House and the homes of the city's prominent citizens, fronting upon the Common; the churches, Library, Hospital, and places of business and amusement. In the Halls of Harvard Collége, Lafayette attended the exercises of Commencement, and was greeted with especial honor as one who had "founded a democratic government under which education best flourishes." Commodore Bainbridge, one of the naval heroes of the War of 1812, received Lafayette at the Charlestown Navy Yard. At Bunker Hill, Lafayette paused at the grave of General Warren; and he went quietly out to Quincy and gladdened the heart of his old friend, ex-President John Adams, then a man of eighty-nine. At Lexington, the militia defiled before Lafayette as he stood beside the pyramid which still marks the place where the first martyrs of American liberty fell, the French hero himself, as the speaker said in his address, "A second and living monument of the Revolution." Boston's farewell banquet was served under an immense tent on the Common, to twelve hundred guests, the center of the table being graced with a silver dish filled with arms, shot, military buttons, etc., collected on Bunker Hill.

A pleasant incident of the return journey to New York is suggested by the illustration of the Deaf and Dumb Asylum of Hartford, Connecticut, the first institution of its kind in the United States, having been opened but seven years before Lafayette's visit by Thomas H. Gallaudet. The unfortunate children who were drawn up in line to greet Lafayette pointed to a banner which they held over their hearts, inscribed with the words, "What others express, we feel." In this city a comrade of Revolutionary days presented to Lafayette the very epaulettes and scarf which he wore upon the field of Brandywine; they still retained traces of his blood. The party made a short stop at New Haven in order to pay a visit to Yale College, before returning to New York.

Lafayette's sail up the Hudson River in the steamboat *James Kent,* accompanied by a number of ladies and gentlemen of New York, was one long gala jaunt. A group of Revolutionary veterans attended the General, and together they spent many hours on deck in enjoyment of the beautiful scenery—the Passes in the Highlands, the mountains, the fertile shores, and the boats of many kinds plying up and down the river. As their vessel passed historic points on the river banks, the company reviewed the events of fifty years before: approaching Tarrytown, they pronounced the names of the three militiamen, John Paulding, David Williams and Isaac Van Wert, who near that spot had taken Major André prisoner, as he was attempting to pass to the English lines with treasonable papers concealed in his boots; a little farther up the river, all eyes turned in the direction of a house standing alone, not far from the river bank—in that house Benedict Arnold had trafficked for the ruin of his country.

At West Point, the party went ashore and were driven in carriages up the hill to the Military Academy, where Lafayette reviewed the cadets, two hundred in number, and partook of their entertainment. Upon the platter pictured in a former chapter is a view of the river bank, the hills and the small group of buildings as they appeared to the guests in 1824. The *James Kent* was four hours late in arriving at Newburgh, and the thousands of people who had gathered to greet Lafayette had become impatient and beyond the control of the officers.

At last, while the General was at dinner, the tumult became so loud that the mayor of the town took Lafayette by the hand, and, preceded by torches, they made their way to an upper balcony of the hotel which overlooked the street.

"Gentlemen," called the mayor to the crowds below, "Do you wish to distress the Nation's Guest?"

"No! No! No!"

"Do you wish that Lafayette should be deprived of his liberty in a country indebted to him for its freedom?"

"No! No! No!"

The people became silent and respectful.

Poughkeepsie, the next landing place, was at that time a town of nearly five thousand inhabitants, and Lafayette was entertained in the very house where Washington, Hamilton, Chancellor Livingston and Mr. Jay had met to discuss the Constitution which afterwards was adopted by the United States. Continuing their voyage, the party spent the night at Clermont, the country residence of Chancellor Livingston, the name of which Robert Fulton gave to the first boat to make the trip by steam upon the Hudson.

As the vessel wound its slow way up the river, glimpses of the Catskill Mountains, which have been presented in the "Tour of the Land," called forth exclamations of delight from the passengers. When, at the village of Catskill, Lafayette was greeted by a soldier who had fought with him on the field of Brandywine, and at Hudson, another veteran handed him a sword which he had once received from Lafayette, with the words: "After my death this sword will change owners, but its destination shall never be changed: it shall always serve in defense of liberty," the General's joy was expressed in tears.

Albany awaited the Guest of the Nation with elaborate festivities, "those who shared with you the toils of the Revolution and still live," as the speaker said, paying him tribute. Lafayette noted important changes in the city which, as a village upon the frontier of a vast wilderness half a century before, had served him for army headquarters. Now it was rich and powerful, the seat of government of New York State, with a population of 16,000 people. Ex-Governor DeWitt Clinton, of Erie Canal fame, accompanied Lafayette to Troy, where the citizens bore the General upon their shoulders, and the fair members of the Troy Female Seminary wept tears of joy over him.

Shortly after his return to New York, Lafayette set out upon his third excursion, this time through the States of the South and the West. Like the New England and the Hudson River journeys, this, too, was marked by a succession of festivities and of reunions of old companions-in-arms, at many places memories of the Revolution and of his friend Washington crowding upon him.

LANDING OF LAFAYETTE AT CASTLE GARDEN

(*Clews*)

DEAF AND DUMB INSTITUTE AT HARTFORD, CONN., WHOSE
INMATES GREETED LAFAYETTE
(*Ridgway*)

LAFAYETTE AT THE TOMB OF FRANKLIN
(*Wood*)

GENERAL LAFAYETTE'S VISIT TO AMERICA

At Bergen, in New Jersey, a cane made from a branch of the apple tree under which he had once breakfasted with Washington was presented to him: Princeton University made him a member of one of its societies: and at Trenton, an elaborate entertainment befitting the historic character of the place was in waiting.

Upon his approach to Philadelphia, it seemed to Lafayette that the entire population of the city had come out to meet him. He drove past several groups of men representing the different trades, in the center of each corps being a workshop in which the workmen were busy at their employments, each shop bearing a banner decorated with portraits of Washington and Lafayette, and the legend, "To their wisdom and courage we owe the free exercise of our industry." As Lafayette passed the shop of the printers, a freshly printed "Ode to Lafayette" was tossed into his coach and copies were scattered among the crowd. After driving through thirteen triumphal arches, Lafayette found himself in front of Independence Hall, where, at the foot of the statue of Washington, he received a welcome to the city of Penn —the city in which, in the year 1777, he had pledged himself to devote his life and his fortune to a cause then almost desperate.

With his usual eagerness to look upon the changes which nearly half a century had brought to the American cities, Lafayette spent much time apart from the gayeties prepared for him in visits to the public institutions of Philadelphia. He was interested in the Library building, in the Pennsylvania Hospital and the United States Bank, all of which we have already looked upon in the illustrations of a former chapter. The pictures of the Dam and Waterworks on the Schuylkill River present the identical sight which Lafayette drove out to see, and over the mechanical skill of which he marveled. Remembering Lafayette's affection for Benjamin Franklin, the English potters printed sets of dishes with a fanciful scene supposed to represent the French hero mourning at the tomb of his old Philadelphia friend.

Upon the battlefield of Brandywine, Lafayette pointed out to his son the exact spot where the British army crossed the river in 1777, and the principal places where the patriot army had maneuvered and fought and where, when wounded, his own blood had been shed. The picture of Gilpin's Mills, in another chapter, was taken upon the estate of Gideon Gilpin, at whose home Lafayette was cared for when wounded, and where upon this visit he found Mr. Gilpin, his former host, an aged and invalid man.

Baltimore greeted her distinguished guest by sending out to meet him at Fort McHenry a company of her soldiers who, in the War of 1812, had gallantly defended that fortress from the British guns. As Lafayette approached the gates of Baltimore, twenty-four young women, armed with lances inscribed with the names of the twenty-four States, crowned him with laurel. Views of early Baltimore which have been shown include the Battle Monument, the Exchange, the University, Almshouse, etc. While in Baltimore, Lafayette attended the annual Fair of the Farmers of Maryland, and distributed the prizes for the best livestock, he himself being presented with a young bull, some heifers, wild turkeys and hogs for his estate in France. At the Society's banquet Lafayette proposed the following suggestive toast: "To the seed of American liberty transplanted to other shores—choked until now, but not destroyed, by European weeds; may it germinate and spring up anew, more vigorous, and less degenerate, and cover the soil of the two hemispheres."

From Baltimore to Washington the Nation's Guest traveled by carriage, and entered the capital city accompanied with a long escort. They proceeded at once to the Capitol, where Congress formally welcomed them, then to the President's House, where President Monroe presented them to the members of his official and domestic families. In his wanderings about the city Lafayette found many evidences of the disastrous British occupation in the War of 1812, the President's House and the Capitol having been since rebuilt. The remainder of the winter of 1824-5, with the exception of an excursion to Yorktown, saw the nation's guests in Washington,

fêted and honored.   The scene in the House of Representatives upon the occasion of Lafayette's introduction
was one long remembered—the members of the Senate
were also assembled in the House, and as Lafayette entered and passed to the center of the Hall, all rose and
listened to Henry Clay's words of greeting.   The line
"Republicans are not always ungrateful," which appears
on one old jug, has reference to the act of Congress in
presenting Lafayette, in recognition of his services to
the cause of liberty, the sum of $20,000 and an estate
of 240,000 acres of our public lands.   The famous Monroe Doctrine was discussed in Congress that winter, and
the French guests were interested listeners to the de-
bates.

Lafayette sailed down the Potomac to pay a visit to
Mount Vernon, the former home of Washington.   Three
nephews of Washington greeted the French party and
welcomed them to the estate, at the same time presenting Lafayette with a ring containing locks of the hair
of their illustrious uncle and his wife, and engraved
with the words, "Pater Patriae, Mount Vernon, 1776
and 1824."   George Washington Lafayette was much
affected as he strolled about the estate which twenty-
eight years before had been his home for two years,
while terror reigned in France and while his father was
a prisoner of state in Austria.   A visit to the Tomb of
Washington ended their stay at Mount Vernon.   Can

we not picture to ourselves the little procession as it wound its slow way from the mansion to the cypress grove not far away, where stood the Tomb so sacred to their eyes? Lafayette entered the enclosure alone and returned with his face wet with tears; then he took his son by the hand, and together they passed through the gate and laid wreaths upon the last resting places of their old friends, George and Martha Washington. Slowly, thoughtfully, the little band found its way down to the river bank, each with a branch of cypress in his hand, and in silence they boarded the waiting vessel. The fanciful view with which the English potters commemorated this solemn scene, a man in foreign dress seated before a tomb marked "Washington," is quite out of keeping with the setting of the original occurrence.

Yorktown awaited its hero with banners flying and streets thronged with people gathered from all the countryside. Under an arch erected upon the site of the English redoubt which he had formerly carried at the head of the American troops, Lafayette, crowned with laurel, addressed the assemblage in the name of the "Sons of the Mountains." He reviewed Revolutionary days and talked over old campaigns with former companions-in-arms, one of whom affectionately entreated him not to return to Europe, but to remain in America where "in every heart you have a friend." By chance,

Lafayette was lodged in Yorktown in the very house which Cornwallis had occupied forty-three years before, and, while rummaging in the cellar, one of his men came upon a large chest of candles which had been left there since the English officer's time. The candles were carried to the camp upon the Common and arranged in a large circle, and to the light of their burning dancing went on all the evening—a ball in Yorktown in 1824 by the light of Cornwallis' candles being so unique an occurrence that the old soldiers were unwilling to retire until the candles were all consumed. Small English cream jugs of copper luster ware picture the hero of Yorktown with two angels about to place a crown upon his brow, the reverse of the jug (shown in a previous chapter) bearing the scene of the surrender of the English sword.

Two ex-presidents of the United States were at the time of Lafayette's visit upon their estates in Virginia—Thomas Jefferson at Monticello, and James Madison at Montpelier. Can we not picture to ourselves the welcome which awaited their old French friend at these homes, and the long visits, far into the night, when bygone issues of the nation were recalled, and the newly arisen problem of slavery was debated?

In response to the urgent appeal of the people of the South and the West, Lafayette set out from Washington upon a tour of those sections of the country. His party traveled by carriage and horses, often, when the roads

LAFAYETTE PITCHER
"The Nation's Guest"
"As Brave and as Disinterested as Washington"

LAFAYETTE CROWNED AT YORKTOWN
(The reverse of this specimen is shown in Chapter IX)

were impassable, by horses alone, and at times they were obliged to cross swollen streams over trunks of fallen trees, in this way making a slow and difficult passage through the pine forests and sandy plains of North and South Carolina; upon the larger rivers and the lakes they took advantage of the newly inaugurated steamboat travel. At Camden, South Carolina, Lafayette assisted in dedicating a monument to Baron de Kalb, he who, like Lafayette, had come from Europe to America in the cause of liberty. At Savannah, Georgia, the citizens were awaiting Lafayette's arrival to unveil monuments to General Greene, a Revolutionary hero of the South, and to General Pulaski, a Polander who had given his life for the freedom of the nation. After a night spent at an Indian Agency in the heart of the Georgia forest, where the Indians called Lafayette the "White Father" and "A Messenger from the Great Spirit," the party pressed on to the Alabama River, where they exchanged carriages for a steamboat which carried them to New Orleans. In New Orleans, originally settled by French people, the greetings, "Vive la liberté, Vive l'ami de l'Amérique, Vive Lafayette," were pleasant and familiar sounds.

Up the Mississippi River, bordered with plantations and thick forests and bristling with dangerous snags, they sailed to St. Louis, the western limit of our territory. Thence, turning their faces eastward, they took a steamer bound up the Ohio River to Pittsburgh, Pennsylvania. At the village of Erie, on Lake Erie, memories of Commodore Perry's victory awaited them in a banquet spread under a tent made of sails of English ships which Perry had captured in the Battle of Lake Erie. At Buffalo, Lafayette met the Indian chief Red Jacket, whom he had known in 1784. "Time has changed us much," said Lafayette. "Oh," cried Red Jacket, "time has not been so severe with you as with me: he has left you a smooth face and a head well covered with hair, while I—look!" And, taking off his handkerchief, he showed a forehead entirely bald. Lafayette, to soften the feelings of the aged chief, then removed his blond wig and exhibited to the astonished Indian a poll as bare as his own.

After a short visit to Niagara Falls, Lafayette hastened his journey through New York State by the Erie Canal, so as to reach Boston in time to assist in the celebration of the fiftieth anniversary of the Battle of Bunker Hill.[1] He was the honored guest upon that famous 17th day of June, 1825. Never had the old city seen such a procession, 17,000 men in line! Two hundred officers and soldiers of the Revolution and forty veterans of the Battle of Bunker Hill were among those who filed from the Common across the river to the site

[1] A view of the Monument which he helped to dedicate has been presented in a previous chapter.

of the historic battle. Lafayette was the hero of the day.

"Fortunate, fortunate man," said Daniel Webster in that immortal address which every school boys knows, "Heaven saw fit to ordain that the electric spark of liberty should be conducted, through you, from the Old World to the New."

Lafayette reached New York in time to celebrate the forty-ninth anniversary of the Declaration of Independence, then he went to Washington, to sail thence for home. Upon September 8, 1825, the ship *Brandywine* with the French guests on board, sailed out from the mouth of the Potomac River towards the center of a brilliant rainbow, one end of which rested upon the shore of Maryland and the other upon that of Virginia—the last triumphal arch raised in America in honor of the great Frenchman.

Lafayette returned to La Grange, his estate near Paris, and there, surrounded with his children and his grandchildren, he passed in peace and quiet the remaining ten years of his life. La Grange, as the illustrations show, is a feudal château of stone, three stories high and flanked with five round towers. The entrance was once over a drawbridge spanning a deep moat, but the moat has been filled in on two sides. The estate is beautifully laid out with ancient woodlands, ponds and gardens, broad roadways winding through avenues of apple and chestnut trees. Lafayette's library is in the tower, and there visitors are shown the mementoes which he carried home from his famous visit to America.

"The vain wish has sometimes been indulged," said Henry Clay in his speech of welcome to Lafayette "that Providence would allow the patriot, after death, to return to his country and to contemplate the changes which had taken place—to view the forests felled, the cities built, the mountains leveled, the canals cut, the highways constructed, the progress of the arts, the advancement of learning, the increase of population."

To General Lafayette in this visit was given the rare fortune to realize the full measure of this prayer.

It is of interest to add that at the time of the present writing, the great European conflict being at its height, the memory of General Lafayette and of the services which he rendered to the patriot cause in time of its greatest need is honored by the establishment of a "Lafayette Fund" by the people of the United States, with which to contribute supplies for the soldiers of France fighting, in their turn, for the existence of their Republic.

THE ERIE CANAL AT BUFFALO
(*R. S.*)

CHAPTER XIV

OPENING OF THE ERIE CANAL

ALMOST as great in number as the cities which disputed the honor of Homer's birthplace, were the claimants of the original idea of the Erie Canal. George Washington, making a tour of New York State shortly after the close of the Revolutionary War, was perhaps the first one to suggest a waterway as a means of more ready communication between the Eastern States and the vast rich lands of the little known West; but actual work was not begun, however, until many years later, after much heated debate over the subject of routes and the manner of building. Finally, the Erie Canal, as brought to a successful construction through the enterprise of Governor DeWitt Clinton and at the expense of New York State alone, astonished the world, for it was an undertaking of such magnitude that the like of it had hitherto been accomplished only by the greatest empires of the Old World and by means of the labor of slaves.

It is but natural, therefore, that the unique spectacle of the celebration of the opening of the great waterway, upon a stage stretching from Buffalo to New York,

before an audience composed of a large part of the population of the State, should appeal to English artists in
search of American views, and that their sketches should
be used to decorate the pottery of Staffordshire. It is
with pride mingled with wonder and no little amusement that one reviews the story of the opening celebration, as it is recorded in the old-china illustrations.

The celebration began at Buffalo, the junction of the
canal and Lake Erie, continued at each little hamlet
and city along the banks, culminating at last in a blaze
of glory and patriotism as the waters from the Great
Lakes were mingled with the Atlantic in New York
harbor. No resplendent Doge of Venice standing upon
the prow of his gayly bedecked Bucentaur and casting
the jeweled ring into the waters of the Adriatic, thereby
symbolizing the marriage of Venice to the sea, was ever
more proud than was Governor Clinton as, standing
upon a primitive canal boat draped with the Stars and
Stripes, he poured a barrel of Lake Erie water into the
Atlantic Ocean, thereby accomplishing the union of our
West and East.

The first illustration presents a view of the harbor
entrance of the canal at Buffalo, with sail boats in the
bay, low warehouses on the dock, and a packet boat
upon the canal, which sailors are tying to the warf.
The study of this scene kindles one's imagination, and
in fancy he hears the pealing of the bells at nine o'clock

GOVERNOR CLINTON—JEFFERSON—WASHINGTON
Inside of Vegetable Dish
(*Stevenson*)

THOMAS JEFFERSON—LAFAYETTE—CLINTON
Inside of Vegetable Dish
(*Stevenson*)

THE AQUEDUCT BRIDGE AT
ROCHESTER, N. Y.
(*Wood*)

THE AQUEDUCT BRIDGE OVER THE GENESEE RIVER AT
ROCHESTER, N. Y.
Vegetable Dish

OPENING OF THE ERIE CANAL

upon that beautiful morning of October 26, 1825, and
he beholds the throngs of people gathering at the Court-
house. After prayer has been offered and speeches
have been made, the procession marches to the dock
where the flotilla is in waiting, ready to make the long
voyage down the canal. With something akin to awe
one listens to the sound of that reverberating cannon-
shot, which, fired at Buffalo and repeated in succession
by cannon stationed along the entire length of the canal,
proclaims in one hour and twenty minutes to the people of New York City that the little fleet is under way.
Four gayly bedecked horses then proudly prance along
the tow-path drawing the canal boat *Seneca Chief,*
which bears Governor Clinton and his associates, followed by the canal boats *Superior, Commodore Perry,*
and *Buffalo.* At the end of the procession is *Noah's
Ark,* from the "unbuilt city of Ararat," having on board
a bear, two eagles, two fawns, birds and fish, besides
two Indian boys in native costume—all taken along to
gratify the curiosity of the effete New Yorkers in regard to the wild West.

One smiles at the allegorical picture, painted in honor
of the occasion, which hangs in the cabin of the *Seneca
Chief,* for in it may be seen Hercules resting upon his
favorite club after his labor of finishing the canal, Governor Clinton in a Roman toga standing by his side,
gazing upon the placid water and inviting Neptune and

215

his Naiads, who coyly hang back as if hesitating to approach domains not theirs by right, to enter through the open lock. Upon the deck stand two brightly painted kegs marked "Lake Erie"—the water from the lake which is to be used in the celebration in New York. A quantity of bird's-eye maple and cedar wood is stored below deck for the purpose of making boxes and medals with which to commemorate the coming event. While the little flotilla proceeds on its way to the accompaniment of gay music and the salutes of guns, the citizens of Buffalo repair to the Eagle tavern for a banquet and speeches, the day ending with a grand ball where, an eye-witness tells us, "beauty, vieing conspicuously with wit, contributed to the enlivening enjoyment of the scene."

It is to be regretted that there are no illustrations of the canal at Lockport, for in that village is one of the most difficult and picturesque pieces of engineering to be found the entire length of the canal—the great locks which lift and lower the boats. As the little flotilla passes through the locks the passengers are greeted with salutes of a cannon which Commodore Perry thirteen years before had used in his gallant Battle of Lake Erie, here adding to its service a record of peaceful achievement. The first day of the celebration ends at Lockport with fireworks and illuminations, and a banquet at the tavern where the guests are introduced to a local celebrity—the man who planted the first orchard and built the first frame barn west of Utica.

A number of pieces of pottery record the scenes of the celebration in Rochester. In that city the canal is obliged to pass over the Genesee River, and the necessary aqueduct is a marvel of construction for that early time.

Rochester was an important city of western New York in the year 1825, and had materially aided and encouraged the canal project, therefore her preparations for the celebration of the opening have been elaborate. But alas! rain is pouring down upon the crowds waiting along the banks of the canal for the arrival of the fleet, eager to catch the first glimpse as it comes out of the West. When at last it arrives, the following dialogue takes place between the *Young Lion of the West,* the Rochester boat stationed at the entrance of the aqueduct to challenge all newcomers, and the flagship *Seneca Chief:*

"Who comes there?"

"Your brothers from the West on the waters of the Great Lakes."

"By what means have they been diverted so far from their natural course?"

"By the channel of the Great Erie Canal."

"By whose authority and by whom was a work of such magnitude accomplished?"

"By the authority and the enterprise of the patriotic people of the State of New York."

After the surprising ignorance of Rochester has been thus dispelled, the *Young Lion* gives way, and the flotilla with the Governor in full view floats into the basin amidst the cheers of the wondering crowds. There follows a mass meeting in the church, with appropriate speeches, and at the hotel are held a banquet and a ball. The next morning the fleet, adding to its train the *Young Lion of the West,* bearing the first citizens of Rochester and carrying wolves, foxes, raccoons and eagles from the forests, and Rochester-made cedar tubs, continues its journey.

The china which illustrates the canal scenes of Rochester are beautiful specimens of the early Staffordshire potters' art. Upon it is preserved a view of the old aqueduct which to-day is but a memory, the aqueduct scene being sometimes combined with views of prominent American buildings, or with those of castles and landscapes of England. In the border of the vegetable dish are medallion portraits of George Washington, General Lafayette, DeWitt Clinton and Thomas Jefferson. General Lafayette had visited many of the canal cities while he was the nation's guest but a few months before the celebration, and therefore he is given a place in the illustration; while Washington and Jeffer-

ERIE CANAL AT ALBANY

(*Wood*)

AQUEDUCT BRIDGE AT LITTLE FALLS

(*Wood*)

UTICA INSCRIPTION PLATE
(*Unknown Maker*)

DE WITT CLINTON EULOGY PLATE
(*Unknown Maker*)

son, it is claimed by some, appear through ignorance of the potters in regard to the dates of our political history.

Upon reaching the town of Syracuse, the party is again greeted with speeches and a banquet. At Rome, they are forced to call to mind that Fourth of July of the year 1817, the day the first ground for the section of the canal lying between Utica and Rochester was broken at this place by Governor Clinton. The Romans, for whom the present ceremony is one of mingled emotions, owing to the placing of the new waterway outside the limits of their town instead of inside it as they had wished, undertake to convey their complex feelings in the manner of their reception. The citizens form in line as the little fleet comes in sight, and, to the sound of muffled drums, they convey a black barrel filled with water from the old canal and empty its contents into the new one just completed. Having thus figuratively disposed of their chagrin, they march in quick time back to the tavern and forget their disappointment in hospitable festivities.

The "Utica Inscription" illustration commemorates the opening of the section of the canal between Utica and Rochester, the lines which fill the center recounting the usual list of benefits which this waterway conferred upon the villages through which it passed:

"Utica, a village in the State of New York, 30 years

since a wilderness, now inferior to none in the western section of the State in population, wealth, commercial enterprise, active industry and civil improvement."

The border pictures canal boats, aqueducts and locks, framed in graceful medallions. It is Sabbath day when the flotilla reaches Utica; the company is conducted to services in the meeting house, and later to the old Academy to listen to rousing speeches and songs.

The illustrations which picture the aqueduct at Little Falls, with the Mohawk River raging underneath, seem, like the Rochester aqueduct scenes, to have made strong appeal to the English potters, for they too are accompanied with portraits of our four canal worthies, with sketches of American buildings or with "Picturesque Landskips" and "Romantick Gentlemen's Seats" of old England. At this place occurs another celebration of welcome—lengthy orations and odes of congratulation delivered amid bonfires and illuminations upon the banks of the Mohawk River.

Leaving Little Falls, the gayly bedecked flotilla floats serenely along the man-made river, the guests seated upon the open decks (as quaint views of the celebration preserved in old prints record) enjoying the scenery and returning the huzzas of greeting from the people who line the banks. Whenever they pass through hamlets too small to offer a festival, the "yeomanry," an old chronicle states, "gathered at the banks of the canal and cheered the passing spectacle."

Upon November 2 the fleet reaches Albany, and here a Grand Fête befitting the Capital city of the Empire State awaits the distinguished guests—the illustrations picturing the "Entrance of the Canal at Albany" showing the very arches which were erected for the celebration. The two vessels at the dock, one a freight boat and the other a passenger packet boat, give a clear idea of canal traffic and travel in the early days; while in the background the home of one of Albany's prominent citizens may be seen. The guests repair to the Capitol building and listen to eulogies and to odes, and, as they pass through the streets, they gaze upon large banners and transparencies which blaze the tidings that "The Great Work is Done"; at the evening performance in the theater there is a "Canal Scene," wherein are shown a real canal and locks and horses and passing boats. At Albany the little fleet enters the Hudson River and is taken in tow by the new steamboat, the *Chancellor Livingston* (pictured in a later chapter) heading the procession as admiral and followed by twelve vessels of various types. A sympathetic writer of that time compares the spectacle to a "fleet from the dominion of the Fairies," adding that Alexander of Macedon when he descended the Indus was not more proud than were "these brave Americans sailing down the Hudson River." The population of the villages along the banks give signals of greeting as the fleet passes by, and, when darkness falls, lights and fireworks from the vessels respond to the fireworks and illuminations on shore.

At daylight on November 4, New York is reached, and a three-day celebration takes place, the setting of which may be in part recalled by a study of the illustrations. In a previous chapter a number of New York's important buildings of that day have been shown— Park Theater, Scudder's Museum, the Almshouse, Saint Paul's Chapel, Columbia College, the City Hall, where a public gathering was held and speeches were made in honor of the canal opening, and Castle Garden and the Battery—the site of the closing canal festivities. But many of the scenes of entertainment of those three days are but memory pictures, and cause us to regret that more of them were not secured by the English potter-historians. For what a pity to neglect the pictorial possibilities of the marvelous parade through the streets; of the Grand Canal Ball, with its supper table adorned with a miniature canal boat of maple sugar floating in a pool of Lake Erie water; of the ceremony at the harbor where the "Lord of the Seas" wedded the "Lady of the Lakes," by pouring the water brought from Lake Erie into the Atlantic Ocean, the nuptial rites being completed by sending a keg of sea-water, "Nep-

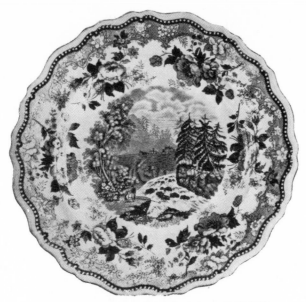

ERIE CANAL AT LITTLE FALLS: HORSES
ON TOW PATH
(*Jackson*)

ENTRANCE OF ERIE CANAL AT ALBANY

tune's Return to Pan," from the ocean to Buffalo, to be emptied into Lake Erie.

In this manner was celebrated the completion of the "big ditch," which skeptics declared "would be filled with the tears of posterity," but which, instead, has so amply justified the sentiment inscribed upon the "Eulogy" plates:

"The Grand Erie Canal, a splendid monument of the enterprise and resources of the State of New York, indebted for its early commencement and rapid completion to the active energies, preëminent talents and enlightened policy of DeWitt Clinton, late Governor of the State."

The journey from Buffalo to New York was made possible in the steam packets upon the canal in six days, at a cost of about eighteen dollars. Commerce was at once stimulated by the new and quicker route to the sea ports; travel was made more convenient for curious foreign tourists who crossed the sea to make the grand tour of the new country, and to look upon the famous cataract of Niagara; emigration was pushed farther westward along the waterway, causing new settlements to be established; and a broader opportunity for education was opened, the young men and women of the western sections being able by means of the canal to attend the schools and colleges of the Eastern States.

But the rapid rate of canal travel was long looked

upon by conservative persons as a fearful danger, and one to be risked only after serious and anxious thoughts of the future. A certain old gentleman of that day, after he had completed a canal journey in safety, penned these lines to a friend: "Commending my soul to God, and asking His defense from danger, I stepped on board the canal boat and was soon flying toward Utica."

CITY OF PITTSBURGH, PA.
("Pennsylvania" Steamboat)
(*Clews*)

CHAPTER XV

THE stories of Colonial America embodied in the decorations of old blue-china conclude with a review of the new modes of travel introduced by our forefathers, for, although theirs was the leisurely day of the stage coach and the sailing vessel, it was their good fortune to witness the dawn of the Age of Steam.

Many persons are familiar with the engraving, frequently found upon old-time parlor walls, of the small boy sitting at a tea-table pressing a spoon over the nose of the kettle and watching the steam lift the lid. The boy was James Watt, who in the year 1774 inaugurated in England trial tests of the strange power he had thus discovered. Half a century later, the people of America were gazing in wonder and awe upon the sight of boats moving up the Hudson River, and of coaches passing over the land, by means of this same magic power.

Success in steam experiment was attained with water-vehicles at a period earlier than with coaches operated upon land, the clumsy little vessels pictured upon the dinner plates sailing the American rivers and lakes a number of years before the whistle of primitive locomotives waked the sleeping echoes in our valleys. The last quarter of the eighteenth century, a number of European and American inventors, mindful of the ancient prophecy that "a steam carriage would one day go almost as fast as birds fly," experimented with the newfound power and turned out eccentric vehicles. In the year 1788, John Fitch, a Philadelphia clock maker, launched a steamboat with a row of propelling paddles on either side (the idea of wheels not occurring to him), and with three ranges of chains, suggested by his trade, along the sides. Failure to interest the public in his experiment brought him but the popular verdict, "Poor fellow! What a pity he is crazy." Another Philadelphian, Oliver Evans, fitted a sort of scow with a steam engine, added paddle wheels to the stern and set it on wheels. He ran this contrivance through the streets of Philadelphia out to the Schulykill River, where he launched it and propelled it down the stream and up the Delaware to the city. About the same time, Colonel Stevens and his son were constructing such marvelous engines in their shops in Hoboken that the fame of the family crossed the seas, and a view of the Stevens mansion, which was considered one of the handsomest homes in America, found its way upon English pottery. The illustration portrays a large Colonial house set in a spacious lawn, shaded with tall pine trees.

But it remained for Robert Fulton, with the aid of

INTRODUCTION OF NEW MODES OF TRAVEL

Chancellor Livingston, to carry to success the experiments of those who had paved the way in steam navigation. Fulton first made trials of steam engines upon the rivers of France, before bringing, in the year 1806, an English engine to New York, where he ordered a hull built for it in the East River shipyards. There the new fangled thing was jeered at and dubbed "Fulton's Folly." And indeed the *Clermont,* as he named the boat for the country home of Chancellor Livingston, was a novel sight—the engine in plain view of the passengers, the boiler set in masonry and covered with a little house like that on a canal boat, the rudder resembling the rudder of a sailing vessel, and huge uncovered paddle wheels revolving heavily upon either side.

Upon a beautiful Sabbath morning in August in the year 1807, the *Clermont* made her trial trip up the Hudson River, her decks filled with Fulton's guests. The ride was a thrilling experience, the passengers all the time fearful for their lives, and the inventor by no means certain that his vessel would move in the water. The *Clermont* started bravely, went a short distance, then stopped. "I told you so," might have been heard among the passengers, but Fulton adjusted the parts and on they went, the machinery groaning and creaking, and the water splashing the deck and mingling with the clouds of cinders from the engine. Soon another trouble presented itself—the captains of sailing vessels, jealous of this new rival in their field, ran into the *Clermont* and then made the accident appear the fault of the new vessel's clumsiness. The fiery object moving up the river struck such terror to the folk along the bank that some of the more ignorant among them fell upon their knees and prayed to be delivered from the monster, while those less timid long looked upon the power obtained from fire and water as of the Evil One. The vessel reached Albany in safety. "I ran it up in thirty-two hours and down in thirty hours. The power of propelling boats by steam is now fully proved," wrote Fulton to a friend, after the accomplishment of the journey.

The success of the *Clermont* paved the way for the construction of other vessels, and the following spring, to the intense delight of the people, the era of steamboat navigation was launched by the establishment of regular sailings between New York and Albany. Little by little, luxurious equipment and furnishings were added to the boats, such as cabins fitted with comfortable beds, bands of music on board, and, an item of especial interest, dining tables were provided with sets of blue dishes ordered from Staffordshire decorated with pictures of the boats. Surviving specimens of these sets are to-day highly prized.

One of the earliest of the Hudson River boats, the steamship *Fulton* (a disputed sketch of which is presented), was considered a very marvel of elegance and

STEVENS MANSION, HOBOKEN, N. J.
(*Stubbs*)

"FULTON" STEAMBOAT

STERN-WHEEL STEAMBOAT
Philadelphia Dam and Waterworks
(*Unknown Maker*)

DARK BLUE CUP AND SAUCER, CALLED "BALTIMORE
AND OHIO RAILROAD"

luxury. "There is not in the whole world such accommodations afloat as the *Fulton* affords," a journal of the day commented, adding the prophecy, "Indeed, it is hardly possible to conceive that anything of the kind can exceed her in elegance and convenience." The *Fulton* was built in the year 1814 and plied between New York and Albany, starting from the foot of Cortlandt Street every Saturday morning and arriving in Albany on Sunday morning, the fare being ten dollars; she had accommodations for 60 passengers. The *Fulton* was the first boat to make the dangerous passage of Hell Gate, as a reward for the feat receiving the name of the inventor. In the "Landing of Lafayette" scene which is presented in a former chapter the steamboat in the center was intended to represent the *Fulton,* but is wrongly drawn, as the real *Fulton* was fitted with one mast only for sails, while she is shown with three; she had but one funnel.

The other large steamboat in the "Landing" scene at the Battery is the *Chancellor Livingston,* the last boat designed by Robert Fulton and not completed until after his death. Another old-china decoration exhibits the *Chancellor Livingston* sailing the Hudson River near the town of Fishkill, a location readily recognized at the present time and one which no doubt appealed for its picturesque beauty to the old-time English artists. The *Chancellor Livingston* measured 165 feet in length, had a draft of seven feet, and her 75 horse-power engine carried her on an average of eight miles an hour. Her sleeping and dining apartments, it is recorded, were noted for their luxury. She was the most powerful and the most elegantly appointed vessel in the world at the time General Lafayette came to America on his famous visit, and for this reason she was chosen to carry the nation's guest in the great "Landing" naval parade.

Another notable steamboat was the *Chief Justice Marshall,* of which there is a sketch preserved upon specimens of her tableware, framed in the familiar border of sea-shells and mosses. The *Chief Justice Marshall* was built in 1825, and, as the large-lettered sign upon her rail announces, she belonged to the "Troy Line" of vessels. The "Union Line" was a rival Hudson River Company and one of its fleet, similar in type to the Troy vessels, is also reproduced. Three examples of early Pennsylvania steamboats appear upon specimens of the dinner service in use in their dining rooms. One of them is a single-funnelled side-wheeler greatly resembling the *Clermont,* from which no doubt it was modeled; this appears in the chapter upon Philadelphia. Another one, here presented, is a stern-wheel vessel; both are represented as steaming past the Dam and Waterworks of the Schuylkill River, near Philadelphia. The third Pennsylvania steamboat, with the name *Pennsylvania* in plain view upon her wheel-box, is fitted with two funnels and is pictured before the city of Pittsburgh, at that time but a small group of buildings at the foot of the mountains on the bank of the Allegheny River. In the view of the harbor of Detroit, Michigan, which a previous chapter presents, a number of other interesting types of primitive American craft may also be seen.

Until the year 1831, all steam-vessels were equipped with one or more masts for sails, the old-time device being retained in order to make use of the wind in case of trouble with the engine, or to attain greater speed. The mania for fast sailing thus early seized upon the people, and racing upon the rivers resulted in many accidents. The first accident occurred in 1830, to the *Chief Justice Marshall,* her boilers bursting as she was leaving the dock at Newburgh one day, many of her passengers being injured. The steamboats upon the western rivers became notorious for racing. To "Never be passed on the river" was the slogan of the Mississippi engineers, and in order to acquire more steam from the blazing pine knots in the furnace they sometimes threw lard and hams into the flames; oft-times the interior of the boat would be destroyed for fuel before port was reached. Bursting of boilers and grounding on snags became such frequent occurrences that upon the Ohio and Mississippi river banks groups of stranded passengers might often have been seen waiting for a passing vessel to pick them up and carry them to their journey's end. General Lafayette, while on his tour of the West in 1824, had a nar-

row escape from drowning in the Ohio River through
the reckless speeding of the small steamboat he was in,
the engineer landing the craft upon a snag in the middle
of the stream. At midnight upon a dark night, Our Nation's Guest, in scant attire, had to be lifted bodily into a
small boat and rowed ashore. A mattress was rescued
from the waves, shelter was found under a tree, and
there the great man was forced to remain until a passing steamer took him aboard. In 1825, "safety barges"
were attached to steamers by cables, and the passengers
occupied them at ease, unworried over the possible bursting of the boiler or the grounding of the steamboat in
front of them.

The change from the old to the new mode of travel
upon land—stage coach and horses to carriages drawn
by steam locomotives—came a few years later than the
change from sailing vessels to steamboats, and the inno-
vation was slower of adoption by our forefathers. The
"Old Style" and "New Style" of travel are curiously
illustrated in a design impressed upon the sides of an old
English pitcher. Underneath the historic dates "1800"
and "1848" are the words "Past" and "Present" and
"The Two Drivers." Upon one side of the pitcher is
pictured a stage-coach driver, a man of rotund figure,
wearing a large hat and carrying a whip; upon the opposite side, a small boy is seen seated in the branches of a

STEAMBOAT "CHIEF JUSTICE MARSHALL,"
"TROY LINE"
(*Wood*)

EARLY STEAMBOAT ON HUDSON, "UNION LINE"
(*Wood*)

BALTIMORE AND OHIO R. R.
(*Wood*)

BALTIMORE AND OHIO R. R.—INCLINED PLANE
(*Wood*)

tree and gazing down in wonder upon a locomotive running over an iron track.

A real personage was the stage coach driver, usually a portly, florid-faced man wearing an air of authority that was most impressive, and, when seated upon his box grasping the reins of his four- or six-in-hand, he was looked up to by the villagers along his route as almost the equal of the squire or the minister.   In addition to carrying passengers, the stage coach driver was accustomed to perform many other duties of various kinds.   He delivered messages, paid bills or collected them, was an agent of banks and brokers—and all of this business he carried in his head, or his hat!   For a stage driver's hat, even in the days when the monstrous bell crown was the fashion, was usually filled with letters and parcels put there for safe keeping, the owner being thus a combined forerunner of the modern postman, expressman and parcel post.   No doubt, had the stage driver been told that one day two parallel iron rails and a tea kettle on wheels would dethrone him from his proud position and render staging unfashionable and almost obsolete, he would have smiled in pity upon the speaker as either a fool or a madman.

Previous to the time locomotives were introduced into America, the country was a maze of stage routes, the year 1811 showing 37,000 miles of post roads, several state roads and a national turnpike, each thoroughfare dotted here and there along its way with roomy, sloping-roofed taverns for the accommodation of travelers. Before the introduction of regular stage routes, the post had been carried by men on horseback, from city to city. In 1755, Benjamin Franklin, who acted as postmaster, gave notice that mail between Philadelphia and New England would start by post once a week, "whereby answers may be obtained to letters between Philadelphia and Boston in three weeks, which used to require six weeks." After the Revolutionary War, a scheme was set on foot to form a line of posts from Falmouth, New England, to Savannah, Georgia, "with cross posts where needful." The first stage between Boston and New York started in June, 1772, to run once a fortnight as "a useful, new, and expensive undertaking," the time required for the journey being thirteen days! A half century later, in 1829, the "Albany Coach" left Boston three times a week, and arrived in Albany on the third day at noon, the distance being 160 miles and the fare six dollars; the "Boston and New York Mail" left Boston daily at ten o'clock in the morning and arrived the second afternoon in New York. The "Pilot Stage" ran from New York to Philadelphia daily in 14 to 16 hours, fare ten dollars, with accommodations in summer for seven passengers. It had connections with another line for Baltimore and Washington, whence still another carried the passengers on to Richmond. Imagination pictures the long, delightful hours of these journeys for indulgence in political discussions or personal gossip, and for enjoyment of the scenery through which the stages passed!

The change from stage coach to steam carriage aroused in the country an opposition similar to that which prevailed when steamboat travel was broached. "What is to become of America," the critics asked, "after the unfortunate country has fed to its locomotives the last pound of its limited supply of coal?" The rapid rate of travel and the shock of the sudden stopping, they argued, could never be endured until we had brains of brass or iron. Tales came from England, where, following the successful experiments of George Stephenson with his "Puffing Billy," steam cars had already been introduced, of the brains of business men becoming so addled by the swiftness of railroad travel that they forgot what they had set out for and had to write home to find out. One elderly gentleman, after a prolonged debauch of railroad travel, dashed his brains against a post and shivered them to pieces, a gruesome story ran. The introduction of steam power was a source of grief to John Ruskin, who saw in it a menace to peace and welfare. The rural villages of this country did not relish the notion of their quiet being disturbed by noisy trains. Daniel Webster drove out one day to Quincy from Boston, to inspect the horse-power railroad in operation at the quarries, and on his way back he shook his head and gave it as his opinion that the frosts on the rails in winter would prove a difficulty which never could be overcome.

In spite of protests, however, the idea of steam travel on land gained friends, and in the summer of 1829 four locomotives were ordered from England for trial on the rails already laid at quarries and mines for cars operated by horses. One of the English engines, the "Stourbridge Lion," was hauled to the tracks of the Delaware and Hudson Railroad near Honesdale, Pennsylvania, and its historic run was made the occasion for a holiday, the entire countryside turning out to witness the trial. No one believed the strange monster would go, even the man who guided her being in doubt, for the timber of the roadway had cracked and warped from the summer's heat, and a thirty-foot trestle over a creek had to be crossed on a curve. "As I placed my hand on the throttle valve handle," he afterwards said, "I was undecided whether I should move slowly or with a fair degree of speed, but preferring, if I did go down, to go handsomely, I started with considerable velocity, passed the curves over the creek safely and was soon out of hearing of the cheers of the vast assemblage. . . . At the end of two or three miles I reversed the valve and returned without accident, having made the first locomotive trip

THE "CHANCELLOR LIVINGSTON" (WITH THREE MASTS AND
ONE FUNNEL) PASSING THE HIGHLANDS, HUDSON
RIVER
(*Wood*)

LEEDS TEAPOT
Fulton's Steamboat Passing West Point
(In Dickins Collection)

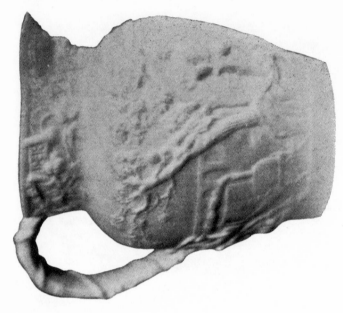

REVERSE
Early Railway Train—" New Style " Travel

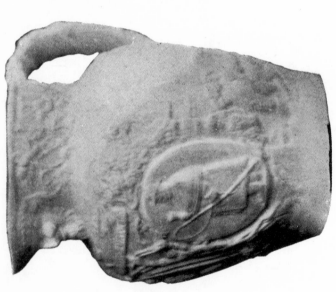

OLD ENGLISH PITCHER
Stage Coach Driver—" Old Style " Travel

on the Western Hemisphere." The "Stourbridge Lion" is now in the National Museum of the Smithsonian Institution in Washington.

The railroad fever then quickly seized upon the people and spread like a contagion; charters for new roads multiplied; iron-banded wooden rails were laid throughout the land; engines were built, odd-looking contrivances, with vertical, bottle-shaped boilers, chimney-like smokestacks and tenders merely an open platform on wheels. Each locomotive originally was given a name, as is the custom with vessels to-day, a custom still in vogue in several countries of Europe. The earliest passenger coaches were modeled after the stage coach, with seats both inside and out, the inside seats being at first arranged around the sides; later on, the center aisle with which we are familiar was adopted, in preference to the English compartment model with a narrow ledge along the outside—a style which continues in use in the Old World.

The two scenes which are framed in the rich shell border of Enoch Wood are of the Baltimore and Ohio Railroad, which was built to connect the eastern States with the semi-wilderness region of the Ohio River. The first scene represents an early locomotive of the English type, drawing a load of freight cars; the second, a stationary engine may be seen at the summit of a hill near the entrance to a mine, with a number of cars running down a very steep grade. The corner stone of the Baltimore and Ohio was laid in Baltimore July 4, 1828, by Charles Carroll, the last surviving signer of the Declaration of Independence, and was an event of great importance, celebrated by a procession, and, it is recorded, by sending to Lafayette (who had visited Baltimore a few years before) a fine pair of specially designed satin shoes, which were placed in the museum at La Grange.

In the year 1829, Peter Cooper built the "Tom Thumb," a model one-horse power engine, and ran it for a short distance upon the tracks of the Baltimore and Ohio, but regular service of railway travel in America was not established until the following year. Peter Cooper describes the "Tom Thumb" thus: "The engine was a very small and insignificant affair. It was made at the time I had become the owner of all the land now belonging to the Canton Company, the value of which I believed depended almost entirely upon the success of the Baltimore and Ohio Railroad. When I had completed the engine I invited the directors to witness an experiment. Some thirty-six persons entered one of the passenger cars, and four rode on the locomotive, which carried its own fuel and water; and made the first passage of thirteen miles over an average ascending grade of eighteen feet to the mile, in one hour and twelve minutes. We made the return trip in fifty-seven minutes." Several of the favored directors, we learn elsewhere, who were aboard the train upon this historic run, took out their notebooks and wrote sentences in them in order to prove that they were able to do so while traveling at such rapid speed.

In the cup and saucer decorations another early locomotive, whether of English or American manufacture is a disputed question, may be seen drawing a passenger car of the stage coach type, a car which closely resembles those which were used upon the tracks of the Mohawk and Hudson River Railroad. The honor of being the first railway line to establish regular train service in America belongs, however, to the Charleston and Hamburg Railroad of South Carolina, with a bottle-shaped vertical engine known as "The Best Friend of Charleston"; this was in the year 1830.

An interesting scene, printed in pale blue and framed in delicate mosses, pictures one of the first railway trains to be run in New York State—without doubt one of the earliest representations of the old DeWitt Clinton engine, the pride of museums and expositions ever since the day she made her historic run from Albany to Schenectady, over the tracks of the Mohawk and Hudson River Railroad. It was a joyous occasion, and not since the opening of the Erie Canal six years previous was there so great excitement. The people of the countryside along the route turned out to view the spectacle, for long distances lining the track on both sides with all sorts of vehicles. Chronicles of the period relate how on the evening of August 8, 1831, the guests who were to board the train on the following morning bought their tickets at the hotel in Albany, and how at daybreak they made their way to the outskirts of the city and were carried up a hill to the place where the train awaited them. The state officials occupied the foremost coaches (some of them stage coaches pressed into service), while as many persons as possible seated themselves along the sides of the cars and upon the roofs, hundreds, however, for lack of room either to sit or stand, being obliged to remain behind. The time came to start; a horn tooted; the engineer, fearful that the load was too heavy for his engine, started with such a jerk that it sent hats flying and people sprawling. Forward the train moved out into the country, the passengers enjoying the novel experience of the rapidly unrolling scenery, when unexpected trouble developed—clouds of sparks streamed from the engine over those who were upon the roofs, setting fire to their clothing, and the umbrellas raised for protection were quickly tossed overboard in flames. The crowds of people along the track cheered lustily the novel spectacle; horses jumped and ran in terror from the snorting monster; at last, the train came to a stop upon the summit of a hill, and the jolted passengers were lowered to the city of Schenectady, their journey at an end. The festivities of celebration continued—music, cannon,

TRAIN ON MOHAWK AND HUDSON RIVER RAILWAY
(C. C.)

salutes, processions, speeches—and the eventful day ended with a banquet where was offered the prophetic toast: "The Buffalo Railroad: May we soon breakfast at Utica, dine at Rochester, and sup with our friends on Lake Erie."

In this manner was ushered in the Age of Steam, that historic era in which sailing vessels and stage coaches, the last mementoes of our Colonial forefathers which English pottery records, gradually gave place to the steam-driven ships and railway trains of the present. At some future time, it will no doubt come to pass that new marvels of science will cause the luxurious trains and steamships of the present day to appear as clumsy and old-fashioned as the little boats and locomotives which are pictured upon the old blue dishes appear to the youthful generation of to-day.

APPENDICES

THE PRESIDENT ROOSEVELT CHINA

APPENDIX I

FOREMOST perhaps among the numerous historical attractions which lure the American pilgrim to Washington is the stately old Mansion which, with one exception, has been the home of all the presidents of the United States. And among the mementos of bygone administrations which the White House shelters at the present time, not the least in popular interest is the collection of specimens of porcelain and glassware which from the earliest days of the Republic graced the table of the Chief Executive. Twenty-four groups, of from one to ten pieces in each group, at the present writing make up the exhibit, the President Johnson administration alone being as yet without representation in the collection; while the President Taft and the President Wilson administrations have continued in use the porcelain selected by Mrs. Roosevelt. The collection is a growing one, however, and in time it is hoped that each administration will, through loan or gift, be adequately represented. The articles are arranged in cabinets upon either side of the Lower Corridor of the White House; while accompanying them hang upon the walls the portraits of six of the former Mistresses of the Mansion—Mrs. Van Buren, a daughter-in-law of President Van Buren, Mrs. Tyler, Mrs. Polk, Mrs. Hayes, Mrs. Harrison, and Mrs. Roosevelt, that of the present Mrs. Wilson being soon to be added to the number. Martha Washington's portrait hangs in the Red Room above, near to that of our first president. A plan is now on foot to place the collection of porcelains and glass in one of the rooms adjoining the Lower Corridor where it now is, building for it permanent and commodious wall cabinets, thereby ensuring greater security for the exhibit as well as, for the visitor, a more satisfactory opportunity for observation and study.

THE BLUE-CHINA BOOK

Like many another enterprise, the idea of forming a collection of china belonging to past presidents long preceded its actual undertaking. Mrs. Hayes and Mrs. Benjamin Harrison, while presiding over the Mansion, each conceived a plan somewhat similar to the one which later on was inaugurated and carried to nearly its present state of completion by Mrs. Roosevelt—to gather together by means of patriotic loan or gift specimens of presidential china which had come into the possession of descendants of the original owners. For, with the revival of interest in all things pertaining to the past history of our country, upon search it was discovered with surprise and dismay that very little of the older pieces of porcelain remained upon the White House pantry shelves, and that a knowledge of their characteristics was therefore in danger of being entirely lost. The cause of this state of things, by the way, may be directly traced to the time of George Washington, for, when he removed the seat of Government from New York to Philadelphia in 1790, Congress enacted a law whereby "the decayed furnishings of the President's House should be sold for refurnishing the new house in Philadelphia." Thereafter, when the city of Washington became the permanent home of the Government, with each incoming administration Congress voted a sum of money (frequently twenty thousand dollars) for fresh furnishings for the President's House, the amount to be expended under the direction and according to the taste of the new Chief Executive and his family. And any of the old furnishings which they might be pleased to consider "decayed" were promptly sold at public sale—carpets, tables, chairs, window-hangings, beds, linen, tableware, etc., etc. This practice led to greater or less alterations in the character of the interior of the mansion with almost every administration, and twice in its history—under President Monroe, after its partial destruction by the fire of the British soldiers in 1814, and under President Roosevelt, who, in his message to Congress submitting the architects' report, declared that it "had become disfigured by incongruous additions and changes"—the White House interior has undergone complete remodeling and refurnishing. At the present time, restored to the plan of James Hoban, its original architect, and made consistent with modern ideas of sanitation, the home of our presidents is one of appropriate dignity and utility. And, in place of the careless and haphazard manner in which it formerly was looked after by the Government, the White House has been put under the direct supervision of the Bureau of Buildings and Grounds.

The White House collection of presidential china, although far from as complete as it eventually will be, is noteworthy in that perhaps to a greater degree than most other displays of historical relics in this country it bears interesting and intimate witness to the progress, halting and varying as it has been, in luxury and in taste of the American people throughout the century and more of national life. For, unlike the existing specimens of Anglo-American pottery which form the special subject of this volume, and which in early years found a place upon the humble tables of the mass of American citizens, the White House collection almost uniformly presents examples of fine and costly porcelains, the choicest output of French, Dutch, English, and Oriental potteries which was brought overseas to grace the boards of our forefathers of wealth and fashion. Exquisite design, color, and form characterize several of the groups belonging to those administrations which were co-temporary with the vogue of French taste in America, due to the close relations with that country growing out of its attitude toward the American struggle for independence, as, for example, some of the Washington, the Madison, and the Monroe pieces. The Polk china, too, with its dainty bird design, displays the same characteristics; while the Pierce and Lincoln groups attract the eye for the broad bands of rich color and the graceful forms which they display. The showy Hayes and Arthur specimens, challenging the beholder to pause and examine, are a reminder of the current styles of interior decoration which were popular in that flamboyant era we have come to designate as mid-Victorian; the Cleveland and Benjamin Harrison groups, on the other hand, claiming attention for the quiet elegance of their decoration, portraying the prevailing taste of the succeeding decade as well as that of their sponsors. And one will pause, as the writer did, before the Roosevelt exhibit, appreciating how distinctly its simple elegance accords with the recognized trend of to-day's thought. Indeed, so expressive not only of the popular inclination of the moment but also of that patriotic ideal which the America of to-day has developed, is the Roosevelt china, that the suggestion has been offered to perpetuate the design for the official White House table, the Taft and Wilson administrations having already signified their approval by merely supplying breakages from it in place of introducing other styles. A piece of china which belonged with every properly planned set in our early Republican times, and one which a later-day mode seems to have relegated to disuse, is the fruit-compote, a number of examples of which may be seen in the collection. This dish consists of a bowl, sometimes round but more often oblong or diamond-shaped, generally of openwork lattice pattern, and set upon a standard from six to ten inches high. Decorated with the same design as the remainder of the set, the compote is an imposing piece, an excellent specimen being the beautiful one illustrated with the Lincoln china. Another piece, which by the way present day fashion is returning to favor, is the pretty little covered custard-cup, an example of which the Lincoln group likewise presents. Also, a punch bowl, decorated to match the other pieces, was oft-times included in old-time sets of porcelain. The Coat of Arms of the United States has been several times fittingly incorporated in the pattern adopted for state sets, the number of stars it displays equaling the number of states in the Union at the time of printing.

Although George Washington died before the completion of the Executive Mansion, in the erection of which he was deeply interested, the story of presidential china properly begins with mention of the wares once used by him, a small number of pieces of which stand at the head of the White House collection. The years of Washington's life spanned the periods between pewter and porcelain as articles of table use in America, the close of the War of the Revolution rather definitely marking the transition.

THE GEORGE WASHINGTON CHINA

THE JOHN ADAMS
GOBLET

THE JEFFERSON STATE SET

THE MADISON CHINA

APPENDIX I

That Washington owned and used pewter, many dinner dishes of that material decorated with his crest and initials remain to attest; while the contents of his camp mess chest, now preserved in the United States National Museum in Washington, D. C., are of pewter. But the war ended and peace restored, our first president had leisure to indulge the fondness which he, in common with Benjamin Franklin, conspicuously possessed for those "little azure-tinted grotesques that, under the notion of men and women, float about uncircumscribed by any element, in that world before perspective—a china teacup." Attactive indeed to Washington must have been the newspaper advertisements of his day announcing the infrequent arrival of vessels from the Orient, and setting forth long lists of cargoes of china, teas, and precious stuffs, to be sold at "Publick Vendue." A letter written by him under date of 1785 is extant, in which he gives orders for the purchase at one of these sales in Baltimore, among other articles, of a "sett of the best Nankin Table China, Ditto—best Evening Cups and Saucers, A sett of large blue and white China, 1 Dozen small bowls blue and white, 6 Wash hand Guglets (small jugs) and Basons, etc., etc." Soon after his inauguration in New York in 1789, Washington established himself in a mansion on Franklin Square which had been repaired and refurnished, and which became known as the President's Palace. In a letter to a friend, a young New York woman of that time writes: "There is scarcely anything talked of now but General Washington and the Palace . . . the best of furniture in every room and the greatest quantity of plate and china that I ever saw . . . " By the time of his return to private life at Mount Vernon, Washington had evidently acquired a goodly quantity of porcelain, for he gave directions for the appropriation of a small room in the remodeled house for "the Sèvres china and other things of that sort which are not in common use." The tableware which *was* in common use both in New York and in Mount Vernon was the blue and white Canton ware which is familiar to all, two pieces of which—a badly cracked platter and a dinner plate—which were purchased at President Washington's sale of household effects when he left New York for Philadelphia in 1790, are to be seen in the White House collection. The remaining articles in the Washington group include a cup and saucer which formed a part of the well-known "white and gold tea-set" belonging to Martha Washington, and a dinner plate of the "Cincinnati set" (to which Order Washington belonged), over the acquisition of which there has been much discussion. It is now agreed that Washington most probably purchased the set himself upon its arrival from China, where quantities of it were decorated with the insignia of the Order from a drawing supplied in America. As may be seen in the illustration, the design which occupies the center of the plate, within a border of blue Oriental scroll and leaf ornaments, consists of a figure of winged Fame in a light green robe and pink scarf, blowing a trumpet and holding suspended from one hand a colored representation of the Society's badge. A plate of the "set given me by Mr. Van Braam," so designated by Martha Washington in her will, and popularly known as "the Martha Washington States" china, is illustrated and described in a former chapter of this volume. A number of pieces of this set are in the National Museum at Washington and other pieces, said to be reproductions, are at Mount Vernon, but the White House collection is without a specimen.

John Adams occupied the President's House (as it was then known) but nine months, completing his term begun in Philadelphia. Unfinished and uncomfortable as the mansion was, (the famous East Room was used to dry the family laundry and fireplaces barely took the chill from the large drafty apartments), nevertheless its levees and state dinners were conducted with the same regard for ceremony for which Washington had established the precedent. While residing abroad, John Adams had made many purchases of furniture and tableware, some of which he doubtless used in Philadelphia and in Washington, but as yet the White House collection contains but two articles with which to commemmorate his administration—the bowl of a cut-glass goblet (the stem and base having disappeared) set in a properly-fitted silver standard, and a framed silhouette of Abigail Adams.

THE PRESIDENT MONROE CHINA

THE JOHN QUINCY ADAMS COLLECTION OF CHINA AND GLASS

THE PRESIDENT JACKSON CHINA AND CANDELABRUM

APPENDIX I

The bowl is etched with floral wreaths festooned from a decorative band, and upon one side is the letter "A." Underneath the letter are the initials S. C. T.—Sarah Corcoran Thom, to whom the goblet was given by a great-grandson of John Adams, who had her initials placed upon it. The goblet was presented to the collection by Mrs. Harry Reade, the daughter of Mrs. Thom. The silhouette is an interesting memento of that period, exhibiting Mrs. Adams in a quaint frilled head-dress. A letter of presentation accompanies the relic, it having originally been a gift to a classmate of Mrs. Adams, a daughter of Jeremiah Bailey, by whom it was given to the donor to the White House collection.

A notion of extreme simplicity in all matters pertaining to the Executive régime has in later years come to be associated with the name of Jefferson, the father of the Democratic party, but a glance at the White House exhibit of his administration goes far to prove that conception erroneous, at least so far as his table appointments were concerned. For as elegant a group of porcelain as the entire collection can boast, together with a time-yellowed family cook-book called "The Virginia Housewife," containing many choice recipes in Jefferson's own hand (among them the writer noted one for a Cabbage Pudding which had come to him from his French cook Petit), occupy an entire shelf. The accommodations in the President's House had become somewhat better by the time Mr. Jefferson moved in than they were during the Adams occupancy, and, in accord with his own personal tastes as well as with his deep-rooted conviction as to the political value of dinners, openhanded hospitality characterized the Mansion during his terms of office; a letter of ex-President Adams in later years declares: "I dined a large company once or twice a week, Jefferson dined a dozen every day." Humboldt, Tom Moore, Jerome Bonaparte, and Tom Paine were among the notables at his table. It has been stated that Jefferson was very fond of olives, figs, mulberries, crabs, venison, oysters, partridges, pineapples and light wines, his household records containing frequent entries of these delicacies. And there are also tales of small dinners in the mansion, when strict privacy was secured by means of a "dumb-waiter" at each guest's chair filled with all necessary articles like extra plates, knives and forks, finger bowls, etc., and by the additional means of a set of revolving shelves placed in the wall, evidently somewhat like the contrivance at the entrance to certain European convents of cloistered nuns to make possible unseen communication with the outside world, whereby fresh viands entered the room as the emptied plates swung around into the pantry. Being a widower, Jefferson's official table was at times presided over by his daughters, but more frequently by the wife of his Secretary of State, Mrs. Madison. Four pieces of a dinner set used upon his table are upon exhibition—a large covered soup-tureen, a large platter, a plate, and the cover of a broken vegetable dish. The porcelain is heavy, a piece of this set being described by Mrs. Earle as of Chinese manufacture of the type erroneously known as Lowestoft. The decoration consists of a wide outer rim and an inner border of deep blue diaper, accentuated by dainty gold bordering lines. The center of the flat pieces and the sides of the tureen and covers bear a blue outlined shield carrying thirteen stars and enclosing a gold letter "J." Above the shield is a blue and gold helmet drawn with visor closed. During Jefferson's term the celebrated De Tuyll silver was purchased in Paris, pieces of which bearing the faint ancestral markings are now in the original chest, and, as the writer observed, upon the sideboard of the private White House dining room. It is claimed that over three hundred pieces of this plate were purchased by Monroe, at Jefferson's request, from a Russian nobleman named De Tuyll, whose financial straits compelled the sacrifice.

James Madison, whose portrait (upon a Liverpool jug) may be found in a previous chapter of this volume, has been described as "a little, apple-faced man with a large brain and pleasant manners but no presence." His wife, "Dolly" Madison, however, "a fine, portly, buxom dame," amply supplied the qualities wanting in her husband, her career as mistress of the Mansion extending over practically four terms and eclipsing that of most of her contemporaries. Her first term as mistress in her

THE PRESIDENT TYLER PLATE

THE PRESIDENT POLK CHINA

THE PRESIDENT PIERCE RED-BANDED SET OF CHINA

THE PRESIDENT LINCOLN CHINA

own right was a continuous blaze of gayety, her toilets, and especially her Paris turbans of unheard-of daring and elegance, having been many times described. State papers show that Mrs. Madison selected a state dining set of porcelain and a quantity of plate for use in the President's Mansion. In the midst of this brilliancy occurred the second War with England, the British soldiers entering Washington in August, 1814, as Mrs. Madison fled leaving the table spread for a dinner prepared in honor of our supposedly victorious officers. A wagon had been hastily heaped with such valuables as could be carried, including the portrait of Washington which now holds the place of honor above the mantel in the Red Room of the White House. The British officers entered, and enjoyed the dinner before giving orders to fire the structure. William Lee, who later on had charge of refurnishing and redecorating the injured building, in his report tells how thorough was the work of vandalism: "There was no recourse in the remnants of glass, earthenware, china, linen, etc., of which scarcely an article would serve; indeed, we may say, there remained none of these articles fit for use." Nevertheless, a number of pieces of a beautiful set of French porcelain now known as the "Dolly Madison china" are claimed to have escaped the catastrophe, and two examples of it—a plate and a tea cup and saucer—are preserved in the collection of presidential ware. Another piece of the same set, which Mrs. Harrison after she became mistress of the Mansion found broken in three parts upon the White House pantry shelves and which she had carefully put together, is an exquisite punch-bowl about two feet in height, the bowl upheld by figures of the three Graces resting upon a standard. Restored to its original beauty, the punch-bowl now adorns a small table in the private White House dining room. The design which this set displays is a dainty one of blue and gold, its distinguishing characteristics being the wide bands filled with small gold dots and bordered with fine blue and gold lines, which encircle each specimen, together with the blue and gold shield-shaped decoration filled with dots which marks the center of the flat pieces. The cup has a deep gold band inside the rim. The two plates of another set in the Madison group upon exhibition in the Corridor are also of French porcelain, the deep buff rings carrying a series of wheel patterns outlined in black, alternating with a conventional branch-like pattern.

President Madison and his family did not again occupy the Mansion, being forced to transfer the Executive home to other quarters upon their return to the partially ruined Capital, and for a year they lived in the Octagon House wherein was ratified the Treaty of Ghent. This house is still preserved in its original form, and in a circular upper room the table upon which the historic document was signed, is shown to visitors. Mr. Monroe came into office as the final repairs were being put upon the President's House, the close of his administration seeing the semi-circular South Portico added to the original front of the mansion, as it appears in the illustration of a previous chapter of this volume, and naturally he impressed his taste upon the refurnishing. A large sum of money was appropriated by Congress, and the newly-elected president, accustomed as he was to life in France and being in sympathy with the prevailing Empire styles in house-interior decoration, ordered in Paris the new furniture, plate, and ornaments of that decorative period. In the bills describing the contents of the 41 packages which arrived at Alexandria from France, one reads of curtains, screens, candelabra, candlesticks, mirrors, lamps, fauteuils, consoles, a "set of table china of gilded porcelain for 30 people," a "dessert service made by Dagoty, with amaranth border and five vignettes representing Strength, Agriculture, Commerce, Art, Science, with Arms of the United States in center," and many other dishes besides. The dining room being as yet unfit for use, state dinners were given in the East Room, which they called "the banqueting hall." The famous "surtout de table," or table plateau, which to this day is occasionally unpacked and placed upon the White House table, was also purchased in France by Monroe at a cost of 6000 francs—a piece of unwarranted extravagance in the eyes of his political critics. Mrs. Taft, in her charming book, "Recollections of Full Years," describes this table piece, which is 13 and one-half feet long and two feet wide, thus: "Based upon oblong plate glass mirrors, each about three feet in length, they (the separate pieces) stretch down the middle of the table, end to end, a perfect riot of festooned railing and graceful figures upholding crystal vases. Then there are large gilded candelabra, center vases and fruit dishes to match . . . appropriate to the ceremony with which a state dinner at the White House is usually conducted." Several of the ornamental clocks, pieces of statuary and bric-a-brac which Monroe purchased now adorn the mantels and cabinets of the state apartments of the White House. Of all the table china which the mansion boasted during this administration, however, but three pieces have as yet found their way back to grace the new collection—a plate and cup and saucer from a tea-set, and a plate from another set. The two match pieces carry a dainty scroll and lattice design in red, blue and gold, while the odd plate shows a dull orange rim in flat tone broken at the edges by six groups of white leaves; the center bears a bunch of flowers.

The John Quincy Adams group, as may be seen in the accompanying illustration, is made up of three tall-stemmed English wine glasses of differing size and form, two salt cellars of Meissen ware bearing the familiar onion pattern, and a dinner plate which was used at state dinners during his term of office. The plate is of French porcelain, the flat rim carrying a decoration consisting of five small panels of pale lavender outlined in gold enclosing two white interwoven figures resembling sea-horses, these alternating with a wheel pattern and scroll in gold. A large gold rosette marks the center.

The disturbing events of Andrew Jackson's terms of office, from the "Pretty Peggy Eaton affair" which disrupted his cabinet at the beginning, to the mammoth 1400 pound gift cheese which, standing in the White House vestibule and served to all comers to his farewell entertainment, gave forth an odor, not of sanctity, but, as one who was present remarked, "like that to which the mephitic gas over Avernus must be faint and inocuous," are well known matters of history. The East Room, which had previously been lighted with candles held in candlesticks nailed to the wall, was now fitted with chandeliers suspended from the ceiling and gleaming with glass prisms. Large gilt-framed mirrors, chairs to match covered with damask, rich window hangings, a Brussels carpet of pronounced pattern, and bouquets of artificial flowers set in painted vases, transformed the room into a reflection of the mode of the period. Jackson also purchased a quantity of tableware, for we read from the accounts covering expenditures for the White House in 1833: "One set of French china, for dinner with the American eagle, $1,500;" "a dessert set, blue and gold, with eagle, $1000;" besides plates, cups and saucers, glass, plate, etc., etc. It may be of interest to know that President Jackson purchased his glassware in Pittsburgh, as Congress had ordered by Act of 1826, but for his porcelains and silks he sent to France. But alas! the freshness of these new furnishings was not to endure, for the mobs of visitors of all ranks of life who, with a practice of democracy exceeding that of Jefferson's day, thronged the receptions of the "Hero of New Orleans," in their boisterous efforts to secure the cake and punch which the waiters were serving upset the trays and deluged the curtains, cushions and carpet, while bits of china and glass were ground underfoot. Like Jefferson, President Jackson was a widower, the lady who presided over his official home being the wife of his secretary (who was Mrs. Jackson's nephew), Mrs. Emily Tennessee Donelson. The first baby said to have been born in the Mansion was the secretary's child, Mary Emily Donelson, and it was her daughter, Miss Mary R. Wilcox, who placed as a memorial to her mother the present interesting exhibit of china, glass, and plate in the White House collection. It includes a two-branched silver candelabra which was presented to General Jackson by Tammany Hall upon the occasion of a visit to that organization, one side of the pedestal bearing the name Andrew Jackson, and the other the inscription: "Our Federal Union; It Must Be Preserved." There are also two round openwork fruit-compotes of white and gold, a silver tea knife, a red Bohemian glass flower-vase, a finger bowl, a cut glass decanter and four wine glasses, in the group. An interesting recent addi-

SPECIMENS OF THE PRESIDENT GRANT COLLECTION

THE FAMOUS HAYES SET OF PRESIDENTIAL CHINA

THE PRESIDENT GARFIELD CHINA

THE PRESIDENT ARTHUR CHINA

tion is the coffee cup and saucer to be seen in the foreground of the illustration, which was commonly used by the President at breakfast during his first administration. The cup is large and flaring at the rim, the gold band being much worn away. We read that Jackson found great solace from the troubles which beset his office in smoking a pipe, sitting by himself in the big south room of the second story and puffing the smoke up the chimney because, as he explained to a visitor, Emily Donelson disliked the smell of tobacco. It perhaps brings the man and his time a little nearer to us to look upon his pipe-bowl of coarse green clay which forms a part of the exhibit.

The single article commemorating Martin Van Buren's occupancy of the historic mansion, an elegant silver water pitcher about ten inches in height, is curiously suggestive of the criticisms of extravagance made by his political enemies, which somehow Jackson seemed to have escaped. But it would appear only natural that a man of Van Buren's type, a bon vivant habituated to luxury, should feel the necessity of thoroughly renovating the mansion after eight years of a régime such as the foregoing had been. The carpets were taken up and cleaned, the furniture was repaired, and much redecorating was done. Quantities of wine glasses and fluted decanters, "blue-edged dishes, blue-printed plates, gold band china coffees, willow plates and dishes," were purchased. The "surtout," or "pictured tray," as it was contemptuously dubbed, was "dressed up" at a cost of $75. Altogether, nearly $27,000 were spent, and a critic in Congress accused the President of maintaining a "royal establishment," in a "palace as splendid as that of the Cæsars and as richly adorned as the proudest Asiatic mansion," the special objects of attack being upon one occasion the silver and gold plate upon the table and the large number of spittoons in the halls and parlors! The silver pitcher was presented to the collection by Mrs. Helen Singleton Green of Columbia, South Carolina, whose aunt, Mrs. Angelica Singleton Van Buren, was mistress of the White House during President Van Buren's administration, and from whom she inherited the relic.

THE BLUE-CHINA BOOK

William Henry Harrison occupied the office of President but one month, and his wife on account of ill health was unable to leave her Ohio home to accompany him to Washington at the time of his inaugural. A plate and a cup and saucer which had been presented to General Harrison at a previous time represent this administration in the White House Collection. They were sent by Miss Mary Reynolds of Washington, District of Columbia, whose mother was a granddaughter of President Harrison. They are of English manufacture, the cream colored surfaces being decorated in black with landscape scenes, which are possibly intended for types of our western country spaces which witnessed his Indian campaigns. An interesting ceramic memento of the lively Harrison political campaign is to be found in the old English pieces of Staffordshire pottery which picture the famous log-cabin, together with the cider barrel which so popularly figured beside it.

President Tyler, who was the first Vice-President to receive promotion to the Presidency in mid-term, is called to our minds by the three objects, a porcelain plate and a pair of Sheffield plate fruit baskets, which make up his exhibit. The fruit baskets are a loan from Judge D. Gardiner Tyler of Williamsburg, Virginia, and are of a peculiar design of twisted cord. They are of special interest from the fact that they were sent, among other valuable articles, by Mr. Tyler in the troublous times of 1862 from his home on the James River to Richmond, Va., for safe keeping, and were burned in the partial destruction of that city by the Northern soldiers in the year 1865. None of the silver remains upon the body of the ware, and both standards have been melted off. The dinner plate is of French porcelain, the rim decoration being a design of wheat and stalk in gold outline, and in the center a bunch of nasturtiums in natural tints upon a chocolate-colored ground. The plate is loaned to the collection by Mrs. William M. Ellis, of Shawsville, Va., the youngest daughter of President Tyler.

The illustration here given of the President Polk relics presents but a partial display of the White House group, the pieces of greatest beauty and interest in it being the tall, diamond-shaped, lattice work fruit-compote and the plate and cup and saucer of a state set. The design upon these pieces is composed of pink, gold-bordered bands broken with vignettes enclosing brilliantly plumaged birds, the plate carrying also a bunch of violet morning glories in the center. They are of old Dresden manufacture, and were presented by Mrs. George W. Fall of Nashville, Tenn., a niece of Mrs. Polk, who is the fortunate possessor of many of the personal relics of the Polk administration. A curious old-time finger and mouth bowl, with a separate compartment for each member to be cleansed, a deep blue Bohemian glass goblet, a small glass vase, and a cut glass wine glass, may also be seen in the illustration; while the White House Collection includes, in addition, two plates of elaborate designs, each one bearing the United States shield in color, and several pieces of white and colored glass.

During President Polk's term of office occurred the war with Mexico, resulting in the annexation of California and the great southwestern area of the United States, and it was a natural consequence that his successor should be a hero of that brilliant campaign. General Zachary Taylor, dubbed by his soldiers "Old Rough and Ready," and his family left their Baton Rouge home with reluctance to take up their residence in the White House, bringing with them, it is said, only a family negro servant, a favorite dog, and the horse the General had ridden through the Mexican War. During the year and a half of the Taylor régime, which was suddenly ended by his death, the East Room was again refurbished to suit the tastes of its good-housekeeping occupants. A new carpet was purchased for it, its walls were redecorated, and gas replaced the candles in the crystal chandeliers. An entire shelf in the White House Collection is filled with Taylor relics, a portion of which were presented by the great-grandchildren of the President, the children of Captain John Taylor Wood, the President's grandson, and another portion by his granddaughter, Mrs. Walter R. Stauffer of New Orleans, La. No porcelain is included in the group, which dis-

THE BLUE-CHINA BOOK

plays a black enameled brooch containing a braided lock of President Taylor's hair, which was once worn by his wife, a decanter and three wine glasses, a pair of silver candlesticks, a pair of Mexican spurs, and the gold head to a walking stick. The unexpired term of President Taylor was filled by Vice-President Millard Fillmore. The Fillmore representation, which by the way it is hoped may some day be augmented by other interesting pieces, is now made up of a large deep-blue Staffordshire platter, a vegetable dish decorated in the green shade of the late period of Staffordshire, and a blue and white Canton soup plate, the gifts of Mrs. E. B. Terry and Miss Cornelia Burtis of Buffalo.

One of the distinctive exhibits in the collection is that of the Franklin Pierce administration, being a large group of the beautiful red-banded porcelain which graced the White House table during his term of office. The most striking piece, as is usual in the earlier groups, is the fruit-compote, this one being of the round, lattice work variety, with bands of the rich deep red which characterize the set encircling the standard and the bowl. A graceful gravy-boat and tray, two plates, a covered oval vegetable dish, a tea cup and saucer and a preserve dish complete the group in the collection, which vies in beauty and in popular interest with the Jefferson and the Lincoln exhibits. It is also of interest to recall the fact that to President Pierce the field of American letters is no doubt indebted for much of the work of Nathaniel Hawthorne. The author was a classmate and personal friend of the President, who gave him the appointment of consul at Liverpool, and thereby enabled him to make those European studies with the rich result of which the world is familiar.

James Buchanan was a bachelor, which possibly may have something to do with the meagerness of his display now in the White House, three pieces of porcelain only marking his administration. One of them is a plate which belonged to a Sèvres banquet set purchased by him from an early French minister to this country, and which was presented to the collection by the President's nephew and ward, Mr. James Buchanan Henry of An-

260

napolis, Md., to whom it descended. The plate has a deep pinkish lavender rim outlined on either edge with heavy bands of gold, while the center carries tall growing tulips and a drooping tree set upon a terrace overlooking distant hills. A tea cup and saucer and a small coffee cup and saucer complete this exhibit.

With the exception of the Roosevelt porcelain, no other exhibit elicits so many expressions of admiration from passing visitors as does the Lincoln group, which was selected from the remains of a state set chosen by Mrs. Lincoln. It is of Haviland make, and wide bands of crimson-lilac edged with lines of plain gold and of dots, together with a spirited representation of the United States Arms in bright colors upon a gold-clouded ground, characterize the decoration. The dish-forms are likewise arresting, the plates being scalloped, the water pitcher graceful, and the compote high and imposing. The little custard-cup is unique in the collection, and a large punch bowl which lack of space does not now permit of exhibiting will be added as soon as more commodious quarters are prepared. Large quantities of this set, most of it damaged by breakage, have survived to grace private collections of historic porcelains, the Dickins loan collection in the National Museum in Washington, D. C., possessing a large number of Lincoln pieces. Vice-President Andrew Johnson, who served out Lincoln's unexpired term of office as President of the United States, is as yet without representation in the White House Collection of Presidential china.

A peculiar interest attaches to the President Grant exhibit of specimens of a state set ordered for his administration, for it is the first one which attempts to incorporate in the decorative design a motif wholly characteristic of this country. While the porcelain is of French manufacture, each piece carries a natural spray of American wild flowers, a wide variety of our common flora being reproduced. The encircing bands are of buff color, edged with gold lines and broken with a small colored reproduction of the United States shield. The old-time fruit-compote marks the end of that style of dish in the exhibit. It has been stated that upon the occasion of Nellie Grant's wedding in the White House, an additional quantity of this set, minus the shield and flowers, was ordered.

Perhaps no more striking example of the popular taste of a period will it be possible to find among any group of historic relics than is to be seen in the specimens of porcelain selected from the state set which was ordered for the White House by Mrs. Hayes, the largest set, it is claimed, ever brought into the Executive Mansion, Mrs. Hayes having an additional sideboard made to accommodate it. The Hayes group is never overlooked by passersby, and the comments one hears upon the decorations vary with the art education of the beholder. The porcelain is Limoges, but both forms and decorations were designed by the American artist, Theodore Davis, his name together with a colored reproduction of the Great Seal of the Republic being put upon the back of all original pieces. Here is realism in decorative art carried far; Flaubert, one may venture to suggest, transmuted into porcelain. The forms are varied to suit special uses, while the scheme of design embraces no less ambitious a field than the reproduction of the flora and fauna of the United States, the present exhibit having been selected largely from the latter division. The post of honor is held by a large turkey platter bearing what at first glance appears to be a genuine barnyard fowl, strutting in a snow-covered field, against a Turneresque sky, with rows of Thanksgiving-time trees marking the far horizon. "A turkey! Isn't that beautiful!" exclaimed a small boy in the writer's hearing, the bird no doubt connoting in his mind the annual American feast. A game-plate beside the platter, with wild deer roaming a valley between Swiss-like mountains, calls to mind a Landseer or a Rosa Bonheur canvas, while the small plate which seemingly holds a snowshoe in raised gold upon a pink ground was thus designed to heighten the enjoyment of ices served upon it. Two shell-shaped plates bear ocean scenes, while the small coffee cup and saucer are odd in conception, the saucer having a raised coiled stem in which to set the cup. The handled dish and tray showing a dainty seashell decoration in natural tints is perhaps the most modest and attractive of the group. Naturally, no display of wine glasses marks this cold water administration.

The few months which James A. Garfield and his family spent in the historic mansion saw no additions to the White House table service, but in the year 1907 Mrs. Garfield sent to the collection at Washington three pieces of a Haviland dinner set which for many years had been in the family—a low fruit dish, a salad bowl and a plate. The buff colored band upon them is edged with a conventional design in flat gold, and each piece is marked with the letter "G." A well-painted bunch of grapes fills the center of the fruit dish. Chester A. Arthur, who took up the reins of government upon President Garfield's tragic death, was, like President Van Buren, fond of the luxuries of life and of entertaining, and during his régime the White House received a strong impress of his personal taste. Twenty-four wagon loads of furniture and other White House furnishings which he considered "decayed" were sold at public auction, 5000 persons attending, the bidding spirited and the prices high. A motley array was thus disposed of—the entire furniture of the East Room, carpets, parlor sets, mattresses, chandeliers, bedroom sets, tables, lace curtains, lead piping, stoves, etc., etc., the lot realizing about $6000. Under the direction of Mr. Louis Tiffany of New York, the state apartments were then freshly decorated and refurnished, the opalescent screen of Tiffany glass, which remained until the Roosevelt day, being at this time set between the long corridor and the vestibule. President Arthur was fond of music, of cozy dinners, and of intimate social entertainments, and the private dining room which he regularly used was made elegant according to the ideas of the day, with heavy gold paper, hangings of pomegranate plush, and crimson-shaded lights. The new president had another sideboard made to match the one that was ordered by Mrs. Hayes, and upon it were displayed specimens of the Hayes set of porcelain. The tableware which he himself added, if one may judge from the plates which identify his administration, was in keeping with the general decorative scheme he introduced. Vivid color and large patterns mark the decorations, one plate bearing a single rose branch in the center around which butterflies are hovering. Another shows two cherubs sporting in a field of daisies, while the surface of still another is entirely covered with decorative motives verging toward the center, the colors being deep blue and pink.

Before Mrs. Cleveland entered the old mansion as a bride and its mistress, a general housecleaning had taken place, including much redecorating, cleaning of carpets and repainting. A large order for a service of glassware, about fifty dozen pieces, the records show, was given. Comparatively little new porcelain was purchased for the table, that which Mrs. Cleveland selected being of simple and exquisite taste, the examples in the collection eliciting much admiration from visitors. The plates are of Wedgwood and Minton manufacture, the plain centers bordered with narrow bands of color, scarlet, green, robin's egg blue, etc., upon the outer rim. One dainty plate carries a narrow wreath of tiny daisies in white enamel outlined with a narrow pink line and bordered on either side with a conventional pattern in raised gold. Upon their return to Washington for the second term, the Clevelands for a great part of the time occupied a suburban home, the administrative offices of the Government having encroached to such an extent upon the living quarters that the White House was inadequate for family life. The suggestion was made at this time to provide a separate building for the Executive Offices, but nothing was done in the matter, however, until Mr. Roosevelt came into power.

Like the Cleveland exhibit, that of the Benjamin Harrison administration declares a taste simple and refined. Mrs. Harrison, being artistic and original, designed the decorations for the new china herself, using a combination of the goldenrod (which she wished to have adopted as the national flower) and Indian corn, which appears in flat gold over the underglaze blue rims of two of the plates, and over the outer white rim of the center plate, as they are arranged in the illustration. A row of golden stars lines the inside of the plates, while upon each center is embla-

THE PRESIDENT CLEVELAND CHINA

THE BENJAMIN HARRISON CHINA

THE PRESIDENT McKINLEY CHINA

zoned the United States Seal in color. Three pieces of exquisite glass are included in this exhibit.

The McKinley administration is represented in the collection by an interesting exhibit of three plates and two cups and saucers, selected from different sets which the family used in the White House. One plate has a bluish green rim overlaid with a pattern in flat gold, another is decorated with Dresden-like festoons of flowers, while the third displays a row of large pink roses upon the rim and a conventional gold pattern in the center. One cup and saucer matches the plate first described, while the second carries a row of pink rosebuds as a motif.

Whatever comments of praise or curiosity the other exhibits may draw from the stream of visitors from all parts of the country who pass through the Lower Corridor, one hears little but unstinted praise for the Roosevelt china, even from the less discerning. While engaged in making a study of the collection, it was the writer's pleasure to linger near the cabinet which contains this group and listen to the remarks expressed with no fear of lèse majésté. "Very plain china," a woman ventured, who evidenty would prefer upon her own table the more showy specimens she had just passed on her way to the glories of the East Room above. "Yes, but he is a plain man," a masculine voice at her side explained. "She had it made in Paris!" volunteered a knowing one. "Plain and elegant" were often upon the lips. One enthusiastic admirer of the ex-President exclaimed with fervor: "The Roosevelt china is all right!" Mr. and Mrs. Roosevelt were fond of and justly appreciated the possibilities of the White House as a national home for this great Republic, and to them is due much praise for its complete restoration to suitable service, as well as to the historic form of its original designers. So thorough was the work of restoration and improvement during their régime that in all probability the old mansion, so indelibly impressed with the intimate and varied associations of more than a century of public life in a newly established country, will remain for many years in its

THE BLUE-CHINA BOOK

present state.   In the general scheme of restoration, it was but
fitting that a distinctive table service of porcelain should be
included.   The subject was given careful consideration by Mrs.
Roosevelt, who, out of a large number of designs submitted by
noted factories and distinguished decorators, selected the simple
Colonial pattern upon Wedgwood ware which the illustration
presents.   The design is traced in flat gold and each piece carries
a correct representation of the Great Seal of the United States,
as it was adopted in the year 1782.   As may be observed in
some of the other exhibits, peculiar liberties have at times been
taken in the presentation of this national emblem, but the Seal
as it appears upon the Roosevelt china may be studied as correct.
The Roosevelt design is protected by patent and copyright for
the exclusive use of the Executive Mansion.

As has already been stated, Mrs. Taft admired the china of
her predecessor in power, and merely filled up broken sets to a
number necessary for 100 covers.   She enjoyed using the old
historic pieces in the mansion at small dinners and luncheons,
there being a sufficient quantity of plates of the Lincoln set
upon the shelves of the mezzanine floor of the White House
pantry to serve a course for thirty persons.   The present Wilson
administration likewise follows precedent in the use of the
Roosevelt porcelain.

APPENDIX II

CHECKING LIST OF AMERICAN VIEWS FOUND UPON ENGLISH OLD POTTERY

Reprinted from "Anglo-American Pottery" by permission of the author, DR. EDWIN ATLEE BARBER.

FOLLOWING the titles of the American views in the list below, names or initials frequently appear in brackets. These, sometimes together with the title of the decoration on the face, the collector will find either printed or impressed upon the back of many pieces of Staffordshire pottery; and they are the surest means of identification.

Wood refers to Enoch Wood, who began potting in Burslem in 1783, the firm name being at various times Wood and Caldwell, Enoch Wood & Co., and Enoch Wood & Sons. The great bulk of their output has the name Enoch, or E. Wood & Sons, either impressed or stamped on the back. Sometimes the name is accompanied with a wreath, scroll, or eagle, and the motto, E Pluribus Unum. The most characteristic Wood border on American views is the Sea-Shell Pattern. The scroll-medallion design containing inscriptions, which frames the Landing of the Pilgrims engraving, is also by Wood; and the one composed of a beautiful flower and foliage combination which circles the various views upon Lafayette's estate in France. At a later date, the firm used colors other than deep blue—brown, red, light blue, green, etc.—for American views. They also produced much scenery of countries other than America: England, Italy, Africa, India, etc., as well as a series of Scriptural designs.

The potter *A. Stevenson* made many beautiful sets, some of his American views being painted from nature by the artist W. G.

Wall, whose name frequently appears upon the back. His borders are flower wreaths and scrolls.

James Clews was a prolific potter, using various border designs, the two best known American ones being the "States," with festoons containing names of fifteen States, and that around the Landing of Lafayette print. His later American output appears in various colored prints, such as the "Picturesque Views" series of Hudson River scenery, copied from Wall's paintings and bordered with a device of birds and flowers. In addition to views of English cathedrals and castles, Clews issued three popular sets which are highly prized by old-china lovers—the Dr. Syntax, the Don Quixote, and the Sir David Wilkie series. The characteristic Clews mark is a circle impressed in the biscuit, with a crown inside, and the words, "Clews Warranted Staffordshire."

J. & W. Ridgway refers to an important pottery conducted by the brothers John and William Ridgway, which turned out a set of dark blue designs called "Beauties of America." The border is easily identified, being a series of rose leaf medallions. In 1830, the firm dissolved, and John Ridgway issued among others the Log-Cabin view with the Columbian star border, during the W. H. Harrison campaign of 1840. This is found in black, brown, pale blue, etc. William Ridgway, a brother of John, also turned his attention to the American market, his prints being of a late period of Staffordshire in the colors of that time. A narrow lace or moss border belongs to him.

The name *Joseph Stubbs* stands for a series of handsome dark blue American designs, enclosed in a border emblematic of early America, an arrangement of flowers and scrolls bound together by eagles with half spread wings. Dr. Barber states that all pieces bearing this border are known to have been made by Stubbs.

S. Tams & Co. used for a border device a very graceful arrangement of growing trees, with the foliage meeting at the top. The Tams specimens are printed in a rich deep blue.

The name *T. Mayer* on the back, and the three border stripes which call to mind the stripes woven in certain rugs of Turkish make, the center one carrying a running vine of trumpet flowers

APPENDIX II

and leaves, mark the important series put out by the firm of that name. A reproduction of the Arms of the original States of the Union characterizes the center of the plates and platters.

The letters *R. S. W.*, or *R. S. & W.*, or simply *R. S.*, stand for Ralph Stevenson and Williams, potters of Cobridge, Staffordshire. The well-known acorn and oak leaf border belongs to them, also a beautiful wreath of vine leaves, and a lace border of a later period. The Erie Canal at Buffalo illustration in Chapter XIV is a Ralph Stevenson design printed in purple.

The pottery under the name of *William Adams,* or *W. Adams & Sons,* is printed in deep blue as well as in the tones characteristic of the later period of Staffordshire manufacture for the American market. They turned out a series of American views in various borders, as well as the Columbus series which are described in chapter VII of this volume.

The *Rogers* mark indicates a small group of Boston views done in deep blue by the Burslem pottery works of John and George Rogers, the firm later on becoming John Rogers and Son.

E. J. Phillips & Co. had a pottery at Longport in the Staffordshire country, their characteristic American view being the Franklin's Tomb design. Very little is known of them.

J. & J. Jackson used a pretty floral device for a border and printed in red, light blue, lilac, black, brown, etc., a long list of American scenes of great interest and value to the collector, the number including the early view of the White House in Washington which is reproduced in this volume.

The name *Godwin* refers to the potter Thomas Godwin, who used a characteristic border device of convolvulus and nasturtiums. The prints appear in green, brown, light blue, etc.

Davenport is the mark found in pieces made by the firm of Davenport and Co. at Longport, Staffordshire. They turned out excellent pottery, but, unlike their contemporaries in the same field, they did not cater to the American market to any great extent. Dr. Barber mentions but one specimen with this mark, a view of the city of Montreal.

C. M. stands for Charles Meigh, who between 1830 and 1840

269

produced a set of American views in various colors, bordered with fine mosses and chickweed.

T. G. or *Thomas Green* is the potter who is mentioned in another part of this volume as the one whose sole output for this country deals with the Treaty of William Penn with the Indians. These prints appear in the various lighter shades and black.

J. H. & C., or *Joseph Heath & Co.,* are best known here for their Richard Jordan design, a pretty landscape scene displaying a roadway leading to the residence, a fine one for that day, of the eminent Quaker preacher, Richard Jordan, at Newton, Gloucester County, N. J. A figure in Quaker hat and clothing appears in the foreground. Other views of this country were also turned out by the Heath pottery.

Edwards, or *J. & T. Edwards,* as the firm was known, sent over a small number of American views in the late colors, showing the "Boston Mails" series of steamships in the border.

John Tams printed in light blue, under commission by a wealthy citizen of Philadelphia, two souvenir designs upon china, one being a portrait of Henry Clay, " Star of the West," and the other that of William Henry Harrison, " Hero of the Thames, 1813."

M. V. & Co., Mellor, Venables & Co., of Burslem, did a series of American views in various colors, within a border of medallions containing the Arms of the early States.

J. B. According to Dr. Barber, these initials are not positively identified. The firm produced the American design known as the "Texian Campaign."

F. M. & Co., Francis Morley and Co., were potters at Hanley, England, and but one design, "American Marine," in various colors within a border of ships and cordage is known to have come from them.

G. L. A. & Bro., George L. Ashworth and Brother, succeeded the above-mentioned firm in the year 1859, and continued to print the same design.

T. F. & Co., Thomas Ford and Co., Hanley, England, fur-

POTTERS' MARKS

1. *Clews*   2. *G. L. Ashworth & Bro.*   3. *Clews*   4. *R. Hall*
5. *Enoch Wood*   6. *R. Hall*   7. *W. Adams*

APPENDIX II

nish a blue design of the American eagle with a shield standing upon a globe.

C. C. Dr. Barber states that several Staffordshire potters might claim these initials, but in the absence of positive knowledge the name of the maker cannot be stated definitely. The border device is designated on the back of these pieces as "Catskill Moss."

In addition to his marked pieces, the collector will find many of his specimens unmarked. Two reasons account for this. First, not all pieces of a set were originally marked, and second, a large number of finely drawn and printed American views are still, owing to the absence of distinguishing marks and to unidentified borders, included in a separate list of "Unknown Makers."

The collector of to-day will be confronted with many forgeries of the favorite old prints. Until recent years, it has been impossible for potters to reproduce the deep rich blue of Old Staffordshire, but at the present time, reproductions of the most sought after designs are so skillfully executed as to make detection the work of an expert. The Pennsylvania Museum of Philadelphia, in order to instruct the student of ceramics, has had placed a number of originals and forgeries side by side, each with its true designation. The American-made dishes of to-day, while very like in every other respect, are as a rule heavier in weight than the English originals.

DESIGNS IN DARK BLUE

Albany
Albany (Wood)
Albany, Dutch Church
American Heroes—Washington, etc.
American Villa
Arms of the U. S.

Baltimore
Baltimore, Alms House
Baltimore, Court House

Baltimore, Exchange
Baltimore, Exchange (R. S. W.)
Baltimore, Masonic Hall
Baltimore and Ohio R. R., Inclined Plane (Wood)
Baltimore and Ohio R. R. (Wood)
Belleville on the Passaic River (Wood)
Boston, Alms House (Ridgway)
Boston, Alms House (R. S.)
Boston, Athenæum (Ridgway)
Boston, Court House (Ridgway)
Boston, Court House (R. S. W.)
Boston Harbor
Boston, Hospital (Ridgway)
Boston, Hospital (R. S.)
Boston, Insane Hospital (Ridgway)
Boston, Lawrence Mansion (R. S.)
Boston, Massachusetts Hospital (R. S.)
Boston, Mitchell and Freeman's China and Glass Warehouse
  (Adams)
Boston, Nahant Hotel, near (R. S. W.)
Boston, Nahant Hotel, near (Stubbs)
Boston, Octagon Church (Ridgway)
Boston, State House (Ridgway
Boston, State House (R. S. W.)
Boston, State House (Wood)
Boston, State House (Rogers)
Boston, State House (Stubbs)
Boston State House, Chaise (Rogers)
Boston, State House, Cows (Rogers)
Boston, St. Paul's Church (Ridgway)
Brooklyn Ferry (R. S.)
Buenos Ayres
Bunker Hill, Battle (R. S.)

Cadmus (Trefoil Border)
Cadmus (Wood)

APPENDIX II

Catskill, Hope Mill (Wood)
Catskill House, Hudson (Wood)
Catskill Mountains (Wood)
Catskills, Pass in the (Wood)
Catskills, Pine Orchard House (Wood)
Charleston, Exchange (Ridgway)
Charleston, Exchange (R. S.)
Chillicothe
Clinton (St. Paul's Church, N. Y.; Rochester)
Columbia College (Clews)
Columbia College (R. S.)
Columbia College (R. S. W.)
Columbia College (Stevenson)
Columbus, Ohio
Connecticut, Arms of (Mayer)
Connecticut, Arms of (Oliver Stoke)
"Constitution" and "Guerrière" (Wood)

Delaware, Arms of (Mayer)
Detroit

Erie Canal, Albany
Erie Canal, Albany (Clews)
Erie Canal, Albany (Wood)
Erie Canal, DeWitt Clinton Eulogy
Erie Canal, Little Falls, N. Y.
Erie Canal, Little Falls (Wood)
Erie Canal, Rochester, N. Y.
Erie Canal, Rochester (Wood)
Erie Canal, Utica
Erie Canal Views

Fishkill, Near
Fort Gansevoort (R. S.)
Fort Gansevoort (Stevenson)
Franklin's Morals

Franklin's Tomb (Phillips)
Franklin's Tomb (Wood)
Fulton's Steamboat

Georgia, Arms of (Mayer)
Gilpin's Mills (Wood)
Governor's Island (Stevenson)
Greensburg, Tappan Zee from (Wood)

Harrisburg, Pa., Capitol at
Hartford Deaf and Dumb Asylum (Ridgway)
Hartford, State House
Harvard College (Ridgway)
Harvard College (R. S. W.)
Harvard University
Highlands at West Point (Wood)
Highlands, Hudson (Wood)
Highlands near Newburg (Wood)
Highlands, North River (Stubbs)
Hobart Town
Hoboken, N. J. (Stubbs)
Hudson and Sacandaga, Junction of (Stevenson)
Hurlgate, East River (Stubbs)

Indianapolis

Jefferson (Columbia College)
Jefferson, Clinton (Albany)
Jefferson, Clinton (Massachusetts Hospital)
Jefferson, Clinton (Park Theater, N. Y.)
Jefferson, Lafayette (Covetham)
Jefferson, Lafayette (Washington, Capitol)

Lafayette (Stevenson)
Lafayette (Clews)
Lafayette and Washington

APPENDIX II

Lafayette, Landing of (Clews)
Lafayette, "Republicans Are Not Always Ungrateful"
Lafayette, "Welcome Lafayette, the Nation's Guest"
Lafayette, "Welcome to the Land of Liberty"
Lake George (Wood)
Lake George, On the Road to (Stevenson)
Lexington, Transylvania University (Wood)
Livingston, Chancellor (Wood)
Louisville
Louisville, Marine Hospital (Wood)

Macdonough's Victory (Wood)
Marshall, Chief Justice (Wood
Maryland, Arms of (Mayer)
Massachusetts, Arms of (Mayer)
Mendenhall Ferry (Stubbs)
Montmorenci, Fall of (Wood)
Mount Vernon (Washington Mounted)
Mount Vernon (Washington with Horse)
Mount Vernon (Wood)
Mount Vernon, near Washington (Ridgway)
Mount Vernon, Seat of Washington

New Jersey, Arms of (Mayer)
New York Alms House (Clews)
New York, Alms House (Ridgway)
New York, Alms House (R. S.)
New York, Alms House (Stevenson)
New York, American Museum (R. S. W.)
New York, Arms of (Mayer)
New York, Battery (R. S.)
New York Bay (Clews)
New York Bay (Stubbs)
New York Bay (Wood)
New York, Castle Garden (Trefoil Border)
New York, Castle Garden Battery (Wood)

New York, Catholic Cathedral (Stevenson)
New York, Church, Dr. Mason's (Stevenson)
New York, Church, Dr. Mason's (Stubbs)
New York, City Hall (Clews)
New York, City Hall (Ridgway)
New York, City Hall (R. S.)
New York, City Hall (Stevenson)
New York, City Hall (Stubbs)
New York, City Hotel (R. S. W.)
New York, Esplanade, Castle Garden (R. S.)
New York from Brooklyn Heights (Clews)
New York from Brooklyn Heights (Stevenson)
New York, from Weehawk (Stevenson)
New York, Fulton Market (R. S.)
New York, Hospital (R. S.)
New York, Insane Asylum (Clews)
New York, Park Theatre (R. S. W.)
New York, St. Patrick's Cathedral
New York, St. Paul's (R. S. W.)
Niagara (Stevenson)
Niagara Falls (Wood)
Niagara, Table Rock (Wood)
North Carolina, Arms of (Mayer)

Passaic Falls (Wood)
Peace and Plenty (Clews)
Pennsylvania, Arms of (Mayer)
Perry Memorial (Clews)
Perry Memorial (Stevenson)
Philadelphia
Philadelphia, A View near
Philadelphia, Bank of the United States (Stubbs)
Philadelphia, Dam and Water Works (Side Wheel)
Philadelphia, Dam and Water Works (Stern Wheel)
Philadelphia, Fairmount, near (Stubbs)
Philadelphia, Library (Ridgway)

Philadelphia, Masonic Temple
Philadelphia, Pennsylvania Hospital (Ridgway)
Philadelphia, Staughton's Church (Ridgway)
Philadelphia, United States Hotel
Philadelphia, Upper Ferry Bridge (Stubbs)
Philadelphia, Water Works (R. S. W.)
Philadelphia, Woodlands, near (Stubbs)
Pilgrims, Landing of (Wood)
Pittsfield, Winter View (Clews)
Prentiss, Henry, and His Employ

Quebec
Quebec (Wood)

Rhode Island, Arms of (Mayer)
Richmond

Sandusky
Savannah, Bank (Ridgway)
Savannah, Bank (R. S.)
Ship of the Line (Wood)
South Carolina, Arms of (Mayer)
States (Clews)
Steamship, American Flag (Wood)

Trenton Falls (Wood)
Troy from Mt. Ida (Stevenson)

Union Line (Wood)
University of Maryland

Virginia, Arms of (Mayer)

Wadsworth Tower (Wood)
Washington (City)
Washington and Lafayette

Washington and Lafayette (R. S. and W.)
Washington, Capitol (Ridgway)
Washington, Capitol (R. S.)
Washington, Capitol (R. S. W.)
Washington, Capitol (Wood)
Washington, Clinton (Boston Hospital)
Washington, Clinton (City Hotel, N. Y.)
Washington, Clinton (Faulkbourn Hall)
Washington, Clinton (Niagara)
Washington, Clinton (Park Theater)
Washington, Clinton (Washington, Capitol)
Washington, from Mount Vernon
Washington, full length with scroll (Wood)
Washington, Jefferson (Capitol, Washington)
Washington, Lafayette (City Hotel)
Washington, Lafayette (Washington, Capitol)
Washington, Lafayette, Jefferson, Clinton (Faulkbourn Hall)
Washington, Lafayette, Jefferson, Clinton (Little Falls)
Washington, Lafayette, Jefferson, Clinton (Niagara)
Washington, Lafayette, Jefferson, Clinton (Park Theater, Albany, N. Y.)
Washington, Lafayette, Jefferson, Clinton (Rochester)
Washington, Lafayette, Jefferson, Clinton (Windsor Castle, Albany, N. Y.)
Washington, Lafayette, Jefferson, Clinton (Writtle Lodge)
Washington, White House (Wood)
Washington's Tomb (Wood)
West Point, Military Academy (Wood)
Wright's Ferry, Susquehanna

DESIGNS IN VARIOUS COLORS

Alabama (Bodley and Co.)
Albany
Albany (Jackson)
Albany, City Hall

APPENDIX II

Albany Theater (1824)
Albany, Thorps and Sprague
Allegheny, Penitentiary (Clews)
"America," Eagle, etc. (T. F. and Co.)
America, Triumphant
America, Whose Militia, etc.
American Flag and Liberty Cap
American Heroes—Van Rensselaer, etc.
American Marine (Ashworth)
American Marine (F. M. and W.)
Anti-Slavery
Arms of the United States (Buzzard and Cannon)
Arms of the United States (Hammersley)
Arms of the United States (Hand Colored)

Bainbridge
Baker's Falls, Hudson (Clews)
Baltimore
Baltimore (C. M.)
Baltimore (Godwin)
Baltimore, Battle Monument (Jackson)
Boston and Bunker Hill (Godwin)
Boston, Bunker Hill Monument
Boston, Court House
Boston from Chelsea Heights (C. C.)
Boston, from Dorchester Heights (C. M.)
Boston, Hancock House (Jackson)
Boston Mails, Gentlemen's Cabin (Edwards)
Boston Mails, Ladies' Cabin (Edwards)
Boston Mill Dam (C. M.)
Boston, State House
Boston, State House (Jackson)
Brooklyn Ferry (Godwin)
Brown
Buffalo on Lake Erie (E. W. and S.)

Caldwell, Lake George (M. V. and Co.)

Caldwell, Lake George (W. Ridgway)
Capitol Buildings, States (M. V. and Co.)
Catskill Mountain House (Adams)
Catskill Mountain House (Jackson)
Catskill Mountains, Pass in (E. W. and S.)
Clay, Henry (Tams)
Columbia Bridge (Godwin)
Columbia Bridge on the Susquehanna (W. Ridgway)
"Columbian Star" (J. Ridgway)
Columbus (Adams)
"Constitution" and "Guerrière"
"Constitution," "Cyane" and "Levant"
"Constitution's" Escape from British Squadron
"Constitution" Leaving Boston Harbor
Constitution of United States
"Constitution" (U. S. S.)
Conway, N. H., View near (Adams)
Cornwallis, Surrender

Decatur (Bust)
Decatur (Free Trade)
Delaware (J. Ridgway)
Delaware Water Gap, Pa. (W. Ridgway)
Dumb Asylum

Eagle on Rock (Wood)
"Enterprise" and "Boxer"
Erie Canal at Buffalo (R. S.)

Fairmount Water Works (Clews)
Fayette the Nation's Guest
Fishkill, Hudson, near (Clews)
Fishkill, Hudson River, from (Clews)
Fishkill, Hudson River, near (E. W. and S.)
Fort Conanicut (Jackson)
Fort Edward, Hudson (Clews)
Fort Hamilton (M. V. and Co.)

APPENDIX II

Fort Hamilton, The Narrows
Fort Hamilton, The Narrows, from (Godwin)
Fort Hamilton, The Narrows, from (W. Ridgway)
Fort Hudson, N. Y. (Yellow)
Fort Millir, Hudson, near (Clews)
Fort Montgomery, Hudson (Clews)
Fort Niagara
Fort Ticonderoga, N. Y. (Jackson)
Franklin (Flying Kite)
Franklin Industries
Franklin's Maxims
Franklin's Proverbs
Fulton's Steamboat (?)

Hadley's Falls, Hudson (Clews)
Harper's Ferry (Adams)
Harper's Ferry, from Potomac Side (W. Ridgway)
Harrison, W. H. (Log Cabin)
Harrison, W. H. (Log Cabin)
Harrison, W. H. (Tams)
Hartford, Connecticut (Jackson)
Harvard College
Harvard College (E. W. and S.)
Harvard Hall, Massachusetts (Jackson)
Hudson City (C. M.)
Hudson, Hudson River (Clews)
Hudson, Hudson River, near (Clews)
Hudson River, View on (Clews)
Hull
Humphreys, U. S. (Adams)

Jackson, "Hero of New Orleans" (Wood)
Jackson, Major-General Andrew (Bust)
Jessup's Landing, Hudson River, near (Clews)
Jones, Captain
Jordan, Residence of the late Richard (J. H. and Co.)

Juniata, Headwaters of (Adams)

Kosciusko's Tomb (C. C.)

Lafayette (Bust and Long Inscription—Auvergne)'
Lafayette (Bust) Embossed Border
Lafayette (Reverse, Cornwallis)
Lafayette and Washington (Raised Border)
Lafayette and Washington (Raised and Splotched Border)
Lafayette, "Welcome L., the Nation's Guest"
Lake George (Adams)
Lake George (Jackson)
Lawrence and Decatur
Lawrence, "Don't Surrender the Ship"
Lexington, Transylvania University (E. W. and S.)
Little Falls, Aqueduct Bridge
Little Falls at Luzerne, Hudson River (Clews)
Little Falls, Mohawk River (Jackson)
Little Falls, N. Y. (C. M.)
Little Falls, N. Y. (M. V. and Co.)
Log Cabin (J. Ridgway)
Lovejoy, 1837

"Macedonian"
Macdonough's Victory on Lake Champlain
Madison, 1815
Merchants' Exchange, New York (Burning)
Merchants' Exchange, New York (Ruins)
Meredith (C. C.)
Monterey (J. H. and Co.)
Monte Video, Ct. (Adams)
Mont Video, Hartford (Jackson)
Montreal (Davenport)
Moral Maxims (Clews)
Mormon
Mount Vernon (Man and Horse)

APPENDIX II

Mount Vernon (M. V. and Co.)
Mount Vernon, Seat of Washington

Natural Bridge, Va. (E. W. and S.)
Newburg, Hudson (Clews)
Newburg, Hudson, View from Ruggles House (W. Ridgway)
Newburg, N. Y. (Jackson)
New Haven, Connecticut (Jackson)
New Haven, Yale College (Jackson)
New Orleans, Old Cathedral
New Orleans (R. S.)
New York, (Adams)
New York, Battery
New York, Battery (Jackson)
New York, Castle Garden (Jackson)
New York, City Hall (C. M.)
New York, City Hall (Jackson)
New York, Coënties Slip
New York from Staten Island (E. W. and S.)
New York from the Bay (Clews)
New York from Weehawken
New York, Hudson (Clews)
Niagara
Niagara Falls (Adams)
Niagara Falls (E. W. and S.)
Niagara Falls (Large House)
Niagara, Fort (Adams)

Odd Fellows (1845)
Ontario Lake Scenery (J. H. and Co.)

Peace, Plenty and Independence
Peekskill Landing, Hudson (W. Ridgway)
Penn's Treaty
Penn's Treaty (T. G.)
Pennsylvania (K. E. and Co.)

Perry (Bust)
Perry (Full length)
Perry (Inscription)
Perry, O. H., Esq.
Perry's Victory, Second View of
Philadelphia, Deaf and Dumb Asylum (Jackson)
Philadelphia, Dumb Asylum
Philadelphia, Fairmount Water Works (Clews)
Philadelphia, Fairmount Water Works (E. W. and S.)
Philadelphia, Girard's Bank (Jackson)
Philadelphia, Pennsylvania Hospital (W. Ridgway)
Philadelphia, Schuylkill Water Works (C. M.)
Philadelphia, Schuylkill Water Works (Godwin)
Philadelphia, The Race Bridge (Jackson)
Philadelphia, The Water Works (Jackson)
Pike
Pittsburg, "Home" and "Lark" Boats (Clews)
Pittsburg, "Pennsylvania" Boat (Clews)
Port Putnam, Hudson, View from (W. Ridgway)

Richmond, Court House (Jackson)
Richmond, Virginia, at (Jackson)

Sacandaga and Hudson, Junction of (Clews)
Sandy Hill, Hudson (Clews)
Saugerties, Iron Works (Jackson)
Shannondale Springs, Virginia (Adams)
Shannondale Springs, Virginia (Jackson)
Shipping Port on the Ohio, Kentucky (E. W. and S.)
Skenectady, Mohawk River (Adams)
Skenectady, New York (Jackson)
Soldiers ("By Virtue and Valor")
States (Wedgwood)

"Texian Campaign" (J. B.)
Trenton Falls (E. W. and S.)

APPENDIX II

Troy, Hudson (Clews)

Undercliff near Cold Spring (W. Ridgway)
"United States" and "Macedonian"
Utica (C. M.)
Utica, New York
Utica, New York (Godwin)

Valley of Shenandoah, from Jefferson's Rock (W. Ridgway)
Virginia (Monument)

Washington and Lafayette "First in War," etc.
Washington (Bust, Military Hat)
Washington (French Portrait)
Washington (Urn Bearing Name)
Washington, Capitol
Washington, Capitol (C. C.)
Washington, Capitol (E. W. and S.)
Washington, Capitol (Godwin)
Washington, Capitol (J. Ridgway)
Washington, Capitol (W. Ridgway)
Washington Crossing the Delaware
Washington, Executive Mansion
"Washington His Country's Father"
Washington Memorial (Red and Green)
Washington, Monument ("Sacred to the Memory")
Washington, President's House (Jackson)
Washington's Tomb, Mount Vernon ("Catskill Moss")
Washington's Tomb, Mount Vernon (M. V. and Co.)
Washington Vase.
Washington, White House
"Wasp" and "Frolic"
"Wasp" and "Reindeer"
West Point, Hudson (Clews)
West Point, Military School (Adams)
White House (M. V. and Co.)

THE BLUE-CHINA BOOK

White Mountains, New Hampshire (Adams)
White Sulphur Springs, Delaware, Ohio (Jackson)
Wilkes Barre, Vale of Wyoming (W. Ridgway)

THE TRUE WILLOW PATTERN

DON QUIXOTE'S ATTACK ON THE WINDMILLS
(*Clews*)

DR. SYNTAX STARTING OUT
(*Clews*)

THE ESCAPE OF THE MOUSE
(*Clews*)

APPENDIX III

THE STORY OF THE WILLOW PATTERN

THE Willow Pattern has been perhaps more popular and more universally familiar ever since the first use of the color blue in English potteries than any other design put upon tableware, but in spite of this fact a surprising amount of ignorance or of half-knowledge concerning it still persists. The Chinese story which inspired the English potter-apprentice Thomas Minton, about the year 1780, to compose and engrave the design to illustrate it may best be given in the form of one of the many delightful bits of verse which formerly were taught to children along with their nursery rhymes:

> " So she tells me a legend centuries old
> Of a Mandarin rich in lands and gold,
> Of Koong-Shee fair and Chang the good,
> Who loved each other as lovers should.
> How they hid in the gardener's hut awhile,
> Then fled away to the beautiful isle.
> Though a cruel father pursued them there,
> And would have killed the hopeless pair,
> But kindly power, by pity stirred,
> Changed each into a beautiful bird.
>
> . . . .
>
> Here is the orange tree where they talked,
> Here they are running away,
> And over all at the top you see
> The birds making love alway."

The large pagoda at the right of the design, as reproduced from an old platter, is the palace of the wealthy Mandarin, while upon the terrace stands the summer house where Koong-Shee, the lovely daughter of the Mandarin, was kept a prisoner in order

THE BLUE-CHINA BOOK

that she might be concealed from Chang, her father's secretary, who loved her and whom she wished to marry. But, as the story runs in "Old China," Chang was poor and the Mandarin had selected a wealthy suitor for his daughter's hand. From her chamber in the prison the unhappy maiden watched the willow tree blossom while yet the peach tree was only in bud, and she wrote verses in which she voiced the hope that before the peach blossoms appeared, she might be free. Chang, however, found means to communicate with Koong-Shee, once by sending a note in a tiny cocoanut shell, which by the aid of a small sail made its way to the captive maiden. Koong-Shee replied by scratching on an ivory tablet the challenge, "Do not wise husbandmen gather the fruits they fear will be stolen?" and, putting the tablet in the boat, she sent it back to her lover.

Chang received the message, entered the Mandarin's garden in spite of the barricades which had been erected to keep him away, and eloped with Koong-Shee. The father gave chase, and there on the bridge the three may be seen—Chang carrying a box of jewels, Koong-Shee with a distaff in her hand, and the angry Mandarin with a whip. The lovers escaped, however, entered the little boat, and sailed away to Chang's house on the island, where they lived happily until the rejected suitor discovered them and burned their home. Then, from out the ashes of Chang and Koong-Shee, who perished in their bamboo grove, there arose two spirits in the form of white doves—the lovers, who forever hover over the scenes of their earthly happiness.

Nearly all of the Staffordshire potters at one time or another made use of the Willow Pattern, or of variants of it. Some of the English designs, erroneously called Willow, have but two men on the bridge, or one man, or they have no boat or birds, being in reality merely arrangements of oriental motifs—trees, pagodas, fences, bridges, etc.—to suit the fancy of individual potters. The borders, too, vary with the pattern in the center, the butterfly, Joo-e dagger, fish-roe, fret, etc., etc., with their own adaptations, offering a separate subject for speculation and identification. The scope of this volume, however, forbids an extended review of this very interesting study of Oriental influence upon the early ceramic art of Europe.

DOCTOR SYNTAX DESIGNS

A very interesting series of dark blue prints on pottery was published by James Clews, after the original designs of the English caricaturist T. Rowlandson. Contrary to the usual method of procedure, rhymes were composed to fit the pictures, the combined product becoming very popular in London. William Combe, an eccentric author who was at the time an inmate of a debtors' prison, pinned the cartoons upon the wall of his cell and penned the verses for them. Blue pottery manufacture being at this time at its height in Staffordshire, the well-known Doctor Syntax was made to cater to the sales of pictured tableware in America. The story goes that the learned Doctor, a poorly paid curate of a small English town, sets out upon his gray mare Grizzle on a "Tour in Search of the Picturesque." In his farewell to his wife Dolly, he explains his purpose:

> "You charm my heart; you quite delight it;
> I'll make a tour — and then I'll write it,
> You well know what my pen can do,
> And I'll employ my pencil too;
> I'll ride and write, and sketch and print,
> And thus create a real mint;
> I'll prose it here, I'll verse it there,
> And picturesque it everywhere."

Then, as the print here presented pictures:

> "At length the ling'ring moment came
> That gave the dawn of wealth and fame.
> Incurious Ralph, exact at four,
> Led Grizzle, saddled, to the door,
> And soon, with more than common state,
> The Doctor stood before the gate.
> Behind him was his faithful wife:
> 'One more embrace, my dearest life;'
> Then his gray palfrey he bestrode,
> And gave a nod and off he rode.

THE BLUE-CHINA BOOK

> 'Good luck! Good luck!' she loudly cried,
> 'Vale! O Vale!' he replied."

According to the illustrated rhymes, a long series of adventures await the traveler—he is attacked by ruffians and tied to a tree; he is rescued by two women who appear on "trotting palfreys"; he loses Grizzle, finding him at last with cropped ears and tail, as he thereafter appears in the illustrations; he visits Oxford, loses his money at races, etc., etc. Finally, he reaches London and arranges with a bookseller for the publishing of his Tour. Then, having created his "mint," he returns to Dolly, who, learning of his success:

> " . . . . started up in joy's alarms
> And clasped the Doctor in her arms."

After several years of happiness, Dolly dies. Doctor Syntax then goes upon a "Tour in Search of Consolation," accompanied by his valet Pat. So successful was this supplementary series that it was quickly followed by a third " Tour in Search of a Wife," wherein after many experiences the sorrowing Doctor secures a mate the equal of his lamented Dolly. His end is an anticlimax—he tumbles into a pond, takes a cold, and dies. A stone is raised to his memory . . .

> "And, as the sculpture meets the eye,
> 'Alas, poor Syntax!' with a sigh,
> Is read by every passer by;
> And wakes the pensive thought, sincere,
> Forever sad! . . . forever dear!"

At least 30 of these prints have been found upon pieces of tableware, the ceramic specimens at the present day almost equaling in value the wonderful old editions of the poem illustrated with the colored engravings.

DON QUIXOTE DESIGNS

A set of at least 21 excellent blue-china prints have been found in this country, reproduced from the engravings of the English artist Robert Smirke, illustrating the adventures of Don Quixote de la Mancha. These also come from the Clews pottery works, and are framed in a handsome deep border composed of a wide-spreading six-scalloped star within the rounded points of which flowers and birds appear.

Transplanted from the barren, sun-scorched hills and plains of their native southland, and set in fresh English landscapes, amid English flowers and trees and English castles, beneath over-clouded English skies, may be found our familiar Spanish friends—the Knight of the Rueful Countenance, the Peasant Maid, Sancho Panza and Teresa his spouse, Rozinante (whose sides "stuck out like the corners of a Spanish real") and Dapple, the Priest, the Barber, the Shepherd boy, the Duke and Duchess, and the alluring Shepherdesses of the Wood. The "enchanted bark" here floats upon a shaded English stream; the wild boar roams a British forest; and the famous windmills sweep their arms through English skies.

Like Doctor Syntax, Don Quixote adventures three times into the world of experience, but, in place of seeking his own personal gain, the dear old Spanish knight has won his way into the hearts of succeeding generations through his generous efforts to teach the ridiculousness of sham and the worth of honesty. The most widely known incident in his travels through an unsympathetic world is that which is pictured in the accompanying illustration—"The Attack Upon the Windmills." Here may be seen Don Quixote and his steed Rozinante prone upon the ground, decidedly worsted in their encounter with the supposed giants of the plain. Coming to their rescue is Sancho Panza, his squire, who accompanies his knight and shares many of his experiences. Sancho's mount is a beloved ass named Dapple, who appears in a number of the pictures. But the knight's chosen lady, the peerless Dulcinea del Toboso, for whose favor all is attempted, remains throughout the series of illustrations, as throughout Cervantes' fascinating pages, a creature of the imagination only, a luring phantom to her deluded lover.

THE BLUE-CHINA BOOK

THE WILKIE SERIES

The art of the painter as well as that of the caricaturist and **of** the illustrator contributed to the decoration of early Staffordshire pottery, the work of no less an artist than Sir David Wilkie being put to that humble use, and thereby introduced into American homes. Seven of Wilkie's best known canvases were reproduced in the pot-works of the enterprising James Clews, all in rich deep blue prints of excellent workmanship. The subjects chosen by the potters are the lowly scenes of country life which the "raw, tall, pale, queer Scotchman" originally loved to observe, and which he depicted in the precise and sober manner of Teniers and of Rembrandt, the two artists whom he at first followed. They exhibit the homely pastimes and customs of the friends and neighbors with whom Wilkie passed his early years, and in them one may learn not a little of the popular English tastes of that day. Later on, after he had made London his home, and after his genius, like Goethe's, had ripened under the influence of the life and art of Italy and Spain, the subjects of his brush became broader in scope, and his manner of expression richer and more free.

The painting which is here presented is entitled, "The Escape of the Mouse." In it may be seen an excited family group of humble station in life, in pursuit of the little intruder who has taken refuge under the chair of the young woman at the spinning wheel. She has turned to watch the dog who heads the chase. One brother pokes under the chair with a broom, while another stands laughing at the spectacle. The mother is seen looking in at the partly opened door. "The Escape of the Mouse" was the artist's diploma picture upon his entrance into the Royal Academy in the year 1811, and upon the walls of that Institution it may still be seen.

APPENDIX IV

Compiled by GEOFFREY A. GODDEN.

THE following checklist gives brief details of the many British potters, or firms, who employed name or initial marks on their wares. The list is arranged in alphabetical order, and where appropriate the reader is given the names of specialist reference books giving detailed information on the potter.

Geoffrey Godden's *Illustrated Encyclopedia of British Pottery and Porcelain* (Crown Publishers, N. Y., 1966) will be found to feature the wares of many of these individuals or firms and the same writer's large *Encyclopedia of British Pottery and Porcelain Marks* (Crown Publishers, N. Y., 1964) will in most cases give further details of the marks employed, while S. Laidacker's privately published *Anglo-American China,* Part I, illustrates many of the American view designs made by British potters. A separate volume by Mr. Laidacker, *Anglo-American China,* Part II, deals with non-American designs, with patterns which were made for the British market (although many of these stock patterns were shipped to North America).[1] Mrs. Elizabeth Collard's *Nineteenth Century Pottery and Porcelain in Canada* (McGill University Press, Montreal, 1967) is a mine of information on wares made

---

[1] W. L. Little's book *Staffordshire Blue* (Batsford, London, 1969) is also a useful source of information on the British market patterns.

THE BLUE-CHINA BOOK

for the Canadian market. In the following list these helpful books are referred to simply as:

> Godden's *Illustrated Encyclopedia*
> Godden's *Encyclopedia of Marks*
> Laidacker, Part I (and/or Part II)
> Collard

While several of the manufacturers listed are not as yet known to have produced earthenwares printed with special American views, they were nevertheless producing the standard range of related blue-printed wares which were shipped to North America in vast quantities in the first half of the nineteenth century.

A. BROS. *See* Ashworth.

ABBEY, Richard. Engraver and printer at Liverpool, c. 1773+. The name "Abbey" is found as a signature mark on some rare specimens. Reference: *The Illustrated Guide to the Herculaneum China and Earthenware Manufactory* by Alan Smith.

ADAMS, Benjamin. Manufacturer at Tunstall, Staffordshire of good quality earthenwares c. 1800–20. The name mark "B. ADAMS" occurs.

ADAMS, William (& Sons). Manufacturers on a large scale of high-class Staffordshire earthenwares of all types from 1769 to the present day. Much good quality blue-printed Adams earthenware was exported to the United States of America. Marks comprise or incorporate "ADAMS," "ADAM & Co," "W. ADAMS & Co," "W. ADAMS & SONS," "W. A. & Co," "W. A. & S." References: *William Adams, an old English Potter* (The Keramic Studio Publishing Co., N. Y., 1904); also Godden's *Encyclopedia of Marks,* Godden's *Illustrated Encyclopedia* and Laidacker, Parts I and II.

ALCOCK, John & George. Manufacturers of earthenware at Cobridge c. 1839–46. Marks incorporate "J. & G. ALCOCK" or "J. & G. A."

APPENDIX IV

ALCOCK, Samuel (& Co.). Large-scale manufacturers of various types of earthenware and porcelain at Cobridge and Burslem, Staffordshire during the period 1828–59. Several different marks incorporate the name in full or the initials "S. A. & Co."

ASHWORTH, G. L. (& Bros.). This Hanley firm succeeded Messrs. Mason, the famous manufacturers of "Patent Ironstone China." Apart from continuing the traditional Mason Ironstone wares, Messrs. G. L. Ashworth & Bros. from 1861 produced a good range of blue-printed Staffordshire earthenware. Marks include "ASHWORTH," "A. BROS," "G. L. A. & BROS." Reference: Geoffrey Godden's *The Illustrated Guide to Mason's Ironstone China.*

B. A. & B. *See* Bradbury, Anderson & Bettanny.

BATKIN, WALKER & BROADHURST. This partnership worked at Lane End, Staffordshire and produced a good range of Staffordshire earthenwares between 1840 and 1845. Some examples bear marks incorporating the initials "W. B. & B."

BAXTER, J. D. This potter worked at Hanley, Staffordshire from 1823 to 1827. Some good blue-printed earthenwares were made, and examples bear the initial mark "J. D. B." or "I. D. B."

BEECH, James. This potter worked at Tunstall, Staffordshire from about 1834 until 1889. Little is known of his wares but some printed earthenwares made for the American market bear "J. B." initial marks and these are believed to relate to this potter.

BELL, J. & M. P. (& Co.). Messrs. J. & M. P. Bell & Co. produced at Glasgow, Scotland from 1842 a varied range of earthenwares including blue-printed designs. Examples bear various marks incorporating the initials "J. B." or "J. & M. P. B. & Co." References: J. A. Fleming's *Scottish Pottery* (Maclehose, Jackson & Co., Glasgow, 1923) and Godden's *Illustrated Encyclopedia.*

BELLE VUE POTTERY, Hull. This Yorkshire pottery produced various earthenwares from about 1802 to 1841. In 1826 William

Bell owned this pottery and the double-bell mark probably dates from this period. The names "Belle Vue" or "Belle Vue Pottery" also occur.

BENTLEY, WEAR & BOURNE. Engravers and printers c. 1813–23; see Introduction to the Dover Edition, p.

B. G. *See* Godwin.

BOYLE, Zachariah (& Sons). This firm produced at Hanley and Stoke, Staffordshire a good range of printed earthenwares between 1823 and 1850. Various printed marks incorporate the initials "Z. B." or "Z. B. & S."

BRADBURY, ANDERSON & BETTANY. This partnership at Longton, Staffordshire produced printed earthenwares between 1844 and 1852. Marks incorporate the initials "B. A. & B."

B. W. & B. *See* Batkin, Walker & Broadhurst.

CAREY, Thomas & John. These potters working at Lane End, Staffordshire produced very good quality earthenwares between about 1823 and 1842. Marks employed incorporate the plural name "CAREYS."

CAREYS. See previous entry.

C & G. *See* Copeland & Garrett.

CHETHAM & ROBINSON. These potters, working at Longton, Staffordshire produced between 1822 and 1837 a good range of printed earthenware. Marks comprise or incorporate the initials "C. & R."

CLEMENTSON, Joseph. This potter produced at the Phoenix Works, Shelton (Hanley), Staffordshire a very good range of earthenwares between 1839 and 1864. Marks incorporate the name or the initials "J. C.," often with the Phoenix-bird motif.

CLEWS, James & Ralph. These potters worked at Cobridge, Staffordshire from c. 1818 to 1834. They produced very good

APPENDIX IV

quality earthenwares including several blue-printed designs depicting American views; name marks occur. References: Laidacker, Parts I & II, where many American subjects are listed, and Godden's *Illustrated Encyclopedia*. N. B.: Clews designs and name marks have been reproduced in the present century.

C. M.

C. M. & S.

C. M. S. & P. *See* Meigh.

COPELAND & GARRETT. This partnership succeeded the famous Spode firm at Stoke. From 1833 to 1847 they were amongst the leading British manufacturers of fine porcelain, stone china and general earthenwares. Although no special pictorial designs appear to have been made for the North American market, a mass of good quality printed Staffordshire earthenware was exported, and bears clear name marks or the initials "C. & G." In 1847 the firm of W. T. Copeland & Sons succeeded this partnership.

C. & R. *See* Chetham & Robinson.

C. & W. K. H. *See* Harvey.

D. *See* Dimmock.

DAVENPORT. The large pottery managed by the Davenports (trading under various styles, such as "W. Davenport & Co.") at Longport in Staffordshire was one of the leading British sources of fine quality porcelain, earthenware and glass. Some printed American-view earthenware was produced but most products depict European or Chinese-styled scenery. Several different marks incorporate the name "Davenport" and although the pottery commenced in 1793, most marked specimens relate to the 1805–1850 period. References: Laidacker, Parts I & II, Godden's *Encyclopedia of Marks* and Godden's *Illustrated Encyclopedia*.

DIMMOCK. Several Staffordshire potters named Dimmock were producing printed earthenwares in the nineteenth century. Thomas Dimmock & Co. of Shelton (Hanley) was one of the larger firms.

THE BLUE-CHINA BOOK

The products are little known, however, as they were often unmarked, but some printed marks incorporating the initial "D" relate to this manufacturer of the 1828–59 period.

EDWARDS, James & Thomas. The Edwardses potted at Burslem, Staffordshire during the 1839–41 period. They produced a good range of general earthenwares, including the popular "Boston Mails" design which was registered in September, 1841. References: Godden's *Illustrated Encyclopedia* and Laidacker, Part I. Examples are marked "Edwards," "J. & T. Edwards" or "J. & T. E."

E. & E. W. *See* Wood.

E. & G. P. *See* Phillips.

E. K. B.
E. K. & Co. *See* Elkin, Knight & Co.

ELKIN, KNIGHT & Co. This firm worked the Foley Pottery at Fenton, Staffordshire from 1822 to 1826. It was succeeded by Messrs. Elkin, Knight & Bridgwood, who continued to 1840. Both partnerships produced good quality printed earthenwares bearing the names in full or the initials "E. K. & Co." or "E. K. B."

ELSMORE & FORSTER. This partnership worked the Clayhills Pottery at Tunstall, Staffordshire during the 1853–71 period (it was succeeded by Thomas Elsmore & Son, 1872–87). Good general Staffordshire pottery was produced, including a design featuring a bust-portrait of George Washington. The name is incorporated in several different marks.

EMBERTON, William (& Co.). William and Thomas Emberton commenced potting at Tunstall, Staffordshire in 1848 and under various changes in trading name the pottery continued until 1888. The general range of printed earthenware was produced and may be marked with the name in full or with the following initials: "W. E." (c. 1851–69), "T. I. & J. E." (c. 1869–82) or "J. E." (c. 1882–8).

APPENDIX IV

E. W. & S. *See* Wood.

F. & Co. *See* Fell.

FELL, Thomas (& Co.). Thomas Fell worked the St. Peter's Pottery at Newcastle-on-Tyne from 1817 to 1890. A varied range of good quality earthenware was produced, including sponged and printed wares for the American market. Examples may be marked "FELL," "FELL & Co.," "F. & Co." or "T. F. & Co." Reference: Godden's *Illustrated Encyclopedia*.

F. M.
F. M. & Co. *See* Morley.

F. & R. P.
F. & R. P. & Co. *See* Pratt.

FURNIVAL, JACOB (& Co.). This firm potted at Cobridge, about 1845 to 1870. Blue-printed Staffordshire earthenwares were produced, often bearing the initial mark "J. F. & Co." and much of this was exported to America.

FURNIVAL, Thomas (& Co.). This firm potted at Hanley, Staffordshire during the 1844–6 period. Printed earthenwares were produced, including one design titled "America" which was registered on November 21, 1846 (Laidacker incorrectly attributes this design to Thomas Ford & Co.). Several differing marks incorporate the initials "T. F. & Co." N. B.: Several later Staffordshire firms use the name FURNIVAL in their marks; cf. Godden's *Encyclopedia of Marks*.

GEDDES, John (& Son). John Geddes worked the Verreville Pottery at Glasgow, Scotland from c. 1806 to 1827. A good range of earthenwares was produced and much of this was exported to North America. Name marks were rarely used; "& Son" was added during the 1824–7 period.

GINDER, Samuel (& Co.). This firm worked the Victoria Pottery at Lane Delph, Staffordshire from 1811 to 1843. Good

THE BLUE-CHINA BOOK

quality printed earthenwares were produced and may bear the name incorporated in printed marks.

G. L. A. & BROS. *See* Ashworth.

GODWIN. Several potters of this name worked in the Staffordshire Potteries during the first half of the nineteenth century. Each produced very good printed earthenwares, although the name of only Thomas Godwin is known to most collectors of American-view pottery. The various potters are listed below; most employed printed marks incorporating their initials. A selection of their products is shown in Godden's *Illustrated Encyclopedia.*

Benjamin Godwin of Cobridge, c. 1834–41: "B. G." initial marks. John & Robert Godwin of Cobridge, c. 1834–66: "J. & R. G." initial marks. Thomas Godwin of Burslem, c. 1834–54: "T. G." initial marks or name in full. Thomas & Benjamin Godwin of Burslem, c. 1809–34: "T. & B. G." or "T. B. G." initial marks, or name in full.

N. B.: Several partnerships incorporate the name GOODWIN. These are not related to the GODWIN family of potters. Details of the Goodwin marks are given in Godden's *Encyclopedia of Marks.* John Goodwin of the Seacombe Pottery, near Liverpool, made good printed wares, much of which was shipped to North America. One of his patterns was the popular "Lasso" design. Marks incorporate the name "Seacombe Pottery," "Goodwin & Co" or "J. Goodwin." Reference: Collard.

GREEN, Thomas. Thomas Green worked the Minerva Pottery at Fenton, Staffordshire from 1847 to 1849, when he was succeeded by M. Green & Co. and in 1876 by T. A. & S. Green. Thomas Green produced good printed earthenwares including table services featuring "Penn's Treaty with the Indians." Name or initial "T. G." marks occur.

HACKWOOD. Several Staffordshire potters of this name pro-

300

APPENDIX IV

duced good quality printed wares for the North American market during the first part of the nineteenth century. Most employed name or initial marks, as detailed below:

Hackwood & Co. of Hanley, c. 1807–27: name or initial "H. & Co." marks. William Hackwood of Hanley, c. 1827–43: name or initial "W. H." marks. William Hackwood & Son of Shelton, c. 1846–9: initial mark "W. H. & S." Hackwood & Keeling of Hanley, c. 1835–6: initial mark "H. & K."

HALL, John (& Sons). John Hall potted at Burslem, Staffordshire from 1814 to 1832. Various earthenwares bear marks incorporating the name "HALL," or "I. HALL" or "I. HALL & SONS" after 1822.

HALL, Ralph (& Co.) (& Son). Ralph Hall & Son potted at Tunstall in Staffordshire from 1822 to 1849. Good printed wares were made, sometimes with American market subjects and these may be marked in the following manner: "R. Hall," "R. Hall & Son," "R. Hall & Co." or "R. H. & Co."

HAMMERSLEY, Ralph (& Son). Ralph Hammersley had works at both Tunstall and Burslem in the Staffordshire Potteries during the 1860–85 period; the firm was then continued under the style Ralph Hammersley & Son until c. 1905. Printed wares were made, much for the North American market; examples bear marks incorporating the initials "R. H." or after 1884 "R. H. & S." Reference: Laidacker, Part II.

HARDING & COCKSON. This partnership worked the Globe Pottery at Cobridge, Staffordshire from 1834 to 1860. Their earthenwares bear marks incorporating the name in full, or the initials "H. & C."

HARVEY, C. & W. K. The Harveys worked several different potteries at Longton, Staffordshire between 1835 and 1853, producing printed and other types of earthenwares. Marks incorporate the name "HARVEY," "C. & W. K. HARVEY" or the initials

THE BLUE-CHINA BOOK

"C. & W. K. H."

H & C. *See* Harding & Cockson.

H. & Co. *See* Hackwood.

HEATH, Joseph (& Co.). There were many Staffordshire potters named Heath. The firm of Joseph Heath & Co. worked the Newfield Pottery at Tunstall, Staffordshire from 1828 to 1841. Good quality printed earthenwares were made and bear marks incorporating the name "J. HEATH & Co." or the initials "J. H. & Co." or "I. H. & Co." Joseph Heath potted at Tunstall from 1845 to 1853, incorporating the name "J. HEATH" in printed marks.

HERCULANEUM POTTERY. This Liverpool pottery was one of the most important producers of British printed earthenwares (from c. 1793 to 1841), shipping its wares from its home port to the American shores. Most of the Herculaneum earthenware was unmarked so that it is seldom correctly identified, although Alan Smith's recent book *The Illustrated Guide to Liverpool Herculaneum Pottery* will be found most helpful and informative.

HICKS & MEIGH and HICKS, MEIGH & JOHNSON. These partnerships managed important factories in High Street, Shelton, in the Staffordshire Potteries from 1804 to 1835, Messrs. Hicks, Meigh & Johnson having continued from 1822. Although these partnerships are mainly known for their fine "Stone China" wares, a good range of printed earthenwares was also made, and examples may bear the name in full, or the initials "H. M. J." or "H. M. & J."

H. & K. *See* Hackwood.

H. M. J.
H. M. & J. *See* Hicks & Meigh.

I. D. B. *See* Baxter.

I. H. & Co. *See* Heath.

APPENDIX IV

I. M.
I. M. & S. *See* Meir.

JACKSON, Job & John. These partners worked the Church Yard Pottery at Burslem from 1831 to the bankruptcy in 1835. They produced very good printed earthenwares including many American views. Marks include "J. & J. Jackson" and "Jackson's Warranted." Reference: Laidacker, Parts I & II.

J. B. *See* Beech and also Bell.

J. C. *See* Clementson.

J. D. B. *See* Baxter.

J. E. *See* Emberton.

J. F. & Co. *See* Furnival, Jacob.

J. & G. A. *See* Alcock, John & George.

J. H. & Co. *See* Heath.

J. M. *See* Meir.

J. & M. P. B. & Co. *See* Bell.

J. M. & S. *See* Meir.

J. R.
J. R. & Co.
J. R. B. & Co. *See* Ridgway.

J. & R. G. *See* Godwin.

J. & T. E. *See* Edwards.

J. W. P.
J. W. P. & Co. *See* Pankhurst.

J. W. R.
J. & W. R. *See* Ridgway.

KEELING, Samuel (& Co.). Samuel Keeling produced general

earthenwares at Hanley, Staffordshire between 1840 and 1850. Marks on printed wares incorporate the name or the initials "S. K. & Co."

MAYER, Thomas. This potter had two potteries, one at Stoke from 1826 to 1835 and one at Longport from about 1836 to 1838. Good quality printed wares were made, including a series of dinner wares bearing representations of the Armorial bearings of various American states. Examples bear marks incorporating the name "T. MAYER." Reference: Laidacker, Parts I & II. N. B.: Several other potters of this famous Staffordshire name were practising their craft in the first part of the nineteenth century; cf. Godden's *Encyclopedia of Marks*.

MEIGH, Charles (& Son). The Meighs worked the Old Hall Pottery at Hanley, where a large and varied range of earthenwares was produced, including some American views. Charles Meigh succeeded his father Job Meigh (c. 1805–35), trading under his own name from 1835 to 1849. From 1850 to 1851 the trading style was Charles Meigh Son & Pankhurst and then Charles Meigh & Son up to March 1861, when the new title "Old Hall Earthenware Co. Ltd." was adopted. Marks include the names in full, or the initials "C. M.," "C. M. S. & P." or "C. M. & S."

MEIR, John (& Son). John Meir worked the Greengates Pottery at Tunstall, Staffordshire from 1812 to 1836, the succeeding firm of John Meir & Son continuing to 1897. A large range of earthenwares was made and bears marks comprising or including "I. MEIR," "J. M.," "I. M." or, after 1836, "MEIR & SON," "J. MEIR & SON," "J. M. & S," "I. M. & S" or "J. M. & SON."

MELLOR, VENABLES & Co. This firm produced earthenwares, Ironstone and china at Burslem, Staffordshire. Examples were made for the American market bearing American views and state arms. This partnership traded from 1834 to 1851, and was succeeded by Messrs. Venables & Baines (1851–3) and then John Venables & Co. during the 1853–5 period. Marks incorporate

APPENDIX IV

the names of these firms, or their initials, such as "M. V. & Co." Reference: Laidacker, Part I.

MORLEY, Francis (& Co.). This potter succeeded Ridgway & Morley (1842–5) and traded from Broad Street, Shelton (Hanley) from 1845 to 1858. Succeeding firms were Morley & Ashworth (1849–61) and then G. L. Ashworth & Bros. (1861 into the twentieth century). All these firms produced good Ironstone-type earthenwares, much of which was exported to North America. Morley marks include the name or the initials "F. M." or "F. M. & Co." Reference: Collard.

M. V. & Co. *See* Mellor, Venables & Co.

PANKHURST, J. W. (& Co.). This firm potted at Hanley in the Staffordshire Potteries. Good printed earthenwares and Iron-stones were produced and bear marks incorporating the name or the initials "J. W. P." or "J. W. P. & Co."

PHILLIPS, Edward & George. These potters worked at Longport in the Staffordshire Potteries from 1822 to 1834; much blue-printed earthenware was made, some for the American market. George Phillips succeeded and potted from 1834 to 1848, making similar wares. Marks include the names, or the initials "E. & G. P."

PODMORE, WALKER & Co. This partnership worked several potteries at Tunstall in the Staffordshire Potteries. A good varied range of earthenwares was made, much of which was exported to America during the period 1834 to 1859. The "& Co" in the firm's title was Enoch Wedgwood and his name "Wedgwood" was often employed by this partnership. In 1860 the firm took the new name "Wedgwood & Co.," a move that subsequently caused much confusion owing to its likeness to the famous Wedgwood firm. Messrs. Podmore, Walker & Co. used the name marks "Wedgwood," "Wedgwood & Co.," the initials "P. W. & Co." or "P. W. & W." Reference: Collard.

THE BLUE-CHINA BOOK

PRATT, F. & R. (& Co.). This firm, which potted at Fenton in the Staffordshire Potteries, is mainly known for its decorative multicolored printed "pot-lids," but during the 1830's and 1840's standard printed Staffordshire earthenwares were produced which bear marks comprising the initials "F. & R. P." or "F. & R. P. & Co."

P. W. & Co.

P. W. & W. *See* Podmore, Walker & Co.

R. H. *See* Hammersley.

R. H. & Co. *See* Hall, Ralph.

R. H. & S. *See* Hammersley.

RIDGWAY. Many Staffordshire firms and potters bore the name Ridgway; the output of the main firm of John & William Ridgway was enormous and very varied. Much of this Ridgway earthenware (and porcelain) was exported to North America. References: Laidacker, Part I, and Collard. The various marks of the different firms are given in Godden's *Encyclopedia of Marks,* and the pre-1850 firms are summarised below:

Ridgway & Abington of Hanley, c. 1835–60. Job Ridgway of Shelton (Hanley), c. 1802–8. Job Ridgway & Sons, c. 1808–13. John Ridgway (& Co.), c. 1830–55. John & William Ridgway, c. 1814–30. John Ridgway, Bates & Co., c. 1856–8. Ridgway, Morley, Wear & Co., c. 1836–42. Ridgway & Morley, c. 1842–5. William Ridgway (& Co.), c. 1830–54. William Ridgway, Son & Co., c. 1838–48.

Various marks were used by these firms, some including their names in full but many others including the initials: "J R," "J. R. & Co.," "J. W. R.," "J. & W. R.," "J. R. B. & Co.," "R. & M.," "W. R.," "W. R. & Co." or "W. R. S. & Co."

R. & M. *See* Ridgway.

APPENDIX IV

ROGERS, John & George. These potters worked the Dale Hall Pottery at Longport, Staffordshire from 1784 to 1814. The firm of John Rogers & Son continued from 1814 to 1836. The Rogerses were famous for the quality of their blue-printed Staffordshire earthenware, some designs being specially made for the American market. The standard mark is the name "ROGERS," impressed. References: Laidacker, Parts I & II, and Godden's *Illustrated Encyclopedia*.

R. S. W.
R. S. & W. *See* Stevenson.

S. A. & Co. *See* Alcock, Samuel.

SHAW, A. (& Co.) (& Son). Anthony Shaw potted at Tunstall in the 1850's and at Burslem, Staffordshire from about 1860 to 1900. Printed earthenwares were produced including "Texian Campaigne" designs. Marks include "Anthony Shaw," "A. Shaw," "Shaw" or "Show." The words "& Son" were added from 1882 to 1898.

S. K. & Co. *See* Keeling.

SPODE. Josiah Spode's pottery at Stoke produced a large range of very fine quality earthenwares and porcelains. The blue-printed wares were probably the finest ever made, although it does not seem that special designs were made for the American market. Nevertheless the standard Spode patterns were undoubtedly exported. Most Spode wares from about 1800 to 1833 bear the simple name mark. Messrs. Copeland & Garrett succeeded Spode.

STEVENSON. Several Staffordshire potters shared this name and produced good quality blue-printed earthenwares for the American market Reference: Laidacker, Parts I and II. The various firms were: Andrew Stevenson of Cobridge, c. 1811–30: name marks occur. Ralph Stevenson of Cobridge, c. 1810–32: name marks or initials "R. S." Ralph Stevenson & Son, c. 1832–5: name marks or initials "R. S. & S." Stevenson, Alcock & Williams of Co-

THE BLUE-CHINA BOOK

bridge, c. 1825: name marks. Stevenson & Williams of Cobridge, c. 1825: name marks or initials "R. S. W." or "R. S. & W."

STUBBS, Joseph. Joseph Stubbs potted at Longport, Staffordshire from 1822 to 1835 (during the period 1828–30 the name Stubbs & Kent was used). Good quality blue-printed earthenwares were made, some designs being made especially for the American market, featuring American views. Name marks were employed. References: Laidacker, Part I.

TAMS. Blue-printed earthenwares occur with the name marks Tams, Tams & Co., S. Tams & Co., Tams & Anderson & Tams. These objects appear to predate 1850 but the contemporary records relating to the Staffordshire Potteries do not list these potters or partnerships. The wares may relate to the predecessors of John Tams of the Crown Pottery, Longton (c. 1875 to the present day). Examples are shown by Laidacker, Parts I & II.

T. & B. G. *See* Godwin.

T. F. & Co. *See* Fell, and also Furnival, Thomas.

T. G. *See* Godwin, and also Green.

T. I. & J. E. *See* Emberton.

W. A. & Co.
W. A. & S. *See* Adams, William.

W. E. *See* Emberton.

WEDGWOOD & Co., of Tunstall. Successors to Podmore, Walker & Co. in 1860, the new firm should not be confused with the main Wedgwood firm. In 1965 this Tunstall firm was retitled "Enoch Wedgwood (Tunstall) Ltd.". Wedgwood & Co. made much printed earthenware especially the "Asiatic Pheasants" pattern, a standard design copied by many other potters.

WEDGWOOD, Josiah (& Sons Ltd.). This internationally known and respected Staffordshire pottery was established in the middle of the eighteenth century. The firm is famous for its black basalts, its coloured jasper wares and the simply decorated creamwares. In the nineteenth century Messrs. Wedgwood produced a range of good quality blue-printed earthenwares. These wares will bear the simple impressed name mark "WEDGWOOD." Most general books on British pottery give a good account of the Wedgwood story and several specialist books will be found in most libraries.

W. H.
W. H. & S. *See* Hackwood.

WOOD, Enoch (& Sons). Enoch Wood was one of the most talented Staffordshire modellers and potters; he was born in January, 1759 and started on his own account in Burslem in 1784. He produced good quality earthenwares of many types until 1790 or 1792, when he joined in partnership with James Caldwell. From this period until July, 1818 they traded as Wood & Caldwell. In 1818 Enoch Wood was joined by his sons and from July 1818 to 1846 they traded as Enoch Wood & Sons. Apart from ornamental wares and figures, the Woods produced much blue-printed and other utilitarian wares during this period. Various name marks were employed, also printed marks incorporating the initials "E. W. & S." or rarely "E. & E. W.". The output of the Enoch Wood pottery was enormous and several designs were engraved for the American market. References: Laidacker, Parts I & II and Godden's *Illustrated Encyclopedia*.

W. R.
W. R. & Co.
W. R. S. & Co. *See* Ridgway.

Z. B.
Z. B. & S. *See* Boyle.

INDEX

Abraham, Plains, of, 8.
"Abundance," 91.
Adair, 189.
Adams, Abigail, 98, 251.
Adams, John, President, 98.
  china of, 250, 251.
  offered design for seal, 151.
  portrait on pottery, 133, 190.
  visited by Lafayette, 198.
Adams, John Quincy, President,
      china of, 255.
  Samuel, 31.
  "Proscribed Patriot," 131.
  William, potter, 107, 269.
Adirondacks, 14.
Adriatic, 214.
Africa, 37, 267.
  pirates of, 174.
Age of Steam, 180, 225, 241.
Albany, 12, 50, 202, 228, 234, 239, 240.
  Dutch Church in, 13.
  Entrance of Erie Canal at, 221.
Alden, John, 114.
Alexander of Macedon, 221.
Alexandria, 174, 175.
Algiers, 174, 175.
Alleghany, "Endless Mountains," 6.
Allegheny, Penitentiary at, 15, 17.
  River, 15, 231.
Allen, Rev. Thomas, 9.
Almshouse, Baltimore, 90, 205.
  Boston, 37.
  New York, 57, 61, 196, 222.
Amazon, 157.
America, early emblems of, 146.
  early immigration to, 4-6, 107-
      123.
  English ideas of early, 4, 108, 117.
  "Map" design of, 7, 96.

America—continued.
  old china views of, 271-286.
  physical aspect of, travel in,
      early, 3-21.
"America" design, 152.
America, South, 112.
"American Marine," 270.
American Museum, New York, 59,
      61.
Amory House, Boston, 27, 28.
André, Major, 142, 200.
Apennines, 6.
"Apotheosis," design, 128, 132.
Ararat, "unbuilt city of," 215.
Architecture, church, colonial (see
      Classic Revival).
  Egyptian, 92.
  Greek, 58, 83.
Arms, of States, 146, 197, 153-157.
  Connecticut, 154.
  Delaware, 157.
  Georgia, 154.
  Maryland, 154.
  Massachusetts, 156.
  New Hampshire, 153.
  New Jersey, 156.
  New York, 156.
  North Carolina, 155.
  Pennsylvania, 155.
  Rhode Island, 153.
  South Carolina, 155.
  Virginia, 157.
Arms of George Washington, 128,
      149.
Arnold, Benedict, 139, 142, 200.
Arthur, President, china of, 263.
Ashworth, G. L. & Bro., potters, 270.
Asia, 37, 112.
Assemblies, Philadelphia, 82.

INDEX

Astor, Hotel, 53.
John Jacob, 56.
Asylum, Deaf and Dumb, Hartford, 199.
Deaf and Dumb, Philadelphia, 76.
Athenæum, Boston, 37.
Austria, emblems of, 146, 192, 206.
Azores, The, 182.

Bainbridge, Commodore, in Algiers and Tripoli, 174, 176, 178.
in battle of *Constitution* and *Java*, 183.
portrait pitcher of, 189.
with Lafayette in Boston, 198.
Baltimore, 16, 88, 89, 90, 98, 99, 204, 205, 234, 249.
Almshouse, 90, 205.
& Ohio R. R., 93, 237, 238.
Battle Monument, 91, 205.
Court House, 90.
Exchange, 90, 205.
Harbor views of, 88.
History of, 88–93.
Hospital, 92, 205.
University of Maryland, 90, 92, 93, 205.
Baltimore, Lord, 89, 154.
Baltimore & Ohio R. R., 93, 237, 238.
Barbadoes, 40.
Barbary, States, 174.
pirates, 175.
Barber, Dr. Edwin Atlee, 267, 268, 269, 270, 271.
Barcelona, 111.
Barnum, P. T., 49, 59.
Baron de Kalb, 209.
Battery, the, New York, 43, 46, 49, 194, 197.
Flagstaff Pavilion on the, 47.
scene of Erie Canal festivities, 222.
Walk, 47, 48.
Beacon Hill, Boston, 24, 30.
Beacon Mall, Boston, 27, 28.
Beacon Street, Boston, 27, 30.
Beatry, 189.

"Beauties of America," series of decorations, 61, 268.
Belgium, 191.
Bellevue, N. Y., 59.
Hospital, 61.
Belt of Peace, 120, 121.
Bemis Heights, 141.
Bennington, Vermont, pottery of, 170.
Bergen, N. J., 203.
Berkshire, Minutemen, 9.
Hotel, 10.
Bermuda, 182.
Blackwell's Island, 61.
Blackstone, William, 23.
Point, 23, 24.
Blakey, 189.
Blue, color on china (see Introduction), 46, 267–271, 287, 289.
love of Franklin for, 158, 159.
love of Washington for, 136, 249.
Bonaparte, Jerome, 251.
Bonheur, Rosa, 262.
Booth, Edwin, 62.
Borders on china (see Introduction), 4, 11, 46, 61, 91, 97, 268.
Baltimore views, 91.
Baltimore & Ohio R. R., 237.
Brandywine River, 140.
"Catskill Moss," 271.
chickweed and moss, 270.
Don Quixote, 291.
eagle designs, 146, 153.
Erie Canal, 218.
Landing of Columbus, 108.
Landing of Lafayette, 194.
Landing of Pilgrims, 115.
Merchants' Exchange, Baltimore, 69.
Penn's Treaty, 117.
"Picturesque Views," 267–271.
Utica Inscription, 220.
Willow, 288.
Boston, 9, 24, 50, 184, 197, 199, 234.
history of, 22–42.
old china views of, 23–42.
Almshouse, 37.
Athenæum, 37.

INDEX

Boston—*continued.*
  Bunker Hill Monument, 139.
  Common, 24–29.
  Court House, 32.
  Fusileers, 144.
  General Hospital, 35.
  Hancock House, 28.
  Harbor, 23.
  Harvard College, 38–42.
  Insane Hospital, 35.
  Lawrence Mansion, 32.
  Mitchell & Freeman's China and
    Glass Warehouse, 36.
  Nahant, 38.
  Octagon Church, 33, 34.
  State House, 27, 29, 198.
  St. Paul's, 33.
"Boston Mails," 270.
Boston Port Bill, 165.
Boston Post Road, 55, 58, 62, 63.
Bowling Green, N. Y., 43, 49, 50, 57.
Boxer, frigate, 186, 187.
Brandywine, Battle of the, 137, 140,
    141, 197, 199, 202.
  47th anniversary of, 196.
  Lafayette visits scene of, 204.
  relics of, 199.
Brandywine, frigate, 211.
Breed's Hill, 137.
Brewster, Elder, 114.
Brick Church, N. Y., 62.
Bridewell, Boston, 27.
  New York, 57.
Broadway, New York, 43, 50, 51, 53,
    55, 71.
  hogs and chimney sweeps on, 50.
  pumps on, 54.
Brooklyn Heights, view of New
    York from, 44, 45.
  Battle of, 137, 140.
Brown, 189, 190.
Brunelleschi, 102.
Buchanan, President, china of, 260.
Buffalo, canal celebration at, 213,
    214, 215, 216, 223.
  Lafayette at, 210.
  Railroad, 241.
  view of harbor of, 269.

Bulfinch, Charles, 30, 32, 34, 35.
Bunker Hill, Battle of, 26, 137, 138,
    198, 199.
  50th anniversary of, 210.
  Monument, 139.
Bureau of Buildings and Grounds,
    Washington, D. C., 247.
Burgoyne, Gen., surrender at Sara-
    toga, 141.
  influence of surrender in France,
    167.

Cadmus, frigate, 193, 194, 195.
Cæsar's Commentaries, 67.
California, annexation of, 259.
  gold in, 17.
Cambridge, Mass., 39.
Camden, S. C., 209.
Canada, 4, 7, 139, 184, 185.
  emblems of, 147.
Canton china, of George Washing-
    ton, 249.
Cape Cod, 113.
Capitol, at Albany, 50, 202.
  at Washington, 96–98, 100, 102, 205.
Caravels, 109, 110, 112.
Cards, Colonial playing, and visit-
    ing, 82.
Carolina, North, 16, 40.
  South, 16, 40.
Carpenters' Hall, Philadelphia, 77.
Carrol, Henry, 53.
Carver, John, 114, 115.
Castle Garden, canal festivities in,
    222.
  fête for Lafayette in, 197.
  history of, 47, 48.
  landing of Lafayette at, 194.
"Catskill Moss," border, 271.
"C. C.," potter, 271.
Ceres, 129, 155, 156.
Champlain, Battle of Lake, 188, 190.
Champlain, founder of Quebec, 8.
Chancellor Livingston, steamboat,
    194, 221, 229.
Chancellor Livingston, 201, 227.
Chang, 287, 288.
Charles II, 72.

313

INDEX

Charleston, S. C., Exchange, 16, 273.
Charleston & Hamburg R. R., 239.
Charlestown, burning of, 139.
navy yard, 184, 198.
Cheese, mammoth, 255.
Chelsea, Boston from, 23.
Chesapeake Bay, 179.
Chesapeake, frigate, 185.
Chief Justice Marshall, steamboat, 230, 231.
China, color blue, manufacture and sale of, prices, etc. (see Introduction).
Franklin's, 75, 169.
in Metropolitan Museum, N. Y., 127.
in National Museum, Washington, D. C., 136.
presidential, in White House, 245–266.
Washington's at Mt. Vernon, 249.
"China Collecting in America," 134.
China, 44, 127, 170.
Church Green, 34.
Churches, architecture of (see Classic Revival in American Architecture).
views of, Albany, 13.
Boston, 33, 34, 198.
New York, 54–57.
Philadelphia, 83.
Cicero, 40.
Cincinnati, Order of the, ensignia on china, 126, 136, 250.
City Hall, N. Y., 46, 52, 58, 59, 60, 69, 101, 195, 222.
City Hall Park, 57, 58.
City Hotel, N. Y., 53, 54, 196.
Classic Revival in American Architecture, 13, 33, 34, 226.
in Boston, 27, 30, 33, 34, 35.
in New York, 52, 55, 56, 58, 60.
in Philadelphia, 80, 83, 85.
in Washington, 101, 102.
Clay, Henry, portrait of, 135.
speech in honor of Lafayette, 206, 212.
"Star of the West," 270.

Clermont, home of Chancellor Livingston, 201.
Clermont, the, steamship, 226, 227.
Cleveland, Grover, President, china of, 264.
Clews, James, potter, 11, 63.
designs of, 268.
Don Quixote designs, 291.
Dr. Syntax designs, 289.
Wilkie designs, 292.
Climate, of America, 3.
of Philadelphia, 73.
Clinton, Castle, 48.
Clinton, DeWitt, Gov., 67, 125, 134, 202, 213, 219.
"Eulogy", 223.
portrait of, 218.
Clinton, Fort, 47, 48.
Clinton, George, 56.
"Clinton, DeWitt," locomotive, 239.
Coach, stage, early railway (see Stage Coach), 237–239.
Coënties Slip, N. Y., 69.
Coffee House Slip, N. Y., 69.
Colonial, styles in architecture (see Classic Revival).
dress (see Styles of Dress).
officers, Washington's farewell to the, 52, 53.
pattern on Roosevelt china, 266.
Colonies, American, 4–7, 107–123.
Colors, on American flag, 147.
on pottery (see Introduction), 46, 117, 267–271.
Columbia College, history of, 63–68.
old china views of, 46, 63–68.
references to, 196, 222.
Columbus, Christopher, discovery of America, 3, 107–113.
landing views on china, 110–112, 269.
references to, 131, 146, 159.
Columbus, Ohio, 16.
Combe, William, 289.
Common, Boston (see Boston), 24–29, 71, 198, 199, 210.
Pittsfield, 9.
Yorktown, 208.

INDEX

Commons, the New York (The Fields), history and views of, 43, 57, 58, 59, 62.
Compact, the *Mayflower*, 114.
Concord, Mass., 26.
Congress, Act of, 150.
Continental, 148.
Hall of, Washington, D. C., 98.
House of Representatives, 205, 206.
Library of, 100.
Second Continental, 166.
Sixteenth, 101.
Connecticut, Arms of, 154.
Historical Society of, 132.
State House of, 10.
Constantinople, 174.
Constitution, The, of the United States, 201.
Constitution, frigate, at Tripoli, 175, 178.
and *Guerriere,* 181.
and *Java,* 183.
in Boston dock, 184, 190.
under Captain Hull, 179, 180.
Coolidge, Joseph, 27.
Cooper, Peter, 93, 238.
Copenhagen, 156.
Copper luster pitcher, 143, 208.
Cornwallis, Lord, at the Brandywine, 141.
house of in Yorktown, 208.
surrender of, 83, 142, 143, 144.
Court House, Baltimore, 90.
Boston, 32.
Cows, in New York, 43, 51, 52, 71, 73.
on Boston Common, 24–26, 31.
Croton Water, 50, 54.
Custard cups, 248, 261.
Custis, John Parke, 65.

Dagoty, 254.
Dam and Waterworks, Philadelphia (see Fairmount), 85, 204, 230.
Dante, 112.
Dapple, 291.

Daughters of the American Revolution, 10.
Davenport & Co., potters, 269.
Davis, Theodore, 262.
Deaf and Dumb Asylum, Hartford, 199.
Debtors' Prison, N. Y., 57, 58.
Decatur, Commodore, 53, 174, 189.
at Tripoli, 176, 177.
battle between *United States & Macedonian,* 182, 183.
Declaration of Independence, 114, 166.
forty-ninth anniversary of, 211.
on blue china, 9, 125.
read in New York, 58.
signed in Philadelphia, 166.
Delaware, River, 6, 72, 73, 84, 117, 226.
Valley of the, 72.
Delaware & Hudson River R. R., 236.
Della Robbia (see Introduction).
Denmark, 156.
Designs, in blue on pottery, 271–278.
in other colors on pottery, 278–286.
D'Estaing, Admiral, 31.
Detroit, view of harbor of, 16, 231.
De Tuyll, Baron, silver in White House, 252.
Diana, Temple of, 58.
Dickens, Charles, in New York, 54.
in Washington, 101.
Dickins, Mrs. F. W., collection of presidential china, 261.
Divine Comedy, 112.
Doge of Venice, 214.
Donelson, Mrs. Emily, 256.
Don Quixote, designs on pottery, 268.
story of, 290, 291.
Dorchester, Boston from, 23.
Dutch, Church in Albany, 13, 14.
emblems, 147, 149.
settlers in Manhattan, 43–47.
settlers in Philadelphia, 72.

315

INDEX

Eagle, in borders and designs on pottery, 115, 129, 146, 215, 268.
  in Great Seal of the United States, 152.
  plumage on Capitol figure at Washington, 102.
Eagle, boat, 38.
Eagle Tavern, Buffalo, 216.
Earle, Mrs. Alice Morse, 134, 252.
East Room of White House, in John Adams' administration, 250.
  in Madison administration, 254.
  in Jackson administration, 255.
  in Taylor administration, 259.
East River, 69.
Eaton, "Peggy," 255.
Edwards, J. & T., potters, 270.
Elijah, 20.
Ellsler, Fanny, 62.
Elm, "Liberty" of Boston, 26.
  Penn's Treaty, 80, 117, 119, 122, 123.
  Pennsylvania Hospital, 123.
  Pittsfield, 9.
  Washington, Washington, D. C., 101.
Emblems, Arms of the Thirteen States, 153–157.
  British, 96.
  earliest of America, 146–148.
  first flag, 149–151.
  of the Republic and the States, 146–157.
  on Staffordshire pottery, 149, 268.
  present flag, 151.
  Seal of the United States, 151–153.
  Spanish, 110.
"Empire" style of house furnishings, 254.
"Endless Mountains," 6, 15.
England, emblems of, 146.
  potteries of (see Introduction).
  potters of, 267–271.
  references to, 63, 77, 115, 117, 142, 155, 161, 225, 236, 291.
Enterprise and *Boxer,* 186.
Ephesus, 58.

"E Pluribus Unum," 102, 151, 152, 189.
Erie Canal, 13, 54, 125, 134, 196, 210.
  celebration of opening of, at Albany, 221.
    at Buffalo, 214, 215, 269.
    at Little Falls, 220.
    at Lockport, 216.
    at New York, 222.
    at Rochester, 217.
    at Rome, 219.
    at Syracuse, 219.
    at Utica, 219.
  story of opening of, 213–224.
Erie, Lake, Battle of, 185, 186.
"Esplanade," N. Y., 47.
"Eulogy" design, 223.
Evans, Oliver, 226.
Exchange, Baltimore, 90, 205.
  Charleston, 16, 273.
Executive Mansion, New York, 50, 246, 249.
  Philadelphia, 75, 246.
  Washington, 94, 95–98, 250–266.

Fairmount Park, Philadelphia, 76, 84.
Fairmount Dam and Waterworks, 84–86, 204, 230.
Fame, figure of, 7, 130.
Father Abraham, 162.
Fauna, on President Hayes china, 262.
Ferdinand, King, 109, 111.
"Fields, The" (see Commons).
Fillmore, Millard, President, china of, 260.
Finger and mouth bowl, 259.
Fire in New York, 69, 70.
Fitch, John, 226.
Flag, adopted by Congress, 149.
  early American, 147.
  made in Philadelphia, 150.
  on vessels, 172.
  origin of, 149–151.
  pine-tree, 8, 130, 147.
  with 15 stars, 136, 150.
  with 48 stars, 151.

316

INDEX

Flagstaff Pavilion, 47.
Flaubert, 262.
Flora, on President Grant china, 261.
on President Hayes china, 262.
on President Benjamin Harrison china, 264.
Florence, 102, 109.
Florida, 4, 5, 17.
Ford, Thomas & Co., potters, 270.
Forgeries of blue china, 271.
Forrest, Edwin, 62.
Fort, Amsterdam, 46.
Clinton, 47, 48.
Gansevoort, 46.
Lafayette, 194.
McHenry, 204.
Niagara, 18.
Foster, James H., 35.
Fountain of Eternal Youth, 5.
France, 6, 16, 56, 133, 146, 147, 158, 173, 205, 247, 254.
Franklin in, 74, 167-169.
on the side of the American Colonies, 141.
Franklin, Benjamin, 56, 78, 84, 131, 151, 159-161, 165, 167, 168, 169, 170, 179, 234.
in Philadelphia, 71, 74, 81, 159.
founder of Philadelphia Library, 77, 160.
Pennsylvania Hospital, 79, 160.
University of Pennsylvania, 160.
on old china, 7, 130, 132, 133, 141, 167, 169, 170, 204.
"Morals," "Proverbs" and "Maxims," 158-171.
Franklin, Mrs. Benjamin, 74.
Fraunce's Tavern, N. Y., 52.
"Freedom," statue of, 102.
Frigates (see War of 1812).
"Frog-Pond," 24.
Fruit-compote, 248, 260, 261.
Fulton, Robert, 201.
trial of the *Clermont*, 226, 227.
Fulton, steamboat, 194, 228, 229.
Fusileers, The Boston, 144.

Gage, General, 138.
Gallaudet, Thomas H., 199.
Gansevoort, Fort, 46.
Garden of Eden, 112.
Garfield, President James A., china of, 268.
Gates, Gen'l, 142.
Genesee, country of, 6.
George II, 64, 65, 78.
III, statue of, 49.
Georgia, Arms of, 154.
early conditions of, 16.
Germany, 146.
Ghent, Treaty of, 33, 191, 254.
Gilpin's Mills, 141, 204.
Gilpin, Gideon, 204.
Girard, Stephen, 80.
Gloucester, Mass., 139.
Goat Island, 19, 20, 21.
Goddard, Nathaniel, 35.
Godwin, Thomas, potter, 269.
Goethe, 292.
Gold in America, 3, 4, 17, 111, 112.
Gore, Gov. Christopher, 28.
Governor's Rooms, N. Y., 60.
Governor's Island, 47.
Governor's House, N. Y., 50.
Grand Opera, first in America, 48.
Grant, Ulysses S., Pres., china of, 261, 262.
Nellie, 261.
Great Lakes, 6, 7, 18, 19, 184.
Green, Thomas, potter, 117, 270.
Greek, in Columbia, 67.
in Harvard, 40.
Griscom, Dr., 59.
Grizzle, 289.
Guerrière and *Constitution*, 181.
Guerrière bound for Russia, 188.

Haiti, 111.
Half Moon, 44.
Hall of Records, N. Y., 58.
Hamilton, Alexander, 69, 197, 201.
Hancock, Dorothy, 31.
Gov. John, 31, 166.
"Proscribed Patriot," 31, 131.
Hancock Mansion, 28.

INDEX

Harding Tavern, 87.
Harrison, Benjamin, Pres., china of, 264.
  Mrs., 245, 246, 253.
Harrison, William H., Pres., china of, 258.
  Hero of the Thames, 1813, 270.
  Log cabin campaign design, 135, 258.
Hartford, Conn., 154, 199.
Harvard College, 10, 63, 67, 71, 198.
  early history and views of, 38–42.
  Halls of, 42.
Harvard, John, 39.
Hawthorne, Nathaniel, 260.
Hayes, Rutherford B., Mrs., 245, 246.
  President, china of, 262.
Heath, Joseph, potter, 270.
Hell Gate, 229.
Hennepin, Father, 19, 20.
Hercules, 151, 215.
"Hero of New Orleans," 256.
Highlands, The, 200.
Hingham, Mass., 13.
"Historical Pitcher of the War of 1812," 190.
Hoban, James, 247.
Hoboken, Stevens mansion at, 226.
Holland, settlers from in Albany, 13.
  in Manhattan, 5.
Holland Land Company, 6.
Holmes, Oliver Wendell, "path," 29.
"Home, Sweet Home," 62.
Homer, 67, 213.
Honesdale, Pa., 236.
Horn of Plenty, 89.
Horseshoe Falls, 19, 20, 21.
Hospital, Baltimore, 90, 92.
  Bellevue, 61, 196.
  Boston General, 35, 198.
  Boston Insane, 35.
  Pennsylvania, 76, 79, 160, 204.
Howe, General, at the Brandywine, 141.
  in Boston, 26.
  in New York, 140.
  in Philadelphia, 83, 141.

Hudson River, 6, 10, 65, 142, 156, 199–202.
  canal boats on, 222.
  steam travel on, 225, 227.
  "Picturesque Views" of, 11.
"Hudson River Portfolio," 11.
Hudson, city of, 202.
  Hendrick, 12, 44.
Hull, Comm. Isaac, 53, 179, 180, 181, 189, 190.
Humboldt, 251.

"Illustrious Moderns," 169.
Independence, Declaration of, 7, 49, 77, 126, 144, 155, 156, 157, 168, 179.
  40th anniversary of, 92.
  49th anniversary of, 211.
  reading of in New York, 58.
  signing of, 166.
Independence Hall, Phila., 203.
India, 109, 118, 267.
Indiana, 11, 151.
Indians, American, 3, 4, 12, 51, 63, 108, 110, 111, 114, 118, 120, 121, 131, 156, 159, 209, 215.
  in Penn's Treaty scene, 118.
  Peace Belt, 120, 121.
Indian Chief Red Jacket, 210.
Indus, The, 221.
Intrepid, The, 176.
Ironsides, Old, 184.
Irving, Washington, 54.
Isabella, Queen, 109, 111, 112.
Italy, 6, 18, 45, 132, 267, 292.
Izard, 189.

Jackson, Andrew, President, pitcher design, 135.
  china of, 255–257.
  "Hero of New Orleans," 191.
Jackson, J. & J., potters, 269.
Japan, 110, 170.
Jardson, 189.
Java, frigate, 183.
Jay, John, 67, 201.

INDEX

Jefferson, Joseph, 62.
Thomas, President, 95, 125, 134, 151, 208, 218, 251.
china of, 251.
Johnson, Andrew, President, 245, 261.
Dr. Samuel, 64.
Jones, Capt. of the *Wasp*, 53, 182, 189, 190.
Capt. Paul, 162.
Jordon, Richard, home of, 270.
Joy, Dr. John, 28.
Juniata, The, 15.
Junto Club, 77, 160.

Kalb, Baron de, 209.
Kean, Edmund, 62.
Kemble, Fanny, 62.
Kentucky, 5, 6, 16, 127, 150, 151.
King Charles II, 72.
Ferdinand, 109, 111.
George II, 64, 65.
George III, 49.
Louis XVI, 141, 167, 168.
King's Chapel, Boston, 33.
College (see Columbia).
Koong-Shee, 287, 288.
Kublai Khan, 109, 110, 111.

"Lady of the Lakes," 222.
Lafayette, General, Tour in America, 1824-5, 192-212.
at Baltimore, 88, 91, 204.
at Boston, 28, 139, 198, 199, 210.
at the Brandywine, 141.
Hudson River sail, 14, 199-202.
at New York, 48, 54, 60, 195, 196, 197.
at Niagara Falls, 18, 210.
at Philadelphia, 74, 86, 203, 204.
at Pittsburgh, 15.
at Mt. Vernon, 127, 206, 207.
at Washington, 101, 102, 205-207.
at Yorktown, 143, 144, 207, 208.
in the South and West, 208-210, 231.

china souvenirs of Tour, 125, 169, 190, 193, 194, 208, 211, 218, 267, 268.
Lafayette, Fort, 194.
"Lafayette Fund," 212.
Lafayette, George Washington, 193, 206.
La Grange, 197, 211, 267.
Lake Erie, Battle of, 185, 186, 241.
Lake George, 15.
Land Companies in America, 5.
Landing of Columbus (see Columbus).
Landing of Lafayette, 194, 268.
Landing of Pilgrims (see "Pilgrims").
Landseer, 262.
La Salle, 19.
Latin, in Columbia, 65, 66.
in Harvard, 40.
Lawrence, Captain, 185, 189.
Lawrence, frigate, 186.
L'Enfant, Major, 95, 96, 104, 126.
Lewis, 189.
Lexington, Battle of, 83, 166.
Kentucky, 17.
Mass., 26, 199.
"Liberty" on china, 7, 77, 126, 128, 130, 144, 147, 148, 151, 155, 156, 157.
"Liberte' des Mers," 168.
Library, Boston, 37, 198.
Columbia, 65.
Philadelphia, 76, 77, 78, 160, 204.
Lincoln, Abraham, President, china of, 261, 266.
Lind, Jenny, 49.
Little Falls, canal at, 220.
Liverpool, pottery of (see Introduction), 26, 95, 144, 153, 165.
"Map" pitcher, 7, 8.
naval pitchers, 172-191.
portrait pitchers, 8, 124-134, 153, 178, 252.
Livingston, Hon. Robert R., 66.
Lockport, canal at, 216.
Locomotive, early models of, 235, 236, 237, 238.

INDEX

Locomotive—*continued*.
 "Best Friend of Charleston," 239.
 "DeWitt Clinton," 239.
 "Puffing Billy," 235.
 "Stourbridge Lion," 236.
 "Tom Thumb," 238.
Log Cabin design, 135, 268.
Lombardy poplars at Columbia, 68.
London, 24, 95, 165.
Longfellow, references to poems of,
 74, 89, 114, 187.
Long Island, 45, 65.
"Lord of the Seas," 222.
Lotteries, 61, 64.
Louis XVI, 141, 167.
Louisiana, 6, 7, 16, 17, 151.
Louisville, Ky., 16.
Lowestoft, so-called, 252.
Luzerne, 14.

Macdonough, Commodore, 188.
Macedonian, frigate, 182, 189, 190.
Madison, "Dolly," 252, 253.
 James, President, 92, 95, 100, 134,
  178, 208, 252.
 china of, 252, 253.
Mall, Beacon Street, Boston, 28.
 Long, Boston, 25, 28.
 Washington, 96, 103, 104.
Manhattan, 5, 45, 63, 71, 147.
 Fort, 46.
Manitou, 12.
"Map," design of America, 7, 130, 147.
 of Washington, D. C., 96.
Marco Polo, 108, 110, 111, 118.
Marie Antoinette, 167.
Marine Hospital, Louisville, Ky., 17.
Marks on Staffordshire pottery, 267–
 271.
Maryland, 40, 205, 211.
 Arms of, 89, 154.
 University of, 92, 93.
Mason, Rev. Dr., 56, 67.
Masonic Temple, Baltimore, 90.
 Philadelphia, 76.
Massachusetts, 9, 22, 23, 51, 115, 144,
 167.
 Arms of, 156.

Massachusetts General Hospital, 35.
Mather, Dr. Cotton, 34.
"Maxims," of Franklin, 161–165.
Mayer, T., potter, 153, 268.
Mayflower, The, 113, 114, 115.
McComb, 189.
McKinley, William, President, china
 of, 265.
McLean, John, 35.
Mediterranean, 175.
Meigh, C., potter, 269.
Mellor, Venables & Co., potters, 270.
Mendenhall Ferry, 87.
Metropolitan Museum, New York,
 127.
Merchants' Exchange, Baltimore, 90,
 205.
 New York, 69.
Mexican War, 259.
Mexico, Gulf of, 7.
Michaux, André, 68.
Michigan, 16.
Military Academy (see West
 Point).
Millir, 189.
Minton, pottery, 264.
 Thomas, 287.
Mirror-knobs, 133.
Mississippi River, 6, 16, 17, 209, 231.
Mitchell & Freeman's China & Glass
 Warehouse, 36.
Mohawk River, 220.
Mohawk & Hudson River R. R., 239.
Monroe, James, President, 193,
 205, 246, 252.
 china of, 254, 255.
"Monroe Doctrine" introduced, 206.
Montgomery, General Richard, 56,
 139.
Monticello, 208.
Montmorenci, Falls of, 8.
Montpelier, 208.
Monument, Battle, at Baltimore, 90,
 91, 92, 205.
 Bunker Hill, Boston, 139.
 Washington, at Baltimore, 91.
 Washington, at Washington, D.
  C., 103, 125–129.

320

INDEX

Moore, Tom, 251.

"Morals" of Franklin, 161–165.

Morley, Francis & Co., potters, 270.

Morningside Heights, 65, 68.

Moses, 151.

Mt. Vernon, 98, 104, 124, 125, 136, 206, 207, 249, 250.

Murray St. Church, N. Y., 56, 67.

Nahant, views of, 38.

Napoleon, 143, 175.

National Museum of Smithsonian Institution, 136, 237, 249, 250, 261.

"Nation's Guest" (see Lafayette).

Naval pitchers, 172–191.

Nelson, Lord, 177, 184.

"Neptune's Return to Pan," 215, 223.

New Amsterdam, 43, 49, 72.

Newburgh, 11, 200, 231.

New Hampshire, 9.
    Arms of, 153.

New Haven, Conn., 10, 199.

New Jersey, 15, 45, 65.
    Arms of, 156.

New Orleans, 6, 16, 209.
    Battle of, 191.

"New Style" travel, 232.

Newtown, Mass., 39.

New York, city of, 40, 43–70, 94, 140, 158, 181, 246, 249.
    old china views of, 44–69.
    Almshouse, 57, 61, 196, 222.
    American Museum, Scudders, 42, 58, 59, 61, 62, 196, 222.
    Battery, 46, 49, 148, 194, 197, 222.
    Brooklyn Heights, 44, 45, 137, 140.
    Castle Garden, 47, 48, 194, 197, 222.
    City Hall, 46, 52, 58, 59, 60, 69, 101, 195, 222.
    City Hotel, 53, 54, 196.
    Columbia, 46, 63–68, 196, 222.
    Esplanade, 47.
    Flagstaff Pavilion, 47.
    Fort Clinton, 47, 48.
    Merchants' Exchange, Burning of, 69.
    Murray St. Church, 56, 67.

Park Theater, 62, 196, 222.

St. Patrick's, 57.

St. Paul's Chapel, 55, 62, 67, 196, 222.

Weehawk, 44, 45.

New York, state of, 6, 199, 202, 210, 213, 222.
    arms of, 56, 156.

Niagara Falls, 17–21, 38, 210, 223.
    in Art, 19–21.
    in Literature, 18.

Niagara, Fort, 18.

Niagara, frigate, 186.

Noah's Ark, canal boat, 215.

North Carolina, 16, 209.
    arms of, 155.

Nova Scotia, 89.

"Octagon Church," Boston, 33.

Octagon House, Washington, D. C., 254.

O'Hara, Gen'l, 143.

Ohio River, 6, 16, 210, 232, 237.
    State of, 151.

"Old China" Magazine, 288.

Old Ironsides, 184.

Olmutz, 196.

Old North Church, Boston, 33, 34.

"Old Ship Meeting House," 13.

"Old Rough and Ready," 259.

Opera, Grand in America, 48, 49.

Old South Church, Boston, 33, 34.

"Old Style" travel on land, 232.

Orange Hotel, Newburgh, 12.

Orinoco River, 113.

Oxford, 290.

Paine, Tom, 251.

Palos, Spain, 109.

Pantheon, 83.

Paris, 68, 95, 211.

Park St. Church, Boston, 27, 32, 33.

Park Theater, N. Y., 62, 196, 222.

Park, City Hall, N. Y., 57, 58, 63.

Park Place, 68.

Park Row, 62.

Parrots, in America, 3, 4.
    in border device, 4, 11.

321

INDEX

Passaic, Falls of, 15.
Patapsco, River, 89.
Paulding, John, 200.
Peace, Belt of, 120, 121.
 Penn's Treaty of, 119-121.
Peale, artist, 128.
Penn, Admiral, 72.
 William, 71, 78, 84, 107, 123, 159.
 old china designs of, 117-119,
 270.
Penn's Treaty with Indians, 117-
 123.
Pennsylvania, 6, 15, 87.
 arms of, 155.
 Hospital, 79, 123, 204.
 Museum, 271.
Perkins, Thomas, 28.
Perry, Commodore, O. H., 185, 186,
 189, 216.
 Memorial, 46, 186.
Perry, Commodore, canal boat, 215.
Petit, cook, 251.
Pewter, 136, 249.
Pewter Platter Alley, 77.
Pewter Platter Inn, 81.
Pharaoh, 151.
Philadelphia, history of, 71-87, 94,
 117, 119, 141, 144, 150, 158, 159,
 181, 203, 204, 226, 234, 246.
 Bank of United States, 76, 80, 204.
 Dam and Waterworks, 85, 204,
 230.
 Fairmount Park, 76, 84.
 Hospital, Pennsylvania, 76, 79,
 160, 204.
 Library, 76, 77, 78, 160, 204.
 Mendenhall Ferry, 87.
 State House, 203.
 Staughton's Church, 83.
 United States Hotel, 82.
 University of Pennsylvania, 160.
 Upper Ferry Bridge, 87.
 "Woodlands," 86.
Philadelphia, frigate, 175-177.
Phillips, E. J. & Co., potters, 269.
 Hon. John, 28.
 Wendell, 28.
Phœnix, 70.

Physick, Dr. Philip Syng, 87.
Pickwick, Mr., 162.
"Picturesque Views," Hudson River
 scenery, 11, 268.
Pierce, Franklin, President, china
 of, 260.
Pike, General, 99, 184, 185, 189.
Pilgrims, story of Landing of, 89,
 107, 113-116, 159.
 old china views of Landing, 114,
 267.
Pincian Hill, Rome, 102.
Pine Orchard House, Catskills, 12.
Pine-tree flag, 8, 130, 147.
Pioneers of America, 107-123.
 Americus Vespucius, 3.
 Columbus, 107-113.
 Dutch, 5, 43-47, 72, 122.
 English, 5, 113-117.
 French, 4, 5.
 Pennsylvania, 117-123.
 Spanish, 5.
Pirates, African, 174, 175.
Pittsburgh, 15, 210, 230, 256.
Pittsfield, Mass., 9.
Pittsfield Elm, 9.
Plains of Abraham, 8.
Plan, of Philadelphia, 72-74.
 of Washington, D. C., 95, 96, 103.
Plutarch, 158.
Plymouth, England, 113.
 Mass., 114, 116.
Plymouth Rock, 114.
Polk, James K., Mrs., 245.
 President, china of, 258, 259.
Polo, Marco, 108, 111, 118.
Pomona, 129.
Porcelain (see Introduction), (see
 China).
 Franklin's fondness for, 133, 158,
 166, 167, 169.
 Washington's fondness for, 259.
 in White House Collection, 245-
 266.
"Poor Richard," 161.
Porter, Capt. 189.
Portrait pitchers, of George Wash-
 ington, 124-134.

INDEX

Portrait, naval, 172–191.
Post Office, New York, 58, 69.
 Washington, D. C., 100.
Post Road, Boston (see Boston).
Potomac, 95, 97, 104, 126, 206.
Potters, Staffordshire (see Intro-
  duction), 267–271.
 marks of, 267–271.
"Potteries, The" (see Introduction).
Poughkeepsie, 201.
Power, Tyrone, 62.
Preble, Commodore, 174–178.
Pesidents of the United States, 245–
  266.
 Mansion (see White House).
Presidential china, White House
  Collection of, 245–266.
 Washington, 248–250.
 John Adams, 250, 251.
 Jefferson, 251, 252.
 Madison, 252–254.
 Monroe, 254, 255.
 J. Q. Adams, 255.
 Jackson, 255–257.
 VanBuren, 257.
 W. H. Harrison, 258.
 Tyler, 258.
 Polk, 258, 259.
 Taylor, 259.
 Fillmore, 260.
 Pierce, 260.
 Buchanan, 260.
 Lincoln, 261.
 Johnson, 261.
 Grant, 261, 262.
 Hayes, 262.
 Garfield, 263.
 Arthur, 263.
 Cleveland, 264.
 B. Harrison, 264.
 McKinley, 265.
 Roosevelt, 265.
 Taft, 266.
 Wilson, 266.
Princeton Univ., 203.
"Proscribed Patriots," 31.
 Pitcher design, 131, 134.
"Proverbs," Franklin's, 161–165.

Provoost, Rev. Dr., 67.
Provost, The, N. Y., 58.
Pulaski, Gen'l, 209.
Punch-bowl, 139, 261.
Puritans (See Pilgrims), 5, 116.
Put-in-Bay, 185.

Quakers, 26, 71, 118.
Quebec, 8, 56, 137, 139.
"Queen's Farm," 63.
Quincy, Josiah, Jr., 28.
 Mass., 198, 235.

Railroads (see Travel).
Raleigh, 131.
Raphael, 133.
Red Jacket, 210.
Red Room, White House, 245, 253.
Red Sea, 151.
Reproductions of designs, 271.
Revolution, War of the (see War
  of the Revolution).
Rhode Island, 9.
 Arms of, 153.
Richmond, Va., 16, 235, 258.
Ridgway, J. & W., potters, 61, 268.
Ripley, 189.
Rivers of America, sketches of (See
  Introduction).
 early knowledge of, 3, 6, 209.
 Alabama, 209.
 Alleghany, 15, 231.
 Brandywine, 117, 141, 204.
 Delaware, 6, 72, 73, 84, 117, 226.
 East, 61, 69, 227.
 Genesee, 217.
 Hudson, 6, 10, 11, 44, 142, 143, 156,
  199–202, 221, 225, 227, 228, 230.
 Juniata, 15.
 Mississippi, 6, 16, 17, 231.
 Mohawk, 220.
 Monongahela, 15.
 Niagara, 18, 19.
 North, 64.
 Ohio, 6, 16, 210, 231, 232, 237.
 Orinoco, 113.
 Patapsco, 89.
 Potomac, 95, 97, 104, 206, 211.

INDEX

Rivers of America, Schuylkill, 73, 84, 85, 86, 87, 204, 226, 230.
Rochester, canal at, 217, 218, 241.
Rogers, J. & G., potters, 269.
Rogers, 189.
Romance, 28, 29, 107, 113, 159.
Rome, Italy, 78, 83, 95, 102, 146, 215.
Rome, N. Y., 219.
Roosevelt, Mrs. Theodore, 245, 246.
  Theodore, Pres., china of, 265, 266.
  Theodore, Pres., remodeled White House, 246, 265.
Ross, "Betsey," 150.
Royal Academy, England, 292.
Rowlandson, T., 289.
Rozinante, 291.
Ruskin, John, 235.
Rutherford, Major Walter, 56.

"Safety barges," 232.
"Sailor Pitchers," 172, 173.
Salem, Mass., 135.
Samoset, Indian, 114.
Sancho Panza, 291.
Sandusky, Ohio, 16.
Saratoga, Battle of, 141.
Saratoga, flagship, 189.
Savage, artist, 128.
Savannah, Georgia, 16, 209, 234.
Schenectady, N. Y., 239, 240.
Schuylkill River, 73, 84, 85, 86, 87, 204, 226.
Scott, 189.
Scriptural designs on pottery, 267.
Scudder's Museum, 42, 58, 59, 62, 196, 222.
Seal, Great, of the U. S., 8, 56, 268, 270.
  adaptations of on china, 152.
  adopted by Congress, 152.
  early designs for, 151.
  on Liverpool pitcher, 129.
  on Presidential china, 248, 254.
  on Lincoln china, 261.
  on Grant china, 261.
  on Hayes china, 262.
  on Benjamin Harrison china, 265.
  on Roosevelt china, 266.

Seneca Chief, canal boat, 215.
Serapis, The, 162.
Shackamaxon, Treaty of, 117.
Shannon, The, 185.
Sims, Joseph, 87.
"Shining Mountains," 17.
Simcoe, Gen'l, 122.
Site, of Baltimore, 89.
  of Boston, 23.
  of New York, 44, 45.
  of Philadelphia, 72, 73.
  of Washington, D. C., 95.
"Sons of the Mountains," 207.
Smirke, Robert, 291.
Smith, Captain John, 89.
Smithsonian Institution (see National Museum).
Snuff-boxes, 168, 181, 184.
"Sons of Liberty," 58.
"Sons of the Mountains," 207.
Socrates, 158.
South America, 37.
South Carolina, 16, 209, 239.
  arms of, 155.
Spain, 5, 6, 109, 110, 146, 291, 292.
Squanto, 114.
Staffordshire, pottery of, when and where made, color, decoration, sold in America, original and present value of, borders, views on, etc. (See Introduction).
  arrival of in Boston, 36.
  list of American views on, 267–286.
  potters of, 267–271.
Stage coach travel, 197, 232, 234.
Stage routes, 233, 234.
Stamp Act, 49, 165, 166.
Standish, Miles, 114.
State House, Boston, 27, 29.
  Philadelphia, 76, 94, 203.
Staten Island, 45, 65.
"States" design, 126, 130, 150, 268.
  Martha Washington, 136.
Staughton's Church, Phila., 83.
  Rev. William, 84.

INDEX

Steamships, early, *Chancellor Livingston,* 229.
  Chief Justice Marshall, 230.
  Clermont, 227.
  Fulton, 194, 228.
  James Kent, 199.
  "Troy Line" of, 230.
  "Union Line" of, 230.
  travel on, 209.
Stephenson, George, 235.
Stevenson potteries, England, 45, 62, 63, 267, 269.
St. Lawrence River, 5, 8.
St. Louis, Mo., 209.
Stonington, Connecticut, Defense of, 187.
"Stourbridge Lion," 236.
St. Patrick's, N. Y., 57.
St. Paul's, Boston, 33.
  Chapel, N. Y., 55, 62, 67, 196, 222.
St. Peter's, Rome, 102.
Streets, city, Baltimore, 88.
  Boston, 22–24, 26, 27, 29, 30, 71.
  New York, 43, 50, 52, 68.
  Philadelphia, 51, 71, 73, 74, 95.
  Washington, 96, 97, 98, 103.
Stuart, Captain, 178, 189.
  Gilbert, 128.
Stubbs, Joseph, potter, 84, 268.
Stuyvesant, Gov. Peter, 43, 46, 49, 51, 72.
Styles in dress in early America, 21, 24, 47, 111, 118, 127.
"Success to the Infant Navy" design, 173.
Superior, canal boat, 215.
"Surtout de table," 254, 257.
Sydney, Algernon, 156.
"Sylvania," 72.
Syntax, Dr., designs on pottery, 268.
  story of, 162, 289, 290.
Syracuse, N. Y., 219.

Table Rock, Niagara Falls, 19.
Taft, Mrs. William H., 254.
  William H., Pres., 245.
  china of, 266.

Tammany Hall, 256.
Tams, John, potter, 135, 270.
  S. & Co., potters, 268.
Tarrytown, N. Y., 200.
Taverns, "Eagle," Buffalo, 216.
  Fraunce's, New York, 52.
  Harding's, Philadelphia, 87.
  Lockport, 216.
  Philadelphia, 53, 54, 81.
  signs, 80, 81.
Tawenna, Indian Chief, 120.
Temple of Fame, 46.
Tennessee, 151.
Teresa Panza, 291.
"Texian Campaign," 270.
Theater, Albany, 279.
  going in Philadelphia, 82.
  Park, New York, 62, 196.
  Scudder's Museum, 59.
Ticknor, George, 28.
Tiffany, Mr. Louis, 263.
  screen in White House, 263.
Tomb, of Franklin, Lafayette at, 169, 204.
  of Washington, 104, 125.
  of Washington, Lafayette at, 127, 206, 207.
Tompkins, Daniel D., 67, 194.
Tom Thumb, General, 59.
"Tom Thumb" locomotive, 93, 238.
Tour, imaginary, of early America, 3–21.
  in search of the Picturesque, 289.
  in search of Consolation, 290.
  in search of a Wife, 290.
  of America by Lafayette in 1824–5, 192–212.
Transylvania University, Lexington, Ky., 17.
Travel, new modes of, 225–241.
  by land, 232–239.
  by water, 225–232.
  references to, 35, 38, 87, 91, 93, 208, 209, 223.
Treaty, Belt of Peace, 120, 121.
  Elm, 122.
  Of Ghent, 33, 54, 191, 254.

INDEX

Treaty, Penn's, with Indians, 107, 117–123, 270.
Penn's Treaty Monument, 123.
with France, 167.
Trenton, N. J., 203.
Tri-Mountain (Tremont St., Boston), 23.
Trinity, Old, New York, 51, 54, 55, 63, 64, 65.
Tripoli, naval engagement, 175, 176, 177.
on Liverpool pitcher, 178.
Tropical scenes in America, 3, 4, 108, 118.
"Troy from Mt. Ida," 14, 46, 202.
Troy Female Seminary, 202.
"Troy Line" of boats, 230.
Trumbull, artist, 128.
Truxton, Com., 173, 174.
Turkey, sultan of, 174.
Tyler, Mrs., John, portrait of, 245.
President, china of, 258.

Ulm, campaign of, 143.
"Union Line" of steamboats, 230.
United States, Bank of, in Phila., 76, 80, 204.
early conditions and map of, 5, 6, 7.
emblems of, 52, 56, 146–157.
Hotel, Philadelphia, 82.
War of France and the, 173.
United States and *Macedonian,* 182.
University, Columbia, 46, 63–68, 196, 222.
Harvard, 10, 38–42, 63, 67, 68, 71, 198.
of Maryland, 90, 92, 93, 205.
of Pennsylvania, 160.
Princeton, 203.
Transylvania, 17.
"Upper Ferry Bridge," 87.
Unknown makers of china decorations, 271.
"Utica Inscription," 219, 241.

Valley Forge, 83, 141.

Van Buren, Mrs., portrait of, 245.
President Martin, china of, 257.
Van Rensselaer, 189.
Van Wert, Isaac, 200.
Venice, 95, 108, 214.
Vermont, 9, 127, 150, 151.
Versailles, 162.
Vespucius, Americus, 3.
Vesuvius, Mt., 18.
Virgil, 67.
Virginia, 5, 6, 16, 40, 143, 208, 211.
Arms of, 157.
sandstone, 97, 102.
"Virginia Housewife," 251.

Wall, W. G., 11, 45, 46, 186, 268.
Wall St., New York, 51, 52, 53, 59, 63, 69, 71.
Wallack, actor, 62.
War of 1812, 16, 53, 91, 99, 135, 179, 190, 204, 253.
story of, 172–191.
Battle of Lake Champlain, 188.
Battle of Lake Erie, 185, 186.
Battle of New Orleans, 191.
Chesapeake and *Shannon,* 185.
Constitution, first engagement of, 179, 180.
Constitution and *Guerrière,* 181.
Constitution and *Java,* 183.
Defense of Stonington, 187.
Enterprise and *Boxer,* 186.
United States and *Macedonian,* 182.
Wasp and *Frolic,* 182.
York, Canada, 184.
War of the Revolution, 66, 122, 165, 199, 213.
Battle of the Brandywine, 141.
Brooklyn Heights, 140.
Surrender at Saratoga, 141.
Surrender at Yorktown, 142, 143.
Treason at Westpoint, 142.
old china views of, 137.
story of, 137–145.
War with Mexico, 259.
Warren, Gen'l, 34, 139, 198.

INDEX

Washington, George, 7, 9, 52, 54, 56, 58, 61, 65, 67, 75, 83, 91, 95, 98, 100, 125, 126, 127, 128, 129, 130, 140, 141, 143, 150, 169, 189, 190, 197, 201, 213, 246, 249.
  Arms of, 149.
  busts, statuettes, medallions of, 133.
  china of in White House, 248–250.
  Erie canal portrait, 218.
  Lafayette at Tomb of, 207.
  Liverpool portraits of, 124–134.
  portrait in White House, 253.
Washington Elm, 101.
  Monument, 103.
"Washington in Glory," 153.
Washington, D. C., 16, 50, 234.
  burning of, 253.
  history of, 94–104.
  old china views of, 100.
  Presidential china in, 245–266.
  President's House (see White House).
Washington, Martha, portrait of in White House, 245.
  "States" china, 136, 150, 250.
  Tomb of, 207.
Wasp and *Frolic,* 182.
Water supply, of New York, 50, 54. of Philadelphia, 84.
Watling's Island, 111.
Watt, James, 225.
Webster, Daniel, 116, 211, 235.
Wedgwood, 169.
Weehawk, New York from, 44, 45.
"Week-day sermons" of Franklin, 71, 161–165.
West, Benjamin, 81, 118, 119, 122.
West Coast, Africa, 37.
West Indies, 37.

West Point, 11, 137, 142, 200.
White House, 97, 102, 103, 126, 192, 205, 246, 247, 264.
  burned, 100.
  East Room of, 250, 254, 255, 259.
  Mrs. Adams in, 98.
  old china view of, 102, 269.
  portraits of mistresses of, 245.
  presidential china in, 245–266.
  rebuilt after fire, 102.
  Red Room in, 245, 253.
  refurnished by Monroe, 246.
  refurnished by Arthur, 263.
  restored by Roosevelt, 265.
White Plains, 140.
Wilkie, Sir David, 268, 292.
Williams, David, 200.
Willow pattern, 257, 287, 288.
Winslow, 114.
Wilson, Woodrow, presidential china of, 266.
  Mrs., portrait of, 245.
Winthrop, Gov. John, 22.
Wolfe, Gen., 8.
Wood, Enoch, potter, 11, 46, 116, 140, 190, 237, 267.
"Woodlands," Philadelphia, 86.
Wren, Sir Christopher, 55.

Xenophon, 67, 158.

Yale College, 10, 199.
"Yankee Doodle," 143.
York, Canada, 99, 185.
Yorktown, Surrender of Cornwallis at, 83, 137, 142, 143, 144, 196.
  visit of Lafayette to, 197, 205, 207, 208.
Young Lion of the West, canal boat, 217.

327

A CATALOGUE OF SELECTED DOVER BOOKS
IN ALL FIELDS OF INTEREST

A CATALOGUE OF SELECTED DOVER BOOKS
IN ALL FIELDS OF INTEREST

AMERICA'S OLD MASTERS, James T. Flexner. Four men emerged unexpectedly from provincial 18th century America to leadership in European art: Benjamin West, J. S. Copley, C. R. Peale, Gilbert Stuart. Brilliant coverage of lives and contributions. Revised, 1967 edition. 69 plates. 365pp. of text.
21806-6 Paperbound $3.00

FIRST FLOWERS OF OUR WILDERNESS: AMERICAN PAINTING, THE COLONIAL PERIOD, James T. Flexner. Painters, and regional painting traditions from earliest Colonial times up to the emergence of Copley, West and Peale Sr., Foster, Gustavus Hesselius, Feke, John Smibert and many anonymous painters in the primitive manner. Engaging presentation, with 162 illustrations. xxii + 368pp.
22180-6 Paperbound $3.50

THE LIGHT OF DISTANT SKIES: AMERICAN PAINTING, 1760-1835, James T. Flexner. The great generation of early American painters goes to Europe to learn and to teach: West, Copley, Gilbert Stuart and others. Allston, Trumbull, Morse; also contemporary American painters—primitives, derivatives, academics—who remained in America. 102 illustrations. xiii + 306pp. 22179-2 Paperbound $3.00

A HISTORY OF THE RISE AND PROGRESS OF THE ARTS OF DESIGN IN THE UNITED STATES, William Dunlap. Much the richest mine of information on early American painters, sculptors, architects, engravers, miniaturists, etc. The only source of information for scores of artists, the major primary source for many others. Unabridged reprint of rare original 1834 edition, with new introduction by James T. Flexner, and 394 new illustrations. Edited by Rita Weiss. 6⅝ x 9⅝.
21695-0, 21696-9, 21697-7 Three volumes, Paperbound $13.50

EPOCHS OF CHINESE AND JAPANESE ART, Ernest F. Fenollosa. From primitive Chinese art to the 20th century, thorough history, explanation of every important art period and form, including Japanese woodcuts; main stress on China and Japan, but Tibet, Korea also included. Still unexcelled for its detailed, rich coverage of cultural background, aesthetic elements, diffusion studies, particularly of the historical period. 2nd, 1913 edition. 242 illustrations. lii + 439pp. of text.
20364-6, 20365-4 Two volumes, Paperbound $6.00

THE GENTLE ART OF MAKING ENEMIES, James A. M. Whistler. Greatest wit of his day deflates Oscar Wilde, Ruskin, Swinburne; strikes back at inane critics, exhibitions, art journalism; aesthetics of impressionist revolution in most striking form. Highly readable classic by great painter. Reproduction of edition designed by Whistler. Introduction by Alfred Werner. xxxvi + 334pp.
21875-9 Paperbound $2.50

VISUAL ILLUSIONS: THEIR CAUSES, CHARACTERISTICS, AND APPLICATIONS, Matthew Luckiesh. Thorough description and discussion of optical illusion, geometric and perspective, particularly; size and shape distortions, illusions of color, of motion; natural illusions; use of illusion in art and magic, industry, etc. Most useful today with op art, also for classical art. Scores of effects illustrated. Introduction by William H. Ittleson. 100 illustrations. xxi + 252pp.
21530-X Paperbound $2.00

A HANDBOOK OF ANATOMY FOR ART STUDENTS, Arthur Thomson. Thorough, virtually exhaustive coverage of skeletal structure, musculature, etc. Full text, supplemented by anatomical diagrams and drawings and by photographs of undraped figures. Unique in its comparison of male and female forms, pointing out differences of contour, texture, form. 211 figures, 40 drawings, 86 photographs. xx + 459pp. 5⅜ x 8⅜.
21163-0 Paperbound $3.50

150 MASTERPIECES OF DRAWING, Selected by Anthony Toney. Full page reproductions of drawings from the early 16th to the end of the 18th century, all beautifully reproduced: Rembrandt, Michelangelo, Dürer, Fragonard, Urs, Graf, Wouwerman, many others. First-rate browsing book, model book for artists. xviii + 150pp. 8⅜ x 11¼.
21032-4 Paperbound $2.50

THE LATER WORK OF AUBREY BEARDSLEY, Aubrey Beardsley. Exotic, erotic, ironic masterpieces in full maturity: Comedy Ballet, Venus and Tannhauser, Pierrot, Lysistrata, Rape of the Lock, Savoy material, Ali Baba, Volpone, etc. This material revolutionized the art world, and is still powerful, fresh, brilliant. With *The Early Work,* all Beardsley's finest work. 174 plates, 2 in color. xiv + 176pp. 8⅛ x 11.
21817-1 Paperbound $3.00

DRAWINGS OF REMBRANDT, Rembrandt van Rijn. Complete reproduction of fabulously rare edition by Lippmann and Hofstede de Groot, completely reedited, updated, improved by Prof. Seymour Slive, Fogg Museum. Portraits, Biblical sketches, landscapes, Oriental types, nudes, episodes from classical mythology—All Rembrandt's fertile genius. Also selection of drawings by his pupils and followers. "Stunning volumes," *Saturday Review.* 550 illustrations. lxxviii + 552pp. 9⅛ x 12¼.
21485-0, 21486-9 Two volumes, Paperbound $7.00

THE DISASTERS OF WAR, Francisco Goya. One of the masterpieces of Western civilization—83 etchings that record Goya's shattering, bitter reaction to the Napoleonic war that swept through Spain after the insurrection of 1808 and to war in general. Reprint of the first edition, with three additional plates from Boston's Museum of Fine Arts. All plates facsimile size. Introduction by Philip Hofer, Fogg Museum. v + 97pp. 9⅜ x 8¼.
21872-4 Paperbound $2.00

GRAPHIC WORKS OF ODILON REDON. Largest collection of Redon's graphic works ever assembled: 172 lithographs, 28 etchings and engravings, 9 drawings. These include some of his most famous works. All the plates from *Odilon Redon: oeuvre graphique complet,* plus additional plates. New introduction and caption translations by Alfred Werner. 209 illustrations. xxvii + 209pp. 9⅛ x 12¼.
21966-8 Paperbound $4.00

DESIGN BY ACCIDENT; A BOOK OF "ACCIDENTAL EFFECTS" FOR ARTISTS AND DESIGNERS, James F. O'Brien. Create your own unique, striking, imaginative effects by "controlled accident" interaction of materials: paints and lacquers, oil and water based paints, splatter, crackling materials, shatter, similar items. Everything you do will be different; first book on this limitless art, so useful to both fine artist and commercial artist. Full instructions. 192 plates showing "accidents," 8 in color. viii + 215pp. 8⅜ x 11¼. 21942-9 Paperbound $3.50

THE BOOK OF SIGNS, Rudolf Koch. Famed German type designer draws 493 beautiful symbols: religious, mystical, alchemical, imperial, property marks, runes, etc. Remarkable fusion of traditional and modern. Good for suggestions of timelessness, smartness, modernity. Text. vi + 104pp. 6⅛ x 9¼. 20162-7 Paperbound $1.25

HISTORY OF INDIAN AND INDONESIAN ART, Ananda K. Coomaraswamy. An unabridged republication of one of the finest books by a great scholar in Eastern art. Rich in descriptive material, history, social backgrounds; Sunga reliefs, Rajput paintings, Gupta temples, Burmese frescoes, textiles, jewelry, sculpture, etc. 400 photos. viii + 423pp. 6⅜ x 9¾. 21436-2 Paperbound $4.00

PRIMITIVE ART, Franz Boas. America's foremost anthropologist surveys textiles, ceramics, woodcarving, basketry, metalwork, etc.; patterns, technology, creation of symbols, style origins. All areas of world, but very full on Northwest Coast Indians. More than 350 illustrations of baskets, boxes, totem poles, weapons, etc. 378 pp. 20025-6 Paperbound $3.00

THE GENTLEMAN AND CABINET MAKER'S DIRECTOR, Thomas Chippendale. Full reprint (third edition, 1762) of most influential furniture book of all time, by master cabinetmaker. 200 plates, illustrating chairs, sofas, mirrors, tables, cabinets, plus 24 photographs of surviving pieces. Biographical introduction by N. Bienenstock. vi + 249pp. 9⅞ x 12¾. 21601-2 Paperbound $4.00

AMERICAN ANTIQUE FURNITURE, Edgar G. Miller, Jr. The basic coverage of all American furniture before 1840. Individual chapters cover type of furniture— clocks, tables, sideboards, etc.—chronologically, with inexhaustible wealth of data. More than 2100 photographs, all identified, commented on. Essential to all early American collectors. Introduction by H. E. Keyes. vi + 1106pp. 7⅞ x 10¾. 21599-7, 21600-4 Two volumes, Paperbound $10.00

PENNSYLVANIA DUTCH AMERICAN FOLK ART, Henry J. Kauffman. 279 photos, 28 drawings of tulipware, Fraktur script, painted tinware, toys, flowered furniture, quilts, samplers, hex signs, house interiors, etc. Full descriptive text. Excellent for tourist, rewarding for designer, collector. Map. 146pp. 7⅞ x 10¾. 21205-X Paperbound $2.50

EARLY NEW ENGLAND GRAVESTONE RUBBINGS, Edmund V. Gillon, Jr. 43 photographs, 226 carefully reproduced rubbings show heavily symbolic, sometimes macabre early gravestones, up to early 19th century. Remarkable early American primitive art, occasionally strikingly beautiful; always powerful. Text. xxvi + 207pp. 8⅜ x 11¼. 21380-3 Paperbound $3.50

ALPHABETS AND ORNAMENTS, Ernst Lehner. Well-known pictorial source for decorative alphabets, script examples, cartouches, frames, decorative title pages, calligraphic initials, borders, similar material. 14th to 19th century, mostly European. Useful in almost any graphic arts designing, varied styles. 750 illustrations. 256pp. 7 x 10.   21905-4 Paperbound $4.00

PAINTING: A CREATIVE APPROACH, Norman Colquhoun. For the beginner simple guide provides an instructive approach to painting: major stumbling blocks for beginner; overcoming them, technical points; paints and pigments; oil painting; watercolor and other media and color. New section on "plastic" paints. Glossary. Formerly *Paint Your Own Pictures.* 221pp.   22000-1 Paperbound $1.75

THE ENJOYMENT AND USE OF COLOR, Walter Sargent. Explanation of the relations between colors themselves and between colors in nature and art, including hundreds of little-known facts about color values, intensities, effects of high and low illumination, complementary colors. Many practical hints for painters, references to great masters. 7 color plates, 29 illustrations. x + 274pp.
                                20944-X Paperbound $2.50

THE NOTEBOOKS OF LEONARDO DA VINCI, compiled and edited by Jean Paul Richter. 1566 extracts from original manuscripts reveal the full range of Leonardo's versatile genius: all his writings on painting, sculpture, architecture, anatomy, astronomy, geography, topography, physiology, mining, music, etc., in both Italian and English, with 186 plates of manuscript pages and more than 500 additional drawings. Includes studies for the Last Supper, the lost Sforza monument, and other works. Total of xlvii + 866pp. 7⅞ x 10¾.
                    22572-0, 22573-9 Two volumes, Paperbound $10.00

MONTGOMERY WARD CATALOGUE OF 1895. Tea gowns, yards of flannel and pillow-case lace, stereoscopes, books of gospel hymns, the New Improved Singer Sewing Machine, side saddles, milk skimmers, straight-edged razors, high-button shoes, spittoons, and on and on . . . listing some 25,000 items, practically all illustrated. Essential to the shoppers of the 1890's, it is our truest record of the spirit of the period. Unaltered reprint of Issue No. 57, Spring and Summer 1895. Introduction by Boris Emmet. Innumerable illustrations. xiii + 624pp. 8½ x 11⅝.
                                22377-9 Paperbound $6.95

THE CRYSTAL PALACE EXHIBITION ILLUSTRATED CATALOGUE (LONDON, 1851). One of the wonders of the modern world—the Crystal Palace Exhibition in which all the nations of the civilized world exhibited their achievements in the arts and sciences—presented in an equally important illustrated catalogue. More than 1700 items pictured with accompanying text—ceramics, textiles, cast-iron work, carpets, pianos, sleds, razors, wall-papers, billiard tables, beehives, silverware and hundreds of other artifacts—represent the focal point of Victorian culture in the Western World. Probably the largest collection of Victorian decorative art ever assembled—indispensable for antiquarians and designers. Unabridged republication of the Art-Journal Catalogue of the Great Exhibition of 1851, with all terminal essays. New introduction by John Gloag, F.S.A. xxxiv + 426pp. 9 x 12.
                                22503-8 Paperbound $4.50

A History of Costume, Carl Köhler. Definitive history, based on surviving pieces of clothing primarily, and paintings, statues, etc. secondarily. Highly readable text, supplemented by 594 illustrations of costumes of the ancient Mediterranean peoples, Greece and Rome, the Teutonic prehistoric period; costumes of the Middle Ages, Renaissance, Baroque, 18th and 19th centuries. Clear, measured patterns are provided for many clothing articles. Approach is practical throughout. Enlarged by Emma von Sichart. 464pp. 21030-8 Paperbound $3.50

Oriental Rugs, Antique and Modern, Walter A. Hawley. A complete and authoritative treatise on the Oriental rug—where they are made, by whom and how, designs and symbols, characteristics in detail of the six major groups, how to distinguish them and how to buy them. Detailed technical data is provided on periods, weaves, warps, wefts, textures, sides, ends and knots, although no technical background is required for an understanding. 11 color plates, 80 halftones, 4 maps. vi + 320pp. 6⅛ x 9⅛. 22366-3 Paperbound $5.00

Ten Books on Architecture, Vitruvius. By any standards the most important book on architecture ever written. Early Roman discussion of aesthetics of building, construction methods, orders, sites, and every other aspect of architecture has inspired, instructed architecture for about 2,000 years. Stands behind Palladio, Michelangelo, Bramante, Wren, countless others. Definitive Morris H. Morgan translation. 68 illustrations. xii + 331pp. 20645-9 Paperbound $2.50

The Four Books of Architecture, Andrea Palladio. Translated into every major Western European language in the two centuries following its publication in 1570, this has been one of the most influential books in the history of architecture. Complete reprint of the 1738 Isaac Ware edition. New introduction by Adolf Placzek, Columbia Univ. 216 plates. xxii + 110pp. of text. 9½ x 12¾. 21308-0 Clothbound $10.00

Sticks and Stones: A Study of American Architecture and Civilization, Lewis Mumford.One of the great classics of American cultural history. American architecture from the medieval-inspired earliest forms to the early 20th century; evolution of structure and style, and reciprocal influences on environment. 21 photographic illustrations. 238pp. 20202-X Paperbound $2.00

The American Builder's Companion, Asher Benjamin. The most widely used early 19th century architectural style and source book, for colonial up into Greek Revival periods. Extensive development of geometry of carpentering, construction of sashes, frames, doors, stairs; plans and elevations of domestic and other buildings. Hundreds of thousands of houses were built according to this book, now invaluable to historians, architects, restorers, etc. 1827 edition. 59 plates. 114pp. 7⅞ x 10¾. 22236-5 Paperbound $3.00

Dutch Houses in the Hudson Valley Before 1776, Helen Wilkinson Reynolds. The standard survey of the Dutch colonial house and outbuildings, with constructional features, decoration, and local history associated with individual homesteads. Introduction by Franklin D. Roosevelt. Map. 150 illustrations. 469pp. 6⅝ x 9¼. 21469-9 Paperbound $4.00

THE ARCHITECTURE OF COUNTRY HOUSES, Andrew J. Downing. Together with Vaux's *Villas and Cottages* this is the basic book for Hudson River Gothic architecture of the middle Victorian period. Full, sound discussions of general aspects of housing, architecture, style, decoration, furnishing, together with scores of detailed house plans, illustrations of specific buildings, accompanied by full text. Perhaps the most influential single American architectural book. 1850 edition. Introduction by J. Stewart Johnson. 321 figures, 34 architectural designs. xvi + 560pp.
22003-6 Paperbound $4.00

LOST EXAMPLES OF COLONIAL ARCHITECTURE, John Mead Howells. Full-page photographs of buildings that have disappeared or been so altered as to be denatured, including many designed by major early American architects. 245 plates. xvii + 248pp. 7⅞ x 10¾.
21143-6 Paperbound $3.50

DOMESTIC ARCHITECTURE OF THE AMERICAN COLONIES AND OF THE EARLY REPUBLIC, Fiske Kimball. Foremost architect and restorer of Williamsburg and Monticello covers nearly 200 homes between 1620-1825. Architectural details, construction, style features, special fixtures, floor plans, etc. Generally considered finest work in its area. 219 illustrations of houses, doorways, windows, capital mantels. xx + 314pp. 7⅞ x 10¾.
21743-4 Paperbound $4.00

EARLY AMERICAN ROOMS: 1650-1858, edited by Russell Hawes Kettell. Tour of 12 rooms, each representative of a different era in American history and each furnished, decorated, designed and occupied in the style of the era. 72 plans and elevations, 8-page color section, etc., show fabrics, wall papers, arrangements, etc. Full descriptive text. xvii + 200pp. of text. 8⅜ x 11¼.
21633-0 Paperbound $5.00

THE FITZWILLIAM VIRGINAL BOOK, edited by J. Fuller Maitland and W. B. Squire. Full modern printing of famous early 17th-century ms. volume of 300 works by Morley, Byrd, Bull, Gibbons, etc. For piano or other modern keyboard instrument; easy to read format. xxxvi + 938pp. 8⅜ x 11.
21068-5, 21069-3 Two volumes, Paperbound $10.00

KEYBOARD MUSIC, Johann Sebastian Bach. Bach Gesellschaft edition. A rich selection of Bach's masterpieces for the harpsichord: the six English Suites, six French Suites, the six Partitas (Clavierübung part I), the Goldberg Variations (Clavierübung part IV), the fifteen Two-Part Inventions and the fifteen Three-Part Sinfonias. Clearly reproduced on large sheets with ample margins; eminently playable. vi + 312pp. 8⅛ x 11.
22360-4 Paperbound $5.00

THE MUSIC OF BACH: AN INTRODUCTION, Charles Sanford Terry. A fine, nontechnical introduction to Bach's music, both instrumental and vocal. Covers organ music, chamber music, passion music, other types. Analyzes themes, developments, innovations. x + 114pp.
21075-8 Paperbound $1.25

BEETHOVEN AND HIS NINE SYMPHONIES, Sir George Grove. Noted British musicologist provides best history, analysis, commentary on symphonies. Very thorough, rigorously accurate; necessary to both advanced student and amateur music lover. 436 musical passages. vii + 407 pp.
20334-4 Paperbound $2.50

JOHANN SEBASTIAN BACH, Philipp Spitta. One of the great classics of musicology, this definitive analysis of Bach's music (and life) has never been surpassed. Lucid, nontechnical analyses of hundreds of pieces (30 pages devoted to St. Matthew Passion, 26 to B Minor Mass). Also includes major analysis of 18th-century music. 450 musical examples. 40-page musical supplement. Total of xx + 1799pp.

(EUK) 22278-0, 22279-9 Two volumes, Clothbound $15.00

MOZART AND HIS PIANO CONCERTOS, Cuthbert Girdlestone. The only full-length study of an important area of Mozart's creativity. Provides detailed analyses of all 23 concertos, traces inspirational sources. 417 musical examples. Second edition. 509pp.

(USO) 21271-8 Paperbound $3.50

THE PERFECT WAGNERITE: A COMMENTARY ON THE NIBLUNG'S RING, George Bernard Shaw. Brilliant and still relevant criticism in remarkable essays on Wagner's Ring cycle, Shaw's ideas on political and social ideology behind the plots, role of Leitmotifs, vocal requisites, etc. Prefaces. xxi + 136pp.

21707-8 Paperbound $1.50

DON GIOVANNI, W. A. Mozart. Complete libretto, modern English translation; biographies of composer and librettist; accounts of early performances and critical reaction. Lavishly illustrated. All the material you need to understand and appreciate this great work. Dover Opera Guide and Libretto Series; translated and introduced by Ellen Bleiler. 92 illustrations. 209pp.

21134-7 Paperbound $1.50

HIGH FIDELITY SYSTEMS: A LAYMAN'S GUIDE, Roy F. Allison. All the basic information you need for setting up your own audio system: high fidelity and stereo record players, tape records, F.M. Connections, adjusting tone arm, cartridge, checking needle alignment, positioning speakers, phasing speakers, adjusting hums, trouble-shooting, maintenance, and similar topics. Enlarged 1965 edition. More than 50 charts, diagrams, photos. iv + 91pp.

21514-8 Paperbound $1.25

REPRODUCTION OF SOUND, Edgar Villchur. Thorough coverage for laymen of high fidelity systems, reproducing systems in general, needles, amplifiers, preamps, loudspeakers, feedback, explaining physical background. "A rare talent for making technicalities vividly comprehensible," R. Darrell, *High Fidelity*. 69 figures. iv + 92pp.

21515-6 Paperbound $1.00

HEAR ME TALKIN' TO YA: THE STORY OF JAZZ AS TOLD BY THE MEN WHO MADE IT, Nat Shapiro and Nat Hentoff. Louis Armstrong, Fats Waller, Jo Jones, Clarence Williams, Billy Holiday, Duke Ellington, Jelly Roll Morton and dozens of other jazz greats tell how it was in Chicago's South Side, New Orleans, depression Harlem and the modern West Coast as jazz was born and grew. xvi + 429pp.

21726-4 Paperbound $2.50

FABLES OF AESOP, translated by Sir Roger L'Estrange. A reproduction of the very rare 1931 Paris edition; a selection of the most interesting fables, together with 50 imaginative drawings by Alexander Calder. v + 128pp. 6½x9¼.

21780-9 Paperbound $1.50

AGAINST THE GRAIN (A REBOURS), Joris K. Huysmans. Filled with weird images, evidences of a bizarre imagination, exotic experiments with hallucinatory drugs, rich tastes and smells and the diversions of its sybarite hero Duc Jean des Esseintes, this classic novel pushed 19th-century literary decadence to its limits. Full unabridged edition. Do not confuse this with abridged editions generally sold. Introduction by Havelock Ellis. xlix + 206pp.   22190-3 Paperbound $2.00

VARIORUM SHAKESPEARE: HAMLET. Edited by Horace H. Furness; a landmark of American scholarship. Exhaustive footnotes and appendices treat all doubtful words and phrases, as well as suggested critical emendations throughout the play's history. First volume contains editor's own text, collated with all Quartos and Folios. Second volume contains full first Quarto, translations of Shakespeare's sources (Belleforest, and Saxo Grammaticus), Der Bestrafte Brudermord, and many essays on critical and historical points of interest by major authorities of past and present. Includes details of staging and costuming over the years. By far the best edition available for serious students of Shakespeare. Total of xx + 905pp.
21004-9, 21005-7, 2 volumes, Paperbound $5.50

A LIFE OF WILLIAM SHAKESPEARE, Sir Sidney Lee. This is the standard life of Shakespeare, summarizing everything known about Shakespeare and his plays. Incredibly rich in material, broad in coverage, clear and judicious, it has served thousands as the best introduction to Shakespeare. 1931 edition. 9 plates. xxix + 792pp.   (USO) 21967-4 Paperbound $3.75

MASTERS OF THE DRAMA, John Gassner. Most comprehensive history of the drama in print, covering every tradition from Greeks to modern Europe and America, including India, Far East, etc. Covers more than 800 dramatists, 2000 plays, with biographical material, plot summaries, theatre history, criticism, etc. "Best of its kind in English," *New Republic*. 77 illustrations. xxii + 890pp.
20100-7 Clothbound $8.50

THE EVOLUTION OF THE ENGLISH LANGUAGE, George McKnight. The growth of English, from the 14th century to the present. Unusual, non-technical account presents basic information in very interesting form: sound shifts, change in grammar and syntax, vocabulary growth, similar topics. Abundantly illustrated with quotations. Formerly *Modern English in the Making*. xii + 590pp.
21932-1 Paperbound $3.50

AN ETYMOLOGICAL DICTIONARY OF MODERN ENGLISH, Ernest Weekley. Fullest, richest work of its sort, by foremost British lexicographer. Detailed word histories, including many colloquial and archaic words; extensive quotations. Do not confuse this with the Concise Etymological Dictionary, which is much abridged. Total of xxvii + 830pp. 6½ x 9¼.
21873-2, 21874-0 Two volumes, Paperbound $6.00

FLATLAND: A ROMANCE OF MANY DIMENSIONS, E. A. Abbott. Classic of science-fiction explores ramifications of life in a two-dimensional world, and what happens when a three-dimensional being intrudes. Amusing reading, but also useful as introduction to thought about hyperspace. Introduction by Banesh Hoffmann. 16 illustrations. xx + 103pp.   20001-9 Paperbound $1.00

POEMS OF ANNE BRADSTREET, edited with an introduction by Robert Hutchinson. A new selection of poems by America's first poet and perhaps the first significant woman poet in the English language. 48 poems display her development in works of considerable variety—love poems, domestic poems, religious meditations, formal elegies, "quaternions," etc. Notes, bibliography. viii + 222pp.

22160-1 Paperbound $2.00

THREE GOTHIC NOVELS: THE CASTLE OF OTRANTO BY HORACE WALPOLE; VATHEK BY WILLIAM BECKFORD; THE VAMPYRE BY JOHN POLIDORI, WITH FRAGMENT OF A NOVEL BY LORD BYRON, edited by E. F. Bleiler. The first Gothic novel, by Walpole; the finest Oriental tale in English, by Beckford; powerful Romantic supernatural story in versions by Polidori and Byron. All extremely important in history of literature; all still exciting, packed with supernatural thrills, ghosts, haunted castles, magic, etc. xl + 291pp.

21232-7 Paperbound $2.00

THE BEST TALES OF HOFFMANN, E. T. A. Hoffmann. 10 of Hoffmann's most important stories, in modern re-editings of standard translations: Nutcracker and the King of Mice, Signor Formica, Automata, The Sandman, Rath Krespel, The Golden Flowerpot, Master Martin the Cooper, The Mines of Falun, The King's Betrothed, A New Year's Eve Adventure. 7 illustrations by Hoffmann. Edited by E. F. Bleiler. xxxix + 419pp. 21793-0 Paperbound $2.50

GHOST AND HORROR STORIES OF AMBROSE BIERCE, Ambrose Bierce. 23 strikingly modern stories of the horrors latent in the human mind: The Eyes of the Panther, The Damned Thing, An Occurrence at Owl Creek Bridge, An Inhabitant of Carcosa, etc., plus the dream-essay, Visions of the Night. Edited by E. F. Bleiler. xxii + 199pp. 20767-6 Paperbound $1.50

BEST GHOST STORIES OF J. S. LeFANU, J. Sheridan LeFanu. Finest stories by Victorian master often considered greatest supernatural writer of all. Carmilla, Green Tea, The Haunted Baronet, The Familiar, and 12 others. Most never before available in the U. S. A. Edited by E. F. Bleiler. 8 illustrations from Victorian publications. xvii + 467pp. 20415-4 Paperbound $3.00

THE TIME STREAM, THE GREATEST ADVENTURE, AND THE PURPLE SAPPHIRE— THREE SCIENCE FICTION NOVELS, John Taine (Eric Temple Bell). Great American mathematician was also foremost science fiction novelist of the 1920's. *The Time Stream,* one of all-time classics, uses concepts of circular time; *The Greatest Adventure,* incredibly ancient biological experiments from Antarctica threaten to escape; The *Purple Sapphire,* superscience, lost races in Central Tibet, survivors of the Great Race. 4 illustrations by Frank R. Paul. v + 532pp.

21180-0 Paperbound $3.00

SEVEN SCIENCE FICTION NOVELS, H. G. Wells. The standard collection of the great novels. Complete, unabridged. *First Men in the Moon, Island of Dr. Moreau, War of the Worlds, Food of the Gods, Invisible Man, Time Machine, In the Days of the Comet.* Not only science fiction fans, but every educated person owes it to himself to read these novels. 1015pp. 20264-X Clothbound $5.00

CATALOGUE OF DOVER BOOKS

LAST AND FIRST MEN AND STAR MAKER, TWO SCIENCE FICTION NOVELS, Olaf Stapledon. Greatest future histories in science fiction. In the first, human intelligence is the "hero," through strange paths of evolution, interplanetary invasions, incredible technologies, near extinctions and reemergences. Star Maker describes the quest of a band of star rovers for intelligence itself, through time and space: weird inhuman civilizations, crustacean minds, symbiotic worlds, etc. Complete, unabridged. v + 438pp. 21962-3 Paperbound $2.50

THREE PROPHETIC NOVELS, H. G. WELLS. Stages of a consistently planned future for mankind. *When the Sleeper Wakes,* and *A Story of the Days to Come,* anticipate *Brave New World* and *1984,* in the 21st Century; *The Time Machine,* only complete version in print, shows farther future and the end of mankind. All show Wells's greatest gifts as storyteller and novelist. Edited by E. F. Bleiler. x + 335pp. (USO) 20605-X Paperbound $2.25

THE DEVIL'S DICTIONARY, Ambrose Bierce. America's own Oscar Wilde—Ambrose Bierce—offers his barbed iconoclastic wisdom in over 1,000 definitions hailed by H. L. Mencken as "some of the most gorgeous witticisms in the English language." 145pp. 20487-1 Paperbound $1.25

MAX AND MORITZ, Wilhelm Busch. Great children's classic, father of comic strip, of two bad boys, Max and Moritz. Also Ker and Plunk (Plisch und Plumm), Cat and Mouse, Deceitful Henry, Ice-Peter, The Boy and the Pipe, and five other pieces. Original German, with English translation. Edited by H. Arthur Klein; translations by various hands and H. Arthur Klein. vi + 216pp. 20181-3 Paperbound $1.50

PIGS IS PIGS AND OTHER FAVORITES, Ellis Parker Butler. The title story is one of the best humor short stories, as Mike Flannery obfuscates biology and English. Also included, That Pup of Murchison's, The Great American Pie Company, and Perkins of Portland. 14 illustrations. v + 109pp. 21532-6 Paperbound $1.00

THE PETERKIN PAPERS, Lucretia P. Hale. It takes genius to be as stupidly mad as the Peterkins, as they decide to become wise, celebrate the "Fourth," keep a cow, and otherwise strain the resources of the Lady from Philadelphia. Basic book of American humor. 153 illustrations. 219pp. 20794-3 Paperbound $1.50

PERRAULT'S FAIRY TALES, translated by A. E. Johnson and S. R. Littlewood, with 34 full-page illustrations by Gustave Doré. All the original Perrault stories—Cinderella, Sleeping Beauty, Bluebeard, Little Red Riding Hood, Puss in Boots, Tom Thumb, etc.—with their witty verse morals and the magnificent illustrations of Doré. One of the five or six great books of European fairy tales. viii + 117pp. 8⅛ x 11. 22311-6 Paperbound $2.00

OLD HUNGARIAN FAIRY TALES, Baroness Orczy. Favorites translated and adapted by author of the *Scarlet Pimpernel.* Eight fairy tales include "The Suitors of Princess Fire-Fly," "The Twin Hunchbacks," "Mr. Cuttlefish's Love Story," and "The Enchanted Cat." This little volume of magic and adventure will captivate children as it has for generations. 90 drawings by Montagu Barstow. 96pp. (USO) 22293-4 Paperbound $1.95

THE RED FAIRY BOOK, Andrew Lang. Lang's color fairy books have long been children's favorites. This volume includes Rapunzel, Jack and the Bean-stalk and 35 other stories, familiar and unfamiliar. 4 plates, 93 illustrations x + 367pp.
21673-X Paperbound $2.00

THE BLUE FAIRY BOOK, Andrew Lang. Lang's tales come from all countries and all times. Here are 37 tales from Grimm, the Arabian Nights, Greek Mythology, and other fascinating sources. 8 plates, 130 illustrations. xi + 390pp.
21437-0 Paperbound $1.95

HOUSEHOLD STORIES BY THE BROTHERS GRIMM. Classic English-language edition of the well-known tales — Rumpelstiltskin, Snow White, Hansel and Gretel, The Twelve Brothers, Faithful John, Rapunzel, Tom Thumb (52 stories in all). Translated into simple, straightforward English by Lucy Crane. Ornamented with headpieces, vignettes, elaborate decorative initials and a dozen full-page illustrations by Walter Crane. x + 269pp.
21080-4 Paperbound $2.00

THE MERRY ADVENTURES OF ROBIN HOOD, Howard Pyle. The finest modern versions of the traditional ballads and tales about the great English outlaw. Howard Pyle's complete prose version, with every word, every illustration of the first edition. Do not confuse this facsimile of the original (1883) with modern editions that change text or illustrations. 23 plates plus many page decorations. xxii + 296pp.
22043-5 Paperbound $2.50

THE STORY OF KING ARTHUR AND HIS KNIGHTS, Howard Pyle. The finest children's version of the life of King Arthur; brilliantly retold by Pyle, with 48 of his most imaginative illustrations. xviii + 313pp. 6⅛ x 9¼.
21445-1 Paperbound $2.50

THE WONDERFUL WIZARD OF OZ, L. Frank Baum. America's finest children's book in facsimile of first edition with all Denslow illustrations in full color. The edition a child should have. Introduction by Martin Gardner. 23 color plates, scores of drawings. iv + 267pp.
20691-2 Paperbound $2.25

THE MARVELOUS LAND OF OZ, L. Frank Baum. The second Oz book, every bit as imaginative as the Wizard. The hero is a boy named Tip, but the Scarecrow and the Tin Woodman are back, as is the Oz magic. 16 color plates, 120 drawings by John R. Neill. 287pp.
20692-0 Paperbound $2.50

THE MAGICAL MONARCH OF MO, L. Frank Baum. Remarkable adventures in a land even stranger than Oz. The best of Baum's books not in the Oz series. 15 color plates and dozens of drawings by Frank Verbeck. xviii + 237pp.
21892-9 Paperbound $2.00

THE BAD CHILD'S BOOK OF BEASTS, MORE BEASTS FOR WORSE CHILDREN, A MORAL ALPHABET, Hilaire Belloc. Three complete humor classics in one volume. Be kind to the frog, and do not call him names . . . and 28 other whimsical animals. Familiar favorites and some not so well known. Illustrated by Basil Blackwell. 156pp.
(USO) 20749-8 Paperbound $1.25

EAST O' THE SUN AND WEST O' THE MOON, George W. Dasent. Considered the best of all translations of these Norwegian folk tales, this collection has been enjoyed by generations of children (and folklorists too). Includes True and Untrue, Why the Sea is Salt, East O' the Sun and West O' the Moon, Why the Bear is Stumpy-Tailed, Boots and the Troll, The Cock and the Hen, Rich Peter the Pedlar, and 52 more. The only edition with all 59 tales. 77 illustrations by Erik Werenskiold and Theodor Kittelsen. xv + 418pp. 22521-6 Paperbound $3.00

GOOPS AND HOW TO BE THEM, Gelett Burgess. Classic of tongue-in-cheek humor, masquerading as etiquette book. 87 verses, twice as many cartoons, show mischievous Goops as they demonstrate to children virtues of table manners, neatness, courtesy, etc. Favorite for generations. viii + 88pp. 6½ x 9¼.
22233-0 Paperbound $1.25

ALICE'S ADVENTURES UNDER GROUND, Lewis Carroll. The first version, quite different from the final *Alice in Wonderland,* printed out by Carroll himself with his own illustrations. Complete facsimile of the "million dollar" manuscript Carroll gave to Alice Liddell in 1864. Introduction by Martin Gardner. viii + 96pp. Title and dedication pages in color. 21482-6 Paperbound $1.25

THE BROWNIES, THEIR BOOK, Palmer Cox. Small as mice, cunning as foxes, exuberant and full of mischief, the Brownies go to the zoo, toy shop, seashore, circus, etc., in 24 verse adventures and 266 illustrations. Long a favorite, since their first appearance in St. Nicholas Magazine. xi + 144pp. 6⅝ x 9¼.
21265-3 Paperbound $1.75

SONGS OF CHILDHOOD, Walter De La Mare. Published (under the pseudonym Walter Ramal) when De La Mare was only 29, this charming collection has long been a favorite children's book. A facsimile of the first edition in paper, the 47 poems capture the simplicity of the nursery rhyme and the ballad, including such lyrics as I Met Eve, Tartary, The Silver Penny. vii + 106pp. 21972-0 Paperbound $1.25

THE COMPLETE NONSENSE OF EDWARD LEAR, Edward Lear. The finest 19th-century humorist-cartoonist in full: all nonsense limericks, zany alphabets, Owl and Pussycat, songs, nonsense botany, and more than 500 illustrations by Lear himself. Edited by Holbrook Jackson. xxix + 287pp. (USO) 20167-8 Paperbound $2.00

BILLY WHISKERS: THE AUTOBIOGRAPHY OF A GOAT, Frances Trego Montgomery. A favorite of children since the early 20th century, here are the escapades of that rambunctious, irresistible and mischievous goat—Billy Whiskers. Much in the spirit of *Peck's Bad Boy,* this is a book that children never tire of reading or hearing. All the original familiar illustrations by W. H. Fry are included: 6 color plates, 18 black and white drawings. 159pp. 22345-0 Paperbound $2.00

MOTHER GOOSE MELODIES. Faithful republication of the fabulously rare Munroe and Francis "copyright 1833" Boston edition—the most important Mother Goose collection, usually referred to as the "original." Familiar rhymes plus many rare ones, with wonderful old woodcut illustrations. Edited by E. F. Bleiler. 128pp. 4½ x 6⅜. 22577-1 Paperbound $1.25

TWO LITTLE SAVAGES; BEING THE ADVENTURES OF TWO BOYS WHO LIVED AS INDIANS AND WHAT THEY LEARNED, Ernest Thompson Seton. Great classic of nature and boyhood provides a vast range of woodlore in most palatable form, a genuinely entertaining story. Two farm boys build a teepee in woods and live in it for a month, working out Indian solutions to living problems, star lore, birds and animals, plants, etc. 293 illustrations. vii + 286pp.

20985-7 Paperbound $2.50

PETER PIPER'S PRACTICAL PRINCIPLES OF PLAIN & PERFECT PRONUNCIATION. Alliterative jingles and tongue-twisters of surprising charm, that made their first appearance in America about 1830. Republished in full with the spirited woodcut illustrations from this earliest American edition. 32pp. 4½ x 6⅜.

22560-7 Paperbound $1.00

SCIENCE EXPERIMENTS AND AMUSEMENTS FOR CHILDREN, Charles Vivian. 73 easy experiments, requiring only materials found at home or easily available, such as candles, coins, steel wool, etc.; illustrate basic phenomena like vacuum, simple chemical reaction, etc. All safe. Modern, well-planned. Formerly *Science Games for Children*. 102 photos, numerous drawings. 96pp. 6⅛ x 9¼.

21856-2 Paperbound $1.25

AN INTRODUCTION TO CHESS MOVES AND TACTICS SIMPLY EXPLAINED, Leonard Barden. Informal intermediate introduction, quite strong in explaining reasons for moves. Covers basic material, tactics, important openings, traps, positional play in middle game, end game. Attempts to isolate patterns and recurrent configurations. Formerly *Chess*. 58 figures. 102pp. (USO) 21210-6 Paperbound $1.25

LASKER'S MANUAL OF CHESS, Dr. Emanuel Lasker. Lasker was not only one of the five great World Champions, he was also one of the ablest expositors, theorists, and analysts. In many ways, his Manual, permeated with his philosophy of battle, filled with keen insights, is one of the greatest works ever written on chess. Filled with analyzed games by the great players. A single-volume library that will profit almost any chess player, beginner or master. 308 diagrams. xli x 349pp.

20640-8 Paperbound $2.50

THE MASTER BOOK OF MATHEMATICAL RECREATIONS, Fred Schuh. In opinion of many the finest work ever prepared on mathematical puzzles, stunts, recreations; exhaustively thorough explanations of mathematics involved, analysis of effects, citation of puzzles and games. Mathematics involved is elementary. Translated by F. Göbel. 194 figures. xxiv + 430pp. 22134-2 Paperbound $3.00

MATHEMATICS, MAGIC AND MYSTERY, Martin Gardner. Puzzle editor for Scientific American explains mathematics behind various mystifying tricks: card tricks, stage "mind reading," coin and match tricks, counting out games, geometric dissections, etc. Probability sets, theory of numbers clearly explained. Also provides more than 400 tricks, guaranteed to work, that you can do. 135 illustrations. xii + 176pp.

20338-2 Paperbound $1.50

MATHEMATICAL PUZZLES FOR BEGINNERS AND ENTHUSIASTS, Geoffrey Mott-Smith. 189 puzzles from easy to difficult—involving arithmetic, logic, algebra, properties of digits, probability, etc.—for enjoyment and mental stimulus. Explanation of mathematical principles behind the puzzles. 135 illustrations. viii + 248pp.

20198-8 Paperbound $1.75

PAPER FOLDING FOR BEGINNERS, William D. Murray and Francis J. Rigney. Easiest book on the market, clearest instructions on making interesting, beautiful origami. Sail boats, cups, roosters, frogs that move legs, bonbon boxes, standing birds, etc. 40 projects; more than 275 diagrams and photographs. 94pp.

20713-7 Paperbound $1.00

TRICKS AND GAMES ON THE POOL TABLE, Fred Herrmann. 79 tricks and games— some solitaires, some for two or more players, some competitive games—to entertain you between formal games. Mystifying shots and throws, unusual caroms, tricks involving such props as cork, coins, a hat, etc. Formerly *Fun on the Pool Table*. 77 figures. 95pp.

21814-7 Paperbound $1.00

HAND SHADOWS TO BE THROWN UPON THE WALL: A SERIES OF NOVEL AND AMUSING FIGURES FORMED BY THE HAND, Henry Bursill. Delightful picturebook from great-grandfather's day shows how to make 18 different hand shadows: a bird that flies, duck that quacks, dog that wags his tail, camel, goose, deer, boy, turtle, etc. Only book of its sort. vi + 33pp. 6½ x 9¼. 21779-5 Paperbound $1.00

WHITTLING AND WOODCARVING, E. J. Tangerman. 18th printing of best book on market. "If you can cut a potato you can carve" toys and puzzles, chains, chessmen, caricatures, masks, frames, woodcut blocks, surface patterns, much more. Information on tools, woods, techniques. Also goes into serious wood sculpture from Middle Ages to present, East and West. 464 photos, figures. x + 293pp.

20965-2 Paperbound $2.00

HISTORY OF PHILOSOPHY, Julián Marías. Possibly the clearest, most easily followed, best planned, most useful one-volume history of philosophy on the market; neither skimpy nor overfull. Full details on system of every major philosopher and dozens of less important thinkers from pre-Socratics up to Existentialism and later. Strong on many European figures usually omitted. Has gone through dozens of editions in Europe. 1966 edition, translated by Stanley Appelbaum and Clarence Strowbridge. xviii + 505pp. 21739-6 Paperbound $3.00

YOGA: A SCIENTIFIC EVALUATION, Kovoor T. Behanan. Scientific but non-technical study of physiological results of yoga exercises; done under auspices of Yale U. Relations to Indian thought, to psychoanalysis, etc. 16 photos. xxiii + 270pp.

20505-3 Paperbound $2.50

Prices subject to change without notice.
Available at your book dealer or write for free catalogue to Dept. GI, Dover Publications, Inc., 180 Varick St., N.Y., N.Y. 10014. Dover publishes more than 150 books each year on science, elementary and advanced mathematics, biology, music, art, literary history, social sciences and other areas.